New Century, Old Disparities

New Century, Old Disparities

GENDER AND ETHNIC EARNINGS GAPS IN LATIN AMERICA AND THE CARIBBEAN

Hugo Ñopo

A COPUBLICATION OF THE INTER-AMERICAN DEVELOPMENT BANK AND THE WORLD BANK

© 2012 Inter-American Development Bank
1300 New York Avenue, NW
Washington DC 20577
Telephone: 202-623-1000
Internet: www.iadb.org
E-mail: res@iadb.org

1 2 3 4   15 14 13 12

A copublication of the Inter-American Development Bank and The World Bank.

The Inter-American Development Bank	The World Bank
1300 New York Avenue, NW	1818 H Street, NW
Washington, DC 20577	Washington, DC 20433

ISBN (paper): 978-0-8213-8686-6
ISBN (electronic): 978-0-8213-9496-0
DOI: 10.1596/978-0-8213-8686-6

Cover: Drew Fasick of the Fasick Group, Inc.

Library of Congress Cataloging-in-Publication Data
New century, old disparities : gender and ethnic earnings gaps in Latin America and the Caribbean /Hugo Ñopo.
    p. cm. — (Latin American development forum series)
   Includes bibliographical references and index.
   ISBN 978-0-8213-8686-6 — ISBN 978-0-8213-9496-0 (electronic)
   1. Sex discrimination against women—Economic aspects—Latin America. 2. Ethnic relations—Economic aspects. 3. Discrimination—Economic aspects—Latin America. I. Ñopo, Hugo.
   HQ1237.5.L29N39 2012
   305.80098—dc23

                                                                2012014249

Latin American Development Forum Series

This series was created in 2003 to promote debate, disseminate information and analysis, and convey the excitement and complexity of the most topical issues in economic and social development in Latin America and the Caribbean. It is sponsored by the Inter-American Development Bank, the United Nations Economic Commission for Latin America and the Caribbean, and the World Bank. The manuscripts chosen for publication represent the highest quality in each institution's research and activity output and have been selected for their relevance to the academic community, policy makers, researchers, and interested readers.

Advisory Committee Members

Alicia Bárcena Ibarra, Executive Secretary, Economic Commission for Latin America and the Caribbean, United Nations

Inés Bustillo, Director, Washington Office, Economic Commission for Latin America and the Caribbean, United Nations

Tito Cordella, Deputy Chief Economist, Latin America and the Caribbean Region, World Bank

Augusto de la Torre, Chief Economist, Latin America and the Caribbean Region, World Bank

Santiago Levy, Vice President for Sectors and Knowledge, Inter-American Development Bank

Eduardo Lora, Chief Economist (a.i.) and General Manager, Research Department, Inter-American Development Bank

Luis Servén, Senior Adviser, Development Economics Vice Presidency, World Bank

Andrés Velasco, Cieplan, Chile

Titles in the Latin American Development Forum Series

New Century, Old Disparities: Gender and Ethnic Earnings Gaps in Latin America and the Caribbean (2012) by Hugo Ñopo

Does What You Export Matter? In Search of Empirical Guidance for Industrial Policies (2012) by Daniel Lederman and William F. Maloney

From Right to Reality: Incentives, Labor Markets, and the Challenge of Achieving Universal Social Protection in Latin America and the Caribbean (2012) by Helena Ribe, David Robalino, and Ian Walker

Breeding Latin American Tigers: Operational Principles for Rehabilitating Industrial Policies (2011) by Robert Devlin and Graciela Moguillansky

New Policies for Mandatory Defined Contribution Pensions: Industrial Organization Models and Investment Products (2010) by Gregorio Impavido, Esperanza Lasagabaster, and Manuel García-Huitrón

The Quality of Life in Latin American Cities: Markets and Perception (2010) by Eduardo Lora, Andrew Powell, Bernard M. S. van Praag, and Pablo Sanguinetti, editors

Discrimination in Latin America: An Economic Perspective (2010) by Hugo Ñopo, Alberto Chong, and Andrea Moro, editors

The Promise of Early Childhood Development in Latin America and the Caribbean (2010) by Emiliana Vegas and Lucrecia Santibáñez

Job Creation in Latin America and the Caribbean: Trends and Policy Challenges (2009) by Carmen Pagés, Gaëlle Pierre, and Stefano Scarpetta

China's and India's Challenge to Latin America: Opportunity or Threat? (2009) by Daniel Lederman, Marcelo Olarreaga, and Guillermo E. Perry, editors

Does the Investment Climate Matter? Microeconomic Foundations of Growth in Latin America (2009) by Pablo Fajnzylber, Jose Luis Guasch, and J. Humberto López, editors

Measuring Inequality of Opportunities in Latin America and the Caribbean (2009) by Ricardo de Paes Barros, Francisco H. G. Ferreira, José R. Molinas Vega, and Jaime Saavedra Chanduvi

The Impact of Private Sector Participation in Infrastructure: Lights, Shadows, and the Road Ahead (2008) by Luis Andres, Jose Luis Guasch, Thomas Haven, and Vivien Foster

Remittances and Development: Lessons from Latin America (2008) by Pablo Fajnzylber and J. Humberto López, editors

Fiscal Policy, Stabilization, and Growth: Prudence or Abstinence? (2007) by Guillermo Perry, Luis Servén, and Rodrigo Suescún, editors

Raising Student Learning in Latin America: Challenges for the 21st Century (2007) by Emiliana Vegas and Jenny Petrow

Investor Protection and Corporate Governance: Firm-Level Evidence across Latin America (2007) by Alberto Chong and Florencio López-de-Silanes, editors

Natural Resources: Neither Curse nor Destiny (2007) by Daniel Lederman and William F. Maloney, editors

The State of State Reform in Latin America (2006) by Eduardo Lora, editor

Emerging Capital Markets and Globalization: The Latin American Experience (2006) by Augusto de la Torre and Sergio L. Schmukler

Beyond Survival: Protecting Households from Health Shocks in Latin America (2006) by Cristian C. Baeza and Truman G. Packard

Beyond Reforms: Structural Dynamics and Macroeconomic Vulnerability (2005) by José Antonio Ocampo, editor

Privatization in Latin America: Myths and Reality (2005) by Alberto Chong and Florencio López-de-Silanes, editors

Keeping the Promise of Social Security in Latin America (2004) by Indermit S. Gill, Truman G. Packard, and Juan Yermo

Lessons from NAFTA: For Latin America and the Caribbean (2004) by Daniel Lederman, William F. Maloney, and Luis Servén

The Limits of Stabilization: Infrastructure, Public Deficits, and Growth in Latin America (2003) by William Easterly and Luis Servén, editors

Globalization and Development: A Latin American and Caribbean Perspective (2003) by José Antonio Ocampo and Juan Martin, editors

Is Geography Destiny? Lessons from Latin America (2003) by John Luke Gallup, Alejandro Gaviria, and Eduardo Lora

About the Author

Hugo Ñopo, a Peruvian national, is a lead research economist in Education at the Inter-American Development Bank (IDB), based in Bogotá, Colombia. Before joining the IDB, he was an assistant professor at Middlebury College, research affiliate at Group for the Analysis of Development (GRADE), and adviser at the Ministry of Labor and Social Promotion in Peru. His research agenda includes gender and racial inequalities in educational systems, labor markets and the access to public services, impact evaluation of public policies, and trust and reciprocity among economic agents. His research has been published in various specialized academic journals and books. Currently, he is also a research affiliate at the Institute for the Study of Labor (IZA).

Contents

FIGURES

Foreword

Socioeconomic inequality is a complex issue that has occupied human thought over the ages. Historically, overcoming inequality has been the battle cry of numerous revolutions and uprisings. In modern times, the study of inequality has been elevated to a major academic enterprise.

Among social scientists, economists bring a unique perspective to this important topic. Their perspective stems from two interrelated features of economic analysis. The first feature is economic theories of inequality, which derive from a common core of insights about the motives of economic agents. These theories include explanations of how inequality can arise from individuals' decisions about investment in human capital and from discrimination against particular demographic groups. The second feature is the body of sophisticated statistical and econometric methodologies for measuring inequality and its components. In the best tradition of economics, empirical methodology is informed by economic models of inequality and discrimination.

Latin America and the Caribbean provide a rich environment for studying social inequality, because historical inequalities along gender and ethnic lines persist, despite positive indicators of economic development. The extent of inequality and its probable causes vary widely across the many countries in the region.

Among the many dimensions of socioeconomic status that one can consider—health, education, earnings—Hugo Ñopo's book places major emphasis on labor market earnings. The book adopts a sophisticated econometric methodology for measuring earnings gaps and applies it consistently across and within countries to measure gender and racial or ethnic differences. The analysis includes a dynamic dimension that sheds light on the evolution of earnings gaps over time. The book offers important insights on economic and political strategies that could be adopted to reduce inequality. As such, it is a must for any academic or policy maker interested in understanding and correcting inequality, with respect to not only Latin America and the Caribbean but also anywhere in the world.

Ronald L. Oaxaca
University of Arizona and Institute for the Study of Labor (IZA)

Acknowledgments

The development of the methodology that is the basis of this book benefited from comments and suggestions by Gadi Barlevy, Fabio Caldieraro, Alberto Chong, Juan Jose Diaz, Mauricio Drelichman, Libertad Gonzalez, Luojia Hu, Zsolt Macskasi, Rosa Matzkin, Bruce Meyer, Lyndon Moore, Andrew Morrison, Dale Mortensen, Jaime Saavedra, Jim Sullivan, Chris Taber, and Maximo Torero. Comments from Luz Karime Abadía, Diego Ángel-Urdinola, Martin Benavides, Matias Busso, Anna Crespo, Mario Cuevas, Chico Ferreira, Miguel Jaramillo, Julia Johannsen, Liuba Kogan, Jorge Lavarreda, Osmel Manzano, Natalia Millan, Ana Maria Muñoz, Maria Beatriz Orlando, Claudia Piras, Rocio Ribero, Cynthia Sanborn, Sergei Soares, Ernesto Stein, and Renos Vakis on different chapters were invaluable. The book also benefited from comments at presentations made at the Latin American and Caribbean Economic Association Meetings, the Latin American Meeting of the Econometric Society, the European Association of Labour Economist Meetings, the Midwest Econometric Group Meetings, the Joint Labor/Public Economics Seminar at Northwestern University, the Group for the Analysis of Development (GRADE), the Institute for the Study of Labor (IZA), Centro de Investigación y Docencia Económica (CIDE), Instituto Tecnológico Autónomo de Mexico (ITAM), the Inter-American Development Bank, the World Bank, Middlebury College, the Universidad de los Andes, the Universidad del Rosario, Universidad Javeriana, Universidad del Pacifico, and Fedesarrollo. Many of the chapters' coauthors also contributed comments and provided research assistance on other chapters.

Felipe Balcázar, Deidre Ciliento, Cristina Gomez, Lucas Higuera, John Jessup, Alejandra Jimenez, Melisa Morales, and Georgina Pizzolito provided valuable research assistance at different stages of this project. The able editorial work of Rita Funaro, Barbara Karni, John Smith, and Janice Tuten is also acknowledged. Centro de Estudios Distributivos, Laborales y Sociales (CEDLAS) at the Universidad de La Plata and Sociometro at the Inter-American Development Bank generously provided the harmonized data sources for this book.

This book was possible thanks to the generous support I received from my supervisors, Eduardo Lora and Marcelo Cabrol, at different stages of this project. Thank you very much! Olga Aguilar, Irma Ugaz, Miski Ñopo, and Maria Ñopo—the women in my life—provided inspiration, support, guidance, and love.

Abbreviations

CASEN   Encuesta de Caracterización Socioeconómico Nacional (National Socioeconomic Characterization Survey; Chile)
CEO   chief executive officer
CLFSS   Continuous Labor Force Sample Survey (Barbados)
ENAHO   Encuesta Nacional de Hogares (National Household Survey; Peru)
ENCOVI   Encuesta Nacional de Condiciones de Vida (National Survey of Living Conditions; Guatemala)
ENEI   Encuesta Nacional de Empleo e Ingresos (National Survey of Employment and Income; Guatemala)
ENEMDU   Encuesta de Empleo, Desempleo, y Subempleo (Survey of Employment, Unemployment, and Underemployment; Ecuador)
ENEU   Encuesta Nacional de Empleo Urbano (National Survey of Urban Employment; Mexico)
GDP   gross domestic product
INEC   Instituto Nacional de Estadísticas y Censos de Ecuador (National Institute of Statistics and Census of Ecuador)
ISCO   International Standard Classification of Occupations
ISIC   International Standard Industrial Classification
PNAD   Pesquisa Nacional por Amostra de Domicilios (National Household Sample Survey; Brazil)
UNICEF   United Nations International Children's Fund

Part I

Overview, Methodology, and Data

1

Overview

Despite sustained economic growth at the end of the 20th and the beginning of the 21st century, Latin America and the Caribbean still faces high inequality and weak indicators of well-being among certain population groups. Women, people of African ancestry, and indigenous peoples are often at the bottom of the income distribution. Growth in gross domestic product, expansion of labor force participation, and (some) increase in formal sector real earnings (ILO 2007) have not been sufficient to remove barriers to access to sustainable income-generating opportunities for these groups (Paes de Barros et al. 2009), among whom unemployment and underemployment rates remain high and the quality of jobs has diminished (Márquez et al. 2007). An increasing share of workers has no access to health or pension benefits, turnover rates have increased, and temporary contracts have become more common (Arias, Yamada, and Tejerina 2004). Within this setup, gender and ethnic earnings gaps persist. Recent decades, however, have seen important changes regarding the situation of women and ethnic minorities in labor markets and, in general, in society (World Bank 2011).

This chapter was adapted from the following sources: "New Century, Old Disparities: Gender and Ethnic Wage Gaps in Latin America," Juan Pablo Atal, Hugo Ñopo, and Natalia Winder, RES Working Paper 4640, Inter-American Development Bank, 2009; "Evolution of Gender Wage Gaps in Latin America at the Turn of the Twentieth Century: An Addendum to 'New Century, Old Disparities,'" Alejandro Hoyos and Hugo Ñopo, IZA Discussion Paper 5086, Institute for the Study of Labor, 2010; "Pushing for Progress: Women, Work and Gender Roles in Latin America," Hugo Ñopo, *Harvard International Review* 33 (2): 315–28, 2011.

Juan Pablo Atal is a graduate student in economics at the University of California, Berkeley, and Natalia Winder is a consultant at UNICEF, Division of Policy and Practice, New York. Alejandro Hoyos is a consultant at the Poverty Reduction and Economic Management Network (PREM) at the World Bank.

Recent Changes on the Situation of Women and Ethnic Minorities

The world, and particularly the region, has experienced important changes in the role of women and men in the past decades. Women's visibility at home, at school, in the labor market, and in society in general has evolved significantly. Concurrently, men's roles have evolved as well. In recent decades, women in Latin America and the Caribbean have seen progress in various dimensions of their social, economic, and political situations. For instance, the number of female presidents democratically elected rose from three in the 1980s to seven in the first decade of the 21st century, and women occupy 20 percent of parliamentary seats and make up 22 percent of elected municipal council representatives (ProLead 2012).

Women's school attainment increased more than that of men. Among people born in 1940, men had nearly one more year of schooling than women (5.8 years compared with 5.0 years); among people born in 1980, women had 0.3 year more education than men (9.5 years compared with 9.2). For the region as a whole, the gender gap in schooling reversed from favoring men to favoring women for the cohort born in 1968. The only countries for which the gap has not reversed are Bolivia and Guatemala, both of which have large indigenous populations.

The global phenomenon of higher schooling attainment among women began earlier in Latin America and the Caribbean than in the rest of the world. These educational advances were observed particularly in the highest levels of education. In 1992, 16.4 percent of working women in the region and 10.7 percent of working men had some (complete or incomplete) tertiary education; by 2007, these figures had risen to 26.1 percent of women and 17.3 percent of men (Duryea et al. 2007).

Women's labor force participation increased in the region, whereas participation of men remained roughly constant.[1] By the beginning of the 1990s, half of women participated in the labor market (worked or looked for work); by 2007, almost two of three women did so in most countries of the region. Most of the increase in women's labor force participation can be explained by the increase in participation of young married women. Men still dominate labor markets, however: three out of five workers in the region are men, and occupational segregation by gender remains high.

The share of female-headed households rose in the past 20 years. By the beginning of the 1990s, women headed 1.2 percent of complete households (households in which both husband and wife are present) and 79.8 percent of single-head households (authors' calculations based on data in household surveys). These percentages increased to 9.2 percent and 82.3 percent, respectively, by the late 2000s. Women are increasingly heading households even when the father of their children is present.

Female-headed households are at both extremes of the income distribution. Some female household heads correspond to the profile of single young professionals or managers with young children. Others correspond to the profile of a low-educated single mother who holds an informal job in the service or commerce sector, has three or more children, and lives at or below the poverty line.

Fertility has declined. In Argentina and Uruguay, fertility rates have decreased since the 1930s. In contrast, Bolivia, Guatemala, Honduras, Nicaragua, and Paraguay still showed high fertility rates in the mid-1990s, although in recent years these rates have also fallen (Ñopo 2011).

Statistics about the presence of children reflect these changes. By the beginning of the 1990s, one in nine working women lived in a household with at least one child age six or younger; by the end of the first decade of the 2000s, that number had been almost halved. A similar situation exists for men: over the same period, the share of men living in households with children fell from 16 percent to 9 percent. This phenomenon, which has been linked to delays in women's age at birth of their first child and higher earnings, suggests an alleviation of household responsibilities related to childbearing and child rearing. For countries that began the demographic transition early, however, responsibilities are shifting to the care of the elderly.

Marriage, education, and work decisions have changed. The most significant increase in labor force participation was among women who married men with more education than themselves and, not surprisingly, women with no children or elderly relatives at home. Women who married men less skilled than themselves were more likely to work than women who married equally skilled men. Relative to women in other regions, skilled women in Latin America and the Caribbean are more likely to marry less skilled men. Ganguli, Hausmann, and Viarengo (2010) reveal that skilled women are less likely than unskilled women or skilled men to be married (or cohabiting). Skilled women who are married are less likely to work than skilled women who are not.

Occupational segregation is particularly high in Latin America (Blau and Kahn 1992). Hierarchical segregation—the fact that managers tend to be men (white) and subordinates women (minorities)—is commonly accepted as the norm in the region's labor markets. The persistence of traditional gender roles may be behind this phenomenon.

The reduction of gender-based segregation in the workplace represents an area in which policy interventions can improve the efficiency of labor markets. Determining whether addressing occupational rather than hierarchical segregation is more effective is one of the areas of policy design to which this book aims to make a contribution.

Latin America and the Caribbean is also a racially and ethnically diverse region, with some 400 ethnic groups (Hopenhayn and Bello 2001). All Latin American countries have indigenous and Afro-descendant populations.[2] Recent progress in the region has not benefited indigenous people or people of African descent (ethnic minorities) as much as whites (ethnic majorities); high inequality remains pervasive (López-Calva and Lustig 2010).

Ethnic minorities have fared worse than women. Across the region, they have higher poverty rates and lower income than whites (Psacharopoulos and Patrinos 1994; Gandelman, Ñopo, and Ripani 2008). They face restricted access to public services, lack of political representation, narrower labor market opportunities, and discrimination (Buvinic, Mazza, and Deutsch 2005; IDB 2008; Thorp 1998). They have weaker health indicators.[3]

Other factors that contribute to this pattern of inequality and poverty include labor force participation in low-productivity and hence poorly remunerated activities (Gaviria 2006). For example, throughout the region, indigenous people are concentrated in informal trade, self-employment, and (for women) domestic service. Indigenous men are concentrated in blue-collar sectors, such as construction and manufacturing, and low-skilled services.

This pattern can be traced largely to lower human capital endowments manifested in poorer educational performance and fewer years of job experience of ethnic minorities (Hernández-Zavala et al. 2006; Solano 2002). Furthermore, returns to education have also been shown to vary substantially across ethnic groups (Gallardo 2006), which explains a large part of the income differences between ethnic minorities and nonminorities.

In this regard, Latin America and the Caribbean have few empirical studies measuring discrimination against indigenous populations and exploring their potential economic costs (Patrinos and Psacharopoulos 1994; Cunningham and Jacobsen 2003; Saavedra et al. 2004; Patrinos and Hall 2006; Inter-American Development Bank 2008). The small number of studies mirrors the limited number of government policies in place to address the inequality between ethnic minorities and ethnic majorities and its impact on the incidence of poverty for the former group.

Overview of the Book

This book presents a regional overview of gender and ethnic disparities in labor earnings during this last turn of the century. After this introduction, chapter 2 presents the methodology adopted by the book and the data sources employed. Chapter 3 then examines education in the region, highlighting the reversal of the gender schooling gap. Nowadays, girls attend more years of schooling than boys. After these three introductory chapters, the book then turns to the analysis of earnings gaps.

Analyses of individual countries and groups of countries appear in chapters 4–16. Chapters 4–12 examine gender earnings gaps. Chapter 4 overviews gender earnings gaps in the region as a whole; chapters 5–12 examine gender earnings gaps in individual countries (Peru, Mexico, Chile, Colombia, Brazil, and Ecuador) and subregions (Central America and the Caribbean). Chapters 13–16 examine ethnic earnings gaps, using the harmonized household surveys described previously. Chapter 13 provides an overview of the issue; the three chapters that follow it examine ethnic earnings gaps in Brazil (chapter 14), Ecuador (chapter 15), and Guatemala (chapter 16). Chapter 17 proposes policy options.

Notes

1. In some other regions of the world, including the countries of the Organisation for Economic Co-operation and Development, labor force participation by men actually dropped.
2. Peru (27 percent of the total), Mexico (26 percent), Guatemala (15 percent), Bolivia (12 percent), and Ecuador (8 percent) account for almost 90 percent of the indigenous and Afro-descendant population in the region.
3. For instance, in Bolivia the provinces with larger proportions of indigenous populations, especially *aymará* and *quechua*, have the worst health indicators in the country: child malnutrition levels are above the national average in the provinces of Inquisivi, Tamayo, and Omasuyo de La Paz (Hopenhayn and Bello 2001), all of which have high indigenous density.

References

Arias, O., G. Yamada, and L. Tejerina. 2004. "Education, Family Background and Racial Earnings Inequality in Brazil." *International Journal of Manpower* 25 (3/4): 355–74.

Atal, J. P., H. Ñopo, and N. Winder, 2009. "New Century, Old Disparities: Gender and Ethnic Wage Gaps in Latin America." RES Working Paper 4640, Inter-American Development Bank, Research Department, Washington, DC.

Blau, F. D., and L. M. Kahn, 1992. "The Gender Earnings Gap: Learning from International Comparisons." *American Economic Review* 82 (2): 533–38.

Buvinic, M., J. Mazza, and R. Deutsch, eds. 2005. *Social Inclusion and Economic Development in Latin America.* Baltimore, MD: John Hopkins University Press.

Cunningham, W., and J. P. Jacobsen. 2003. "Earnings Inequality Within and Across Gender, Racial, and Ethnic Groups in Latin America." Wesleyan Economics Working Paper 2003-001. Wesleyan University, Middletown, CT.

Duryea, S., S. Galiani, H. Ñopo, and C. Piras. 2007. "The Educational Gender Gap in Latin America and the Caribbean." RES Working Paper 4510, Inter-American Development Bank, Research Department, Washington, DC.

Gallardo, M. L. 2006. "Ethnicity-Based Wage Differentials in Ecuador's Labor Market." Master's thesis, Cornell University, Department of Economics, Ithaca, NY.

Gandelman, N., H. Ñopo, and L. Ripani. 2008. "Las fuerzas tradicionales de exclusión: Análisis de la bibliografía." In *¿Los de afuera? Patrones cambiantes de exclusión en América Latina y el Caribe,* 17–34. Washington, DC: Inter-American Development Bank.

Ganguli, I., R. Hausmann, and M. Viarengo. 2010. "'Schooling Can't Buy Me Love': Marriage, Work, and the Gender Education Gap in Latin America."

Faculty Research Working Paper RWP10–032, Harvard University, Kennedy School of Government, Cambridge, MA.

Gaviria, A. 2006. "Movilidad social en América Latina: Realidades y percepciones." Universidad de los Andes, Facultad de Economía, Bogota. http://economia .uniandes.edu.co/content/download/9168/44755/file/movilidad%20social.pdf.

Hall, G., and H. A. Patrinos, eds. 2006. *Indigenous Peoples, Poverty and Human Development in Latin America.* London: Palgrave Macmillan.

Hernández-Zavala, M., H. A. Patrinos, C. Sakellariou, and J. Shapiro. 2006. "Quality of Schooling and Quality of Schools for Indigenous Students in Guatemala, Mexico, and Peru." Policy Working Paper 3982, World Bank, Washington, DC.

Hopenhayn, M., and A. Bello. 2001. "Discriminación étnico-racial y xenofobia en América Latina y el Caribe." Serie Políticas Sociales 47, Comisión Económica para América Latina y el Caribe (CEPAL), Santiago.

Hoyos, A., and H. Ñopo. 2010. "Evolution of Gender Wage Gaps in Latin America at the Turn of the Twentieth Century: An Addendum to 'New Century, Old Disparities.'" IZA Discussion Paper 5086, Institute for the Study of Labor, Bonn, Germany.

IDB (Inter-American Development Bank). 2008. *Economic and Social Progress in Latin America, 2008 Report.* Washington, DC: Inter-American Development Bank.

ILO (International Labour Organization). 2007. *Modelo de tendencias mundiales del empleo.* Geneva: International Labour Organization.

López-Calva, F., and N. Lustig, eds. 2010. *Declining Inequality in Latin America: A Decade of Progress?* Washington, DC: Brookings Institution Press.

Márquez, G., A. Chong, S. Duryea, J. Mazza, and H. Ñopo, eds. *¿Los de afuera? Patrones cambiantes de exclusión en América Latina y el Caribe.* Washington, DC: Inter-American Development Bank.

Ñopo, H. 2011. "Pushing for Progress: Women, Work and Gender Roles in Latin America." *Harvard International Review* 33 (2): 315–28.

Paes de Barros, R., F. H. G. Ferreira, J. R. Molinas Vega, and J. Saavedra Chanduvi. 2009. *Measuring Inequality of Opportunities in Latin America and the Caribbean.* Washington, DC: World Bank.

ProLead. 2012. "Cuál ha sido el impacto de las leyes de cuotas sobre la representación parlamentaria de las mujeres en América Latina." Inter-American Development Bank. http://www.iadb.org/research/geppal/index.cfm.

Psacharopoulos, G., and H. Patrinos. 1994. *Indigenous People and Poverty in Latin America: An Empirical Analysis.* Washington, DC: World Bank.

Saavedra, J., Ñopo, H., and M. Torero. 2004. "Ethnicity and Earning in Urban Peru." IZA Discussion Paper 980, Institute for the Study of Labor, Bonn, Germany.

Solano, E. 2002. "La Población Indígena en Costa Rica según el Censo 2000." Conference paper presented at "Costa Rica a la Luz del Censo 2000," San José, Costa Rica.

Thorp, R. 1998. *Progress, Poverty and Exclusion: An Economic History of Latin America in the 20th Century.* Baltimore, MD: Johns Hopkins University Press.

World Bank. 2011. *World Development Report 2012: Gender Equality and Development.* Washington, DC: World Bank.

2

Methodology and Data

Individuals' earnings differ substantially. Within the vast heterogeneity of earnings there are patterns, of course. Some of these patterns correspond to productivity-related characteristics (individuals earn more the higher their educational achievement, the more experience they have, and so forth), but others do not correspond to those types of productivity-related characteristics.

On average, men earn more than women and whites earn more than ethnic minorities.[1] Gender and ethnicity may be linked indirectly to the extent that on average, men and whites exhibit human capital characteristics that are better rewarded in the labor market than the characteristics of women, people of indigenous descent, and Afro-descendants.

What if these differences in human capital characteristics were removed? Would men still earn more than women and whites more than indigenous people and Afro-descendants? The statistical counterfactual question that has been used to address this issue is "what would the average earnings of a working woman (or ethnic minority) be if her labor market characteristics were equal, on average, to those of a working man (white)?"

This chapter was adapted from the following sources: "Matching as a Tool to Decompose Wage Gaps," Hugo Ñopo, *Review of Economics and Statistics* 90 (2): 290–99, 2008; "New Century, Old Disparities: Gender and Ethnic Wage Gaps in Latin America," Juan Pablo Atal, Hugo Ñopo, and Natalia Winder, RES Working Paper 4640, Inter-American Development Bank, 2009; "Evolution of Gender Wage Gaps in Latin America at the Turn of the Twentieth Century: An Addendum to 'New Century, Old Disparities,'" Alejandro Hoyos and Hugo Ñopo, IZA Discussion Paper 5086, Institute for the Study of Labor, 2010.

Juan Pablo Atal is a graduate student in economics at the University of California, Berkeley, and Natalia Winder is a consultant at UNICEF, Division of Policy and Practice, New York. Alejandro Hoyos is a consultant at the Poverty Reduction and Economic Management Network (PREM) at the World Bank.

The Blinder-Oaxaca Decomposition

Methodologically, the approach to answer such questions has been the Blinder-Oaxaca decomposition. This partitions the average difference in earnings—the earnings gap—into two components, one attributable to differences in observable characteristics and the other that remains after these observable differences are removed (and hence attributable to differences in unobservable elements within the labor markets, including discrimination). This decomposition is performed on the estimated differences in (Mincerian) earnings equations (Blinder 1973; Oaxaca 1973).

The Blinder-Oaxaca decomposition is the prevailing approach in the empirical work on earnings gaps, but the literature has extensively documented its limitations and drawbacks. Three are particularly worth noting. First, the relationship between characteristics and earnings is not necessarily linear, and recent data have been found to violate key implications of the Mincerian model, the key input of the Blinder-Oaxaca decompositions (Hansen and Wahlberg 1999; Heckman, Lochner, and Todd 2003). Second, Blinder-Oaxaca is informative only about the average earnings gap decomposition, providing no clues about the distribution of the differences in pay (Jenkins 1994; DiNardo, Fortin, and Lemieux 1996; Donald, Green, and Paarsch 2000). Third, Blinder-Oaxaca fails to restrict its comparison to comparable individuals, which is likely to substantially upwardly bias the estimators for unexplained differences in pay (Barsky et al. 2002).

Methodology for This Book:
An Extension of the Blinder-Oaxaca Decomposition

The econometric procedure pursued in this book is the one introduced in Ñopo (2008). Conceived as an extension of the Blinder-Oaxaca decomposition using a nonparametric matching approach, this methodology attempts to explore the extent to which gender and ethnic earnings gaps can be attributed to differences in observable characteristics. This alternative approach addresses the traditional Blinder-Oaxaca question not only for averages but also, and more interestingly, for the distribution of earnings, emphasizing the role of gender and ethnic differences in the "common support" of the distribution of observable human capital characteristics.

The proposed methodology yields a more precise measurement of the explained and unexplained components of the earnings gap. It not only decomposes the earnings gap into "endowment" and "unexplained" blocks, it also allows for the exploration of the distribution of the unexplained differences in earnings.

The methodology constrains the comparison of earnings gaps to people with comparable characteristics. In other words, it accounts for the outcomes of minorities and women for whom no whites or men (respectively) with comparable human capital characteristics can be found, an issue often neglected in the earnings gaps literature. Finally, this methodology does not need to assume any sort of functional form for the relationship between characteristics and earnings (such as the Mincerian model).

The methodology works by generating synthetic samples of individuals by matching men (whites) and women (ethnic minorities) with the same observable characteristics. The matching characteristics are discrete, so the match is done perfectly, without using propensity scores or any notion of distance between the characteristics. The basic form of the algorithm is shown below for gender earnings gaps (it works in the same way for ethnic earnings gaps):

- Step 1: Select one woman (without replacement) from the sample.
- Step 2: Select all men who have the same characteristics as the woman selected.
- Step 3: Construct a synthetic individual whose earnings are equal to the average of all of individuals selected in step 2 and "match" him to the original woman.
- Step 4: Put the observations of both individuals (the synthetic man and the woman) in the new (respective) samples of matched individuals.
- Repeat steps 1–4 until it exhausts the original sample of women.

Application of this matching algorithm creates three sets of individuals: one of men whose observable characteristics cannot be matched to those of any women in the sample; one of women whose observable characteristics cannot be matched to those of any men in the sample; and one of matched men and women, in which the distribution of observable characteristics for men is identical to that of women. In this last group, observations for men are weighted in such a way that their joint distribution of observable characteristics mimics the distribution of observable characteristics of matched women. Only comparable individuals are compared. It is possible to calculate the earnings distribution of the sample of women if their observable characteristics resemble those of the sample of men.

The other two sets—of unmatched men and women—make it possible to determine how much of the calculated gap is accounted for by the outcomes of men and women out of the common support. This issue of lack of comparability between some men and women (uncommon supports) has been largely neglected in the gender earnings gap literature. As Ñopo (2008) shows, failure to recognize the lack of common support in some circumstances may lead to overestimation of the unexplained component of the earnings gaps.

The sets of matched and unmatched individuals are compared. The earnings gap (Δ)—the difference in average earnings of men and women, expressed as a percentage of women's average earnings—is then decomposed into four additive elements:

$$\Delta = (\Delta_X + \Delta_M + \Delta_F) + \Delta_0.$$

As in the Blinder-Oaxaca decomposition, one component: Δ_X, is attributed to the differences in observable characteristics between men and women. However, as the matching procedure takes into account the fact that not every combination of characteristics of men is found among women (and vice versa), the computation of Δ_X is restricted to men and women whose characteristics lie in the common support of both characteristics' distributions. Further extending the basic Blinder-Oaxaca approach, instead of controlling for differences in average characteristics of men and women, the matching procedure allows controlling for differences in the distributions of those characteristics.

The second element, Δ_M (Δ_W in the ethnic-based decompositions), is the portion of the earnings gap caused by the existence of men with combinations of characteristics that are not met by any women (for instance, highly educated young workers filling high-profile positions such as chief executive officer [CEO]).

The third element, Δ_F (Δ_{NW} in the ethnic-based decompositions), is the portion of the gap caused by the existence of women with combinations of characteristics that are not met by any men (for instance, old and low-skilled domestic workers). Both Δ_M and Δ_F exist because the supports of the sets of observable characteristics of men and women do not completely overlap.

The element Δ_M is referred to as the "CEO effect"; Δ_F is referred to as the "maid effect." These effects reflect the fact that CEOs tend to be men and not women and maids tend to be women and not men.

Dávila and Pagán (1999) report that Costa Rican and Salvadoran women are underrepresented in occupational categories such as managerial, services, agricultural labor, and laborer occupational categories and overrepresented in professional, administrative support/clerical, and transportation jobs. Hertz et al. (2008) report that working women are underrepresented in managerial positions and overrepresented as service workers, merchants, administrative personnel, and professionals.

Marked differences by economic sector are also apparent. Construction and agriculture are sectors dominated by men, whereas community, social, and personal services are dominated by women. These differences may reflect women's self-selection into segments of the labor market where they enjoy more flexibility to manage their work and household responsibilities. Women may choose to permanently or temporarily withdraw from the labor market or work in occupations with flexible or fewer working hours (Tenjo, Ribero, and Bernat 2006). As a result, they may accumulate less work experience or invest less in education or on-the-job training (Terrell 1992).

The fourth element, Δ_0, is the portion of the gap that cannot be explained by the first three elements. It could be attributable to differences in unobservable characteristics, possibly including discrimination. It is comparable to the component of the earnings gap that reflects the differences in rewards to observable characteristics in the traditional Blinder-Oaxaca approach but restricted to the common support of those characteristics.

In this way, the methodology yields an alternative estimator for the unexplained earnings gap. This estimator attenuates biases and is more informative about the gap distribution, not only its average. The methodology, nonetheless, has some limitations. In addition to the need to define the matching characteristics as categorical variables only, it faces a challenge known as the "curse of dimensionality," which is behind most nonparametric configurations. This "curse" refers to the fact that the likelihood of finding matches of men and women decreases as the number of control variables (the "dimension") increases—a problem, given that researchers would like to use the maximum number of observable characteristics in order to control the scope of the role of unobservable factors in explaining the earnings gap. The curse of dimensionality forces researchers to make a trade-off between the number of control characteristics and the size of the nonoverlapping supports. This tradeoff is expressed in the decomposition exercises described in the following chapters as a shrinkage in the size of the common supports as new observable characteristics are added to the matching configuration.

Two limitations that the approach introduced by this methodology cannot overcome are selectivity and unobservables. Men and women and whites, indigenous people, and Afro-descendants may differ in their decision-making processes about entering the labor markets. Hence, the way in which they select into the active (and employed) labor force may be different. The observed samples of working women and men and whites and ethnic minorities may not be representative samples of the population as a whole. This limitation can be treated with conventional corrections in the regression-based approach (Heckman 1979), but not in a matching-based one.

Another limitation, shared by the regression-based and matching-based approaches is that data on all relevant variables that might affect earnings are not available. Individual abilities and characteristics on which data are not available—including work ethic, commitment, and capacity to work as part of a team—are very relevant for determining earnings. As employers, and labor markets in general, can observe them and reward them appropriately, their effects should be embedded in individuals' earnings. These features are, however, unobservable. In this sense, the estimators reported in this book for the unexplained differences in pay are just that: gaps that cannot be explained on the basis of observable characteristics.[2]

Data

The methodology was applied to nationally representative household survey data. Table 2.1 indicates the years of each survey analyzed in each chapter of this book. These surveys were processed and harmonized by the Research Department of the Inter-American Development Bank and CEDLAS at the Universidad de La Plata to facilitate cross-country comparisons.

Each observation in every household survey has an associated expansion factor that reflects the particularities of the sampling methods involved. The expansion factor can be interpreted as the number of individuals each observation represents; the sum of the expansion factors in any given survey approximates the population size of the country. In this way, pooling the observations in the 18 surveys for the gender studies, each weighted by its expansion factor, creates a sample representative of the working population of Latin America and the Caribbean.

The focus of the analyses is on the working population in each country. The variable of interest is labor earnings, measured as hourly earnings. In the pooled data sets, hourly earnings are measured in terms of 2002 dollars using purchasing power parity (PPP) exchange rates and nominal GDP deflators. Every chapter therefore excludes the population below and above certain ages. Also excluded from the data sets are all observations for which hourly income is missing or negative. For the purpose of the decompositions, only observations with values for every one of the characteristics used as control variables are kept.

As the gender variable is available in all national data sources, the gender earnings gap analysis is performed for the entire sample of countries listed in table 2.1. In contrast, the datasets pooled for the ethnic studies cover only Bolivia, Brazil, Chile, Ecuador, Guatemala, Paraguay, and Peru, which represent about 55 percent of the region's population. The sample used in the ethnic regional analysis is selected in the same way as the gender sample, excluding observations with the same criteria.

Cross-country comparisons of ethnic earnings gaps should be interpreted with caution, because the definition of ethnicity is not the same in all countries. Individuals are classified as either minority or nonminority depending on the ethnic groups each survey considers. Ethnic minorities are defined by individuals' self-assessment of being part of an indigenous group in Bolivia, Chile, Ecuador, Guatemala, and Peru; by skin color in Brazil; and by mother tongue in Paraguay. The details of this classification are presented in table 2.2.

Questions on surveys for educational attainment information are frequently expressed in terms of the grade completed in school or university. Calculating years of schooling—obtained by summing the years completed by each respondent—requires taking into account differences in school systems across countries. After years of schooling are calculated,

Table 2.1 Household Survey Data Used, by Country and Chapter

Country	Survey	Gender chapters				Ethnic chapters	
		Education	Regional	Subregional	Country	Regional	Country
Argentina	Encuesta Permanente de Hogares (EPH)		1992				
	Encuesta Permanente de Hogares-Continua (EPH-C)	2006	2006				
Barbados	Continuous Labor Force Sample Survey (CLFSS)			2004			
Bolivia	Encuesta Nacional de Empleo (ENE)		1997				
	Encuesta Continua de Hogares (ECH)—Mejoramiento de las Encuestas y Medición de las Condiciones de Vida (MECOVI)	2007	2006, 2007			2006	
Brazil	Pesquisa Nacional por Amostra de Domicilios (PNAD)	2008	1992 2007, 2008		1996–2006	2007	1996–2006
Chile	Encuesta de Caracterización Socioeconómica Nacional (CASEN)	2006	1992 2006		1992, 1994, 1996, 1998, 2000, 2003, 2006, 2009	2006	
Colombia	Encuesta Nacional de Hogares — Fuerza de Trabajo (ENH—FT)		1992, 2005		1994–2006		
	Gran Encuesta Integrada de Hogares (GEIH)	2006	2006				

(continued next page)

Table 2.1 Household Survey Data Used, by Country and Chapter (continued)

Country	Survey	Education	Gender chapters			Ethnic chapters	
			Regional	Subregional	Country	Regional	Country
Costa Rica	Encuesta de Hogares de Propósitos Múltiples (EHPM)	2007	1992, 2006, 2007	1995, 2000, 2006			
Dominican Republic	Encuesta Nacional de Fuerza de Trabajo (ENFT)	2007	2000, 2003, 2007				
Ecuador	Encuesta de Condiciones de Vida (ECV) Encuesta de Empleo, Desempleo, y Subempleo (ENEMDU)	2006	1995, 2006, 2007		2003–07	2007	2003–07
El Salvador	Encuesta de Hogares de Propósitos Multiples (EHPM)	2007	1991, 2005, 2007	1995, 2000, 2005			
Guatemala	Encuesta Nacional de Condiciones de Vida (ENCOVI) Encuesto Nacional de Empleo e Ingresos (ENEI)	2006	2000, 2006	2000, 2006, 2004		2006	2000, 2006, 2004
Honduras	Encuesta Permanente de Hogares de Propósitos Multiples (EPHPM)	2007	1997, 2007	1997, 2002, 2007			
Jamaica	Labor Force Survey undertaken by the Statistical Institute (STATIN)			2003			
Mexico	Encuesta Nacional de Ingresos y Gastos de los Hogares (ENIGH) Encuesta Nacional de Empleo Urbano (ENEU)	2008	1992, 2008, 2004		1994–2004		

Table 2.1 Household Survey Data Used, by Country and Chapter *(continued)*

		Gender chapters				Ethnic chapters	
Country	*Survey*	*Education*	*Regional*	*Subregional*	*Country*	*Regional*	*Country*
Nicaragua	Encuesta Nacional de Hogares sobre Medición de Nivel de Vida (EMNV)	2005	1993, 2005	1998, 2001, 2005			
Panama	Encuesta de Hogares, Mano de Obra (EMO) Encuesta de Hogares (EH)	2006	1991 2003, 2006	1997, 2002, 2006			
Paraguay	Encuesta de Hogares (Mano de Obra) (EH) Encuesta Permanente de Hogares (EPH)	2007	2006, 2007			2006	
Peru	Encuesta Nacional de Hogares (ENAHO)	2007	1997 2006, 2007		1997–2009	2006	
Uruguay	Encuesta Continua de Hogares (ECH)	2007	1992 2005, 2007				
Venezuela, RB	Encuesta de Hogares Por Muestreo (EHM)	2006	1992 2004, 2006				

Source: The data sources were compiled and harmonized by the Research Department of the Inter-American Development Bank and CEDLAS.

Table 2.2 Criteria for Classifying Ethnic Groups as "Minorities," by Country

Country		Criterion	Percentage of workers 12–65
Bolivia	Self-declaration	Self-declaration as Quechua, Aymara, Guarani, Chiquitano, Mojeño, or other	52.6
Brazil	Skin color	Self-declaration of skin color as black or brown	48.5
Chile	Self-declaration	Self-declaration as Aymara, Rapa nui, Quechua, Mapuche, Atacameño, Coya, Kawaskar, Yagan, or Diaguita	6.0
Ecuador	Self-declaration	Self-declaration as indigenous, black, mulatto, or other	10.0
Guatemala	Self-declaration	Self-declaration as K'iche', Q'eqchi', Kaqchikel, Mam, Q'anjob'al, Achi, Ixil, Itza', Poqomchi', Chuj, Awakateko, Poqomam, Ch'orti', Jakalteko, Sakapulteco, Mopan, Uspanteko, Tz'utujil, Sipakapense, Chalchiteko, Akateko, Xinka, or Garifuna	35.1
Paraguay	Self-declaration	Self-declaration as Guarani speaking	33.4
Peru	Self-declaration	Self-declaration as Quechua, or Aymara; from Amazonia; or black, mulatto, Zambo, or other	31.3

Source: The data sources were compiled and harmonized by the Research Department of the Inter-American Development Bank and CEDLAS.

new variables for educational attainment are created that consider the same education levels across countries. These are seven dummy variables, one for each of the following levels: no education, primary incomplete, primary complete, secondary incomplete, secondary complete, tertiary incomplete, and tertiary complete or more.

In general, job characteristics include whether or not the individual works in the formal sector, the firm size, the occupation, and the economic sector of the activity. Formal labor is a dummy variable created from information on social security affiliation; it is equal to 1 if the respondent reports paying mandatory social security. Small firm is a dummy variable that takes the value 1 for firms with no more than five workers. Occupation is a variable coded to the one-digit level based on categorizations used in each country, which are frequently based on the International Standard Classification of Occupations (ISCO) international code. The categories included are professionals and technicians, directors and upper management, administrative personnel, merchants and sellers, service workers, agricultural workers and similar, nonagricultural blue collar workers, armed forces, and other occupations not classified in the previous categories. Economic sector is a variable coded to the one-digit level based on categorizations used in each country that are frequently based on the International Standard Industrial Classification (ISIC) international code. The categories included are agriculture, hunting, forestry, and fishing; mining and quarrying; manufacturing; electricity, gas, and water supply; construction; wholesale and retail trade and hotels and restaurants; transport, storage; financing, insurance, real estate, and business services; and community, social, and personal services. In general, sociodemographic variables will be dummies, which take the value of 1 if the condition is met and 0 otherwise.

Notes

1. For simplicity, the term *ethnic minorities* is used to refer to ethnic and racial groups other than whites. In some countries, these groups represent majorities.
2. See Ñopo (2008) for technical details on the matching procedure, a comparison between it and the traditional approach based on linear regressions, and proofs of the asymptotic consistency of the estimators derived from this method. The same procedure is used to decompose gender and ethnic earnings gaps.

References

Atal, J. P., H. Ñopo, and N. Winder, 2009. "New Century, Old Disparities: Gender and Ethnic Wage Gaps in Latin America." RES Working Paper 4640, Inter-American Development Bank, Research Department, Washington, DC.

Barsky, R., J. Bound, K. Charles, and J. P. Lupton. 2002. "Accounting for the Black–White Wealth Gap: A Nonparametric Approach." *Journal of the American Statistical Association* 97 (459): 663–73.

Blinder, A. 1973. "Wage Discrimination: Reduced Form and Structural Differences." *Journal of Human Resources* 7 (4): 436–55.

Dávila, A., and J. Pagán. 1999. "Gender Pay and Occupational-Attainment Gaps in Costa Rica and El Salvador: A Relative Comparison of the Late 1980s." *Review of Development Economics* 3 (2): 215–30.

DiNardo, J., N. Fortin, and T. Lemieux. 1996. "Labor Market Institutions and the Distribution of Wages, 1973–1992: A Semiparametric Approach." *Econometrica* 64 (5): 1001–44.

Donald, S., D. Green, and H. Paarsch. 2000. "Differences in Wage Distributions between Canada and the United States: An Application of a Flexible Estimator of Distribution Functions in the Presence of Covariates." *Review of Economic Studies* 67: 609–63.

Hansen, J., and R. Wahlberg. 1999. "Endogenous Schooling and the Distribution of the Gender Wage Gap." IZA Discussion Paper 78, Institute for the Study of Labor, Bonn, Germany.

Heckman, J. 1979. "Sample Selection Bias as a Specification Error." *Econometrica* 47 (1): 153–61.

Heckman, J., L. Lochner, and P. Todd. 2003. "Fifty Years of Mincer Earnings Regressions." NBER Working Paper 9732, National Bureau of Economic Research, Cambridge, MA.

Hertz, T., A. P. de la O Campos, A. Zezza, P. Winters, E. J. Quiñones, and B. Davis. 2008. "Wage Inequality in International Perspective: Effects of Location, Sector, and Gender." ESA Working Paper 8/08, Food and Agriculture Organization, Agricultural and Development Economics Division, Rome. ftp://ftp.fao.org/docrep/fao/011/ak230e/ak230e00.pdf.

Jenkins, S. P. 1994. "Earnings Discrimination Measurement: A Distributional Approach." *Journal of Econometrics* 61 (1): 81–102.

Ñopo, H. 2008. "Matching as a Tool to Decompose Wage Gaps." *Review of Economics and Statistics* 90 (2): 290–99.

Ñopo, H., and A. Hoyos. 2010. "Evolution of Gender Wage Gaps in Latin America at the Turn of the Twentieth Century: An Addendum to 'New Century, Old Disparities.'" IZA Discussion Paper 5086, Institute for the Study of Labor, Bonn, Germany.

Oaxaca, R. 1973. "Male-Female Wage Differentials in Urban Labor Markets." *International Economic Review* 14 (3): 693–70.

Tenjo, J., R. Ribero, and L. Bernat. 2006 "Evolución de las diferencias salariales de género en seis países de América Latina." In *Mujeres y trabajo en América Latina*, ed. C. Piras, 149–98. Washington, DC: Inter-American Development Bank.

Terrell, K. 1992. "Female-Male Earnings Differentials and Occupational Structure." *International Labor Review* 131 (4–5): 387–98.

3

Gender Differences in Education in Latin America and the Caribbean: Girls Outpacing Boys

Education is fundamental to economic and social development and the end of poverty. Countries with higher average schooling have been more successful in their development paths.

As important as the overall level of education is its distribution. A significant dimension of the distribution of education is gender. In most countries, women attain less schooling than men; the gender gap is wider in developing countries than in developed countries.

Latin America and the Caribbean is an interesting exception, as girls in the region achieve more schooling than boys. In contrast to Africa, Asia, and the Middle East and North Africa, it has achieved gender parity (or a ratio that favors girls) in education. Furthermore, in most countries of the region, there is a reverse gender gap in education. Women have more average years of schooling than their male counterparts (important exceptions are the indigenous communities of Bolivia and Guatemala). These surprising outcomes seem to contradict the standard assumption that parents favor investing in boys' education.

This chapter analyzes the evolution of the gender gap in average years of education for cohorts born between 1940 and 1984. A descriptive cross-country analysis of the changes in the distribution of education by

This chapter was adapted from "The Educational Gender Gap in Latin America and the Caribbean," Suzanne Duryea, Sebastian Galiani, Hugo Ñopo, and Claudia Piras, RES Working Paper 4510, Inter-American Development Bank, Research Department, 2007.

Suzanne Duryea is a lead economist in the Social Sector Unit at the Inter-American Development Bank. Sebastián Galiani is a professor of economics at the University of Maryland. Claudia Piras is a lead social development economist at the Inter-American Development Bank.

gender, cohort, and country is produced using household surveys (for a description of the household surveys used in this chapter and the rest of this book, see chapter 2).

The chapter attempts to answer the following questions: When did the gender gap in schooling close in Latin America and the Caribbean? Was it a uniform process across the region, or did some countries close the gender gap earlier than others? Is the reversal of the gender gap uniformly distributed across education levels, or is it explained mostly by changes among the more educated? Are there remaining gender differences in attendance and attainment among 6 to 20-year-olds by income quintile?

Strengthening girls' education opportunities is a strategic priority in many countries, because societies pay a price for gender inequality in terms of slower growth and reduced income (Dollar and Gatti 1999). Studies of rates of return also document the economic benefits of investing in girls' education (Psacharopoulos and Tzannatos 1992; Psacharopoulos 1994). In addition to generating private returns from labor market participation, women's education yields strong social externalities, including the following:

- Higher levels of education among women reduce fertility (Schultz 1973; Cochrane 1979), which decreases infant mortality and increases life expectancy (Behrman and Deolalikar 1988).
- Mothers' education has important intergenerational effects on the education, health, and well-being of their children (King et al. 1986; Schultz 1988; Strauss and Thomas 1995; Behrman, Duryea, and Székely 1999).
- Adding to a mother's schooling has a larger beneficial effect on a child's health, schooling, and adult productivity than adding to a father's schooling (King and Hill 1993; Schultz 1993).

Advances in the education of women represent one of the biggest success stories in Latin America and the Caribbean. However, little is known about this important and unprecedented accomplishment in the developing world. Most studies that look at educational outcomes have not gone beyond addressing the absence of a gender gap in the region. Knodel and Jones (1996) stress the rapid closure of the gender gap in most of the world, suggesting that the strong emphasis on eliminating gender inequality in schooling is no longer needed, but they do not specifically address the situation in Latin America and the Caribbean. Behrman, Duryea, and Székely (1999) were the first to analyze schooling progress in the region using household surveys. They highlight that for two-thirds of the 18 countries considered, the average years of schooling for women is higher than for men for cohorts born in 1970.

One of the few efforts to look at gender differences in education in Latin America and the Caribbean is Parker and Pederzini (2000), who examine the determinants of the level of education of girls and boys in Mexico and the factors that may explain gender differences. Marshall and Calderón (2005) find that enrollment rates of 6 to 11-year-olds were lower among girls than boys in only 4 of 22 countries considered. The picture changes slightly for older age groups, but in the majority of countries, enrollment rates favored girls. Marshall and Calderón also report lower repetition and drop-out among girls, higher promotion rates, and, in most countries, better grade-for-age outcomes.

Changes in the Gender Education Gap

Figure 3.1 shows the evolution of the average number of years of schooling completed by women and men and the gap between the two by birth year. The data are computed as three-year moving averages (that is, data reported for the 1940 cohort correspond to people born between 1939 and 1941 and so on).

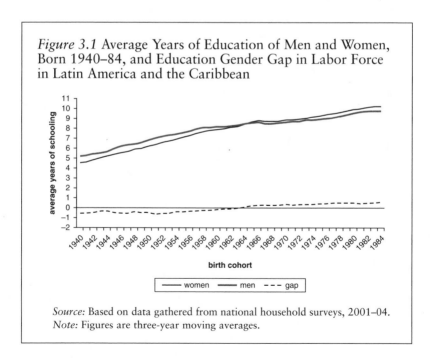

Figure 3.1 Average Years of Education of Men and Women, Born 1940–84, and Education Gender Gap in Labor Force in Latin America and the Caribbean

Source: Based on data gathered from national household surveys, 2001–04.
Note: Figures are three-year moving averages.

Among people born between 1939 and 1941, on average, women attained 4.4 years of schooling and men attained 5.1 years. The gender education gap for this birth cohort was thus 0.7 year in favor of men. For people born between 1983 and 1985 (people who were 21–23 at the time of the surveys), the average schooling attainment was 10.1 years for women and 9.6 years for men; the gender education gap was 0.5 year in favor of women. During this period of four decades, women's schooling attainment increased by 5.7 years while men's attainment increased by 4.5 years. On average, the gender gap has been declining at a rate of about 0.27 years of schooling per decade. Figure 3.1 suggests that gender parity was achieved beginning with the cohort born around 1965.

These average statistics for the region hide intraregional diversity (for graphs for individual countries and descriptions of the data, see Duryea et al. 2007). Table 3.1 reports the birth cohort in which each country achieved gender parity. Six countries (Argentina, Brazil, Colombia, Costa Rica, Panama, and República Bolivariana de Venezuela) achieved parity for cohorts born in the 1950s. The Dominican Republic, Honduras, and Nicaragua achieved parity for cohorts born in the 1960s. Chile, Ecuador, and Paraguay achieved parity for cohorts born in the 1970s (the educational gap in Chile has been close to zero since the mid-1960s). El Salvador, the last country to achieve gender parity, did so for cohorts born in 1984 (but its gap was close to zero for cohorts born in the early 1970s).

The gender gap in educational attainment in Uruguay favors women in all years considered, suggesting that it was the first country in which the gap closed (before the period of analysis). In four countries (Bolivia, Guatemala, Mexico, and Peru), the gender educational gap favored men during the whole period. These countries have the largest shares of indigenous people.

Data are available for two additional birth cohorts for Mexico (2008) and Peru (2007). These data show that Mexico achieved gender parity for the 1985 birth cohort, with the gap for this year equal to 0.10 year favoring women. Peru has an education gender gap that is very close to zero, but it favors men (–0.09) for the last cohort in the survey.

A linear extrapolation of the rate at which the gap has been declining in Bolivia and Guatemala suggests that parity will be achieved in Bolivia for the cohort born in 1999. The trends for Guatemala do not allow estimation of the year at which parity will materialize.

Decomposing Changes in the Gender Education Gap

For Latin America as a whole, the gender gap in schooling attainment has been declining at a rate of about 0.27 year of schooling per decade. Since the mid-1960s, the gap has favored women.

These changes in the average trend are interesting, but it would be even more interesting to understand the segments of the schooling distribution

Table 3.1 Gender Gap in Education in Latin America and the Caribbean for Cohorts Born in 1940 and 1984, by Country *(years)*

Country	Gap for 1940 birth cohort	Birth cohort at which the gap closes	Gap for 1984 birth cohort
Argentina	−0.89	1951	0.69
Bolivia	−2.40	–	−0.19
Brazil	−0.41	1950	0.82
Chile	−0.74	1975	0.18
Colombia	−0.28	1958	0.45
Costa Rica	−0.57	1956	0.54
Dominican Republic	−0.83	1965	0.90
Ecuador	−0.69	1971	0.33
Guatemala	−0.59	–	−0.84
Honduras	−0.53	1968	0.72
Mexico	−0.83	–	−0.13
Nicaragua	−0.88	1966	1.18
Panama	−1.01	1955	0.72
Peru	−1.84	–	−0.17
Paraguay	−0.83	1975	0.65
El Salvador	−1.44	1984	0.11
Uruguay	0.07	++	0.91
Venezuela, RB	−0.84	1955	1.23
Latin America	**−0.65**	**1965**	**0.46**

Source: Based on data from national household surveys, 2001–04.

Note: – = gap has not closed for any of the birth cohorts considered, ++ = gap closed for a previous cohort to the 1940 cohort.

in which changes were most pronounced. For this purpose, the sample was decomposed into four groups: individuals who acquired no education or only incomplete primary education, individuals with complete primary or incomplete secondary education, individuals with complete secondary or incomplete university education, and university graduates (figure 3.2) (see Duryea et al. 2007 for figures by country).

The proportion of women with no schooling or incomplete primary education fell markedly, decreasing at a faster rate than for men. The

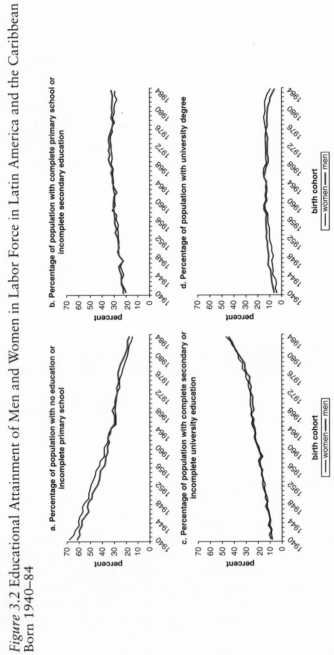

Figure 3.2 Educational Attainment of Men and Women in Labor Force in Latin America and the Caribbean Born 1940–84

Source: Based on data from national household surveys, 2001–04.

proportion of people with complete secondary or incomplete university increased slightly more rapidly for women than for men. At the upper extreme of the distribution, there are three periods with interesting differences. During the first period (cohorts born 1940–60), university graduation rates increased for women. This period was followed by a period (cohorts born 1960–75) of relative stagnation. A third period, starting with cohorts born around 1975, was marked by a decrease in university graduation rates for both women and men, although there are good reasons to attribute the decline to the fact that younger people in these cohorts may still be in school.

Changes in the gender schooling gap between the oldest and the youngest cohort in the sample are decomposed into changes at each educational level. Results are first reported for the components of the educational gap accounted for by each educational level in each birth cohort (figure 3.3). Each component of the education gap for a cohort corresponds to the difference between women's average years of schooling at each educational level weighted by women's participation at that level and men's average years of schooling at each educational level weighted by men's participation at that level.

The gender schooling gap in the 1940 birth cohort is compared with the gender schooling gap in the 1984 cohort in figure 3.4. Each component of

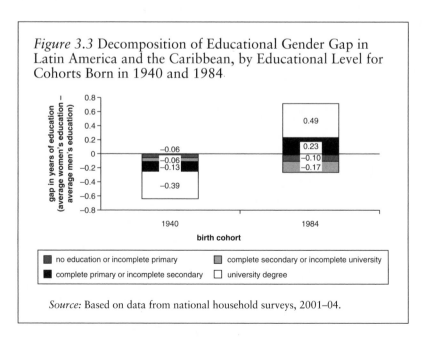

Figure 3.3 Decomposition of Educational Gender Gap in Latin America and the Caribbean, by Educational Level for Cohorts Born in 1940 and 1984

gap in years of education
(average women's education – average men's education)

0.8
0.6
0.4
0.2
0
−0.2
−0.4
−0.6
−0.8

1940   1984

birth cohort

−0.06
−0.06
−0.13
−0.39

0.49
0.23
−0.10
−0.17

■ no education or incomplete primary
■ complete primary or incomplete secondary
▦ complete secondary or incomplete university
☐ university degree

Source: Based on data from national household surveys, 2001–04.

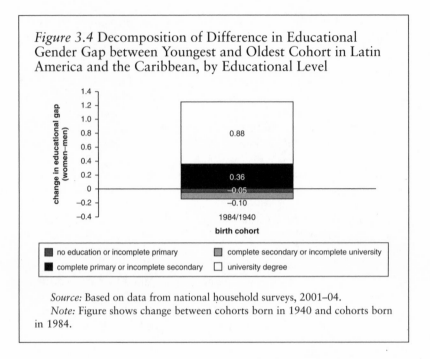

Figure 3.4 Decomposition of Difference in Educational Gender Gap between Youngest and Oldest Cohort in Latin America and the Caribbean, by Educational Level

Source: Based on data from national household surveys, 2001–04.

Note: Figure shows change between cohorts born in 1940 and cohorts born in 1984.

the total is the difference between the gender gap at each educational level for the 1984 cohort, calculated as described before, and the gender gap at the same level for the 1940 cohort.

The gender education gap for the 1940 cohort is –0.65 (the negative sign indicates that it favors men). Decomposition yields gaps of –0.06, –0.06, –0.13, and –0.39 for each of the four education levels. For the cohort born in 1984, the gender education gap is 0.46, favoring women, decomposed as –0.10, –0.17, 0.23, and 0.49. The change in the education gap between the oldest and youngest cohorts is 0.46 – (–0.65) = 0.11, decomposed as –0.05, –0.10, 0.36, and 0.88. Figure 3.4 indicates that changes among university graduates explain 88 percent of the change in the gender gap.

A country-by-country decomposition of the change in the gap reveals some interesting differences across countries (figure 3.5). For most countries, the third and fourth education levels are the most important contributors to the change in the schooling gap. For Ecuador, Honduras, and Peru, the second-level component (complete primary and incomplete secondary) is positive; in Mexico and Chile, the gap is positive but small. In the remaining 13 countries in the region, the gap at this level is negative. In Bolivia, Ecuador, El Salvador, Guatemala, Honduras, Mexico, and

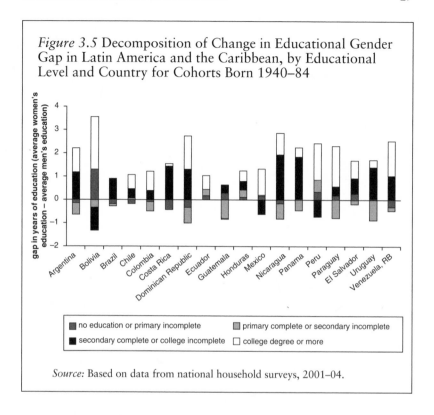

Figure 3.5 Decomposition of Change in Educational Gender Gap in Latin America and the Caribbean, by Educational Level and Country for Cohorts Born 1940–84

Source: Based on data from national household surveys, 2001–04.

Peru, the first-level component (no education and incomplete primary) explains why changes in the gap favor women.

Figure 3.5 reveals polarization in many countries, particularly Argentina, Nicaragua, and Venezuela. These countries exhibit large changes in the gap that favor women at the higher levels of schooling attainment as well as changes at the lower levels of attainment that favor men. Thus, women are falling behind men at low levels of education even as they are surpassing men at higher levels of educational attainment.

The change in the gap between cohorts is decomposed into two components, the probability component and the conditional expectations component. The probability component accounts for the gender difference in the probability of achieving a given educational level. The conditional expectations component accounts for the gender difference in the number of expected years of completed schooling at each level. The probability component is calculated as the sum of the four differences in the percentages of the female and male population at each educational level multiplied by the average years of schooling that men reach by level. The conditional expectations component is calculated as the sum of the four differences in average years of schooling between women and men at each educational level weighted by the percentage of women at each level.

The results are summarized in figure 3.6, which shows that most of the changes in schooling attainment between cohorts occurred as a result of changes in the probability component rather than the number of completed years of schooling at each level. The figure shows that the probability component accounted for 0.90 and the conditional expectations component for 0.19 year of the gap. Thus, changes in gender differences in the probabilities of achieving higher education levels explain four-fifths of the change in the schooling gender gap. Within the changes in probabilities, changes at the completed secondary and completed university levels are most important, although less than a third of the population reaches university. There is thus still much room for improvement in enrollment, attendance, and graduation from the upper levels of education in the region, for women and men alike.

Figure 3.7 decomposes the changes into changes in probabilities and changes in expectations. Only the aggregate changes for each are presented.

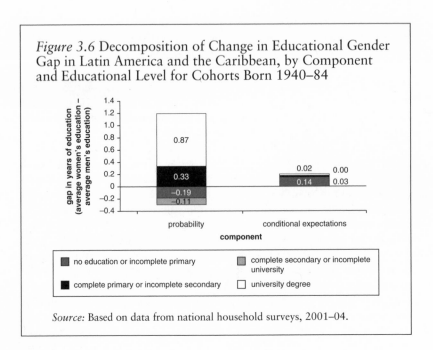

Figure 3.6 Decomposition of Change in Educational Gender Gap in Latin America and the Caribbean, by Component and Educational Level for Cohorts Born 1940–84

Source: Based on data from national household surveys, 2001–04.

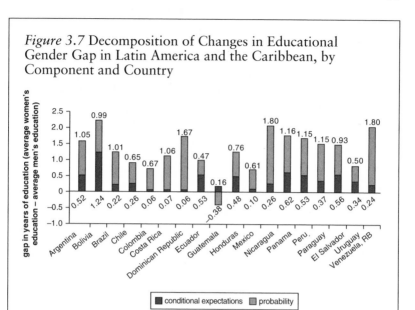

Figure 3.7 Decomposition of Changes in Educational Gender Gap in Latin America and the Caribbean, by Component and Country

Source: Based on data from national household surveys, 2001–04.
Note: Figure shows changes in the educational gender gap between cohorts born in 1940 and cohorts born in 1984.

The results show that change in the probability of attaining a given level of education is the more important of the two component in most countries, as is the case with the aggregate data for the region reported earlier. There are two exceptions to this pattern: Bolivia and Ecuador. Guatemala is the only country displaying a negative change in gender differences in the probability of attaining a particular level of education. It appears to be the only country in the region in which the rate of completion of primary, secondary, and university education grew more rapidly for men than for women. Bolivia experienced the largest changes in the expectations component in the region, followed by Panama and El Salvador.

The gender schooling gap changed at a rapid pace during the past four decades. For the oldest cohort in the data (people born in 1940), the gap in attainment was 0.6 year favoring men. For the youngest cohort (people born in 1984), the gap favored women by almost half a year. During this period, the gap in attainment changed by 0.27 year of schooling per decade in favor of women.

One of the plausible implications of these changes has to do with changes in marriage markets. People across the world are delaying marriage decisions (Schultz 1973; Cochrane 1979; King et al. 1986; Blau, Kahn, and Waldfogel 2000; Saardchom and Lemaire 2005). It would be useful to understand the extent to which this phenomenon is the result of changes in women's and men's schooling and the extent to which other forces are driving these trends.

Gender Differences in Attendance and Attainment among Children of School Age

Although the main focus of this chapter is to explore gender differences in completed average years of schooling across generations, it is instructive to explore the gender gap in children who are still of school age in the countries in which the gap has not yet been closed: Bolivia, Guatemala, Mexico, and Peru. Of particular interest is the role of household income in schooling decisions, given that household economic constraints represent an important barrier to girls' schooling. For young children, it is possible to examine how both attendance and attainment vary by household income level, something that cannot be done in the analysis of adult attainment.[1]

Figure 3.8 presents population-weighted school attendance profiles for 6 to 18-year-olds in Bolivia, Guatemala, Mexico, and Peru by gender and per capita household income quintile. Three income groups are displayed: the bottom 20 percent of the per capita household income distribution, the middle 20 percent, and the top 20 percent. Attendance rates among children 8–11 exceed 95 percent, leaving little room for variation across gender or income group; significant differences in attendance by gender are not evident before age 12. At older ages, there is a slight tendency for boys from the lowest income quintile to have higher attendance rates than girls from the same income group. The opposite pattern is evident at the highest income quintile.

No gender differences in attainment are evident for the middle and top income quintiles; there is, however, evidence of a small gender gap in favor of men in the bottom quintile (figure 3.9).[2] The most striking differences in school attendance (figure 3.8) and attainment (figure 3.9) occurred across income groups rather than by gender, however.

For three out of the four countries that did not close the gender schooling gap (Bolivia, Guatemala, and Peru), it is possible to explore household ethnicity. In Bolivia and Peru, the indigenous classification is based on "mother tongue"; in Guatemala, it is based on self-identification.

Both attendance profiles and schooling attainment vary by gender and ethnicity in these three countries (for graphs for each country, see Duryea

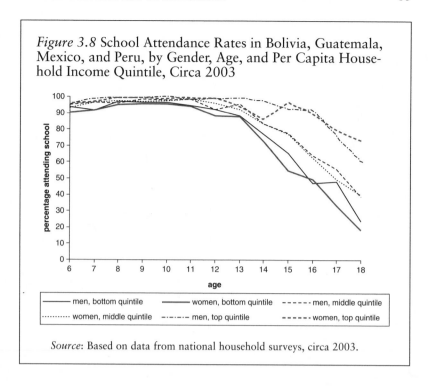

Figure 3.8 School Attendance Rates in Bolivia, Guatemala, Mexico, and Peru, by Gender, Age, and Per Capita Household Income Quintile, Circa 2003

Source: Based on data from national household surveys, circa 2003.

et al. 2007). Attendance rates in Peru exceed 90 percent for children ages 6–13 for all groups. There is quite a bit of noise in the data for ages 14–18, with an unclear pattern in attendance rates for indigenous people. By the age of 19 and 20, it becomes clear that indigenous people attend school at much lower rates than their nonindigenous peers. Nonindigenous women display similar schooling attainment as their male peers. In contrast, indigenous women lag behind their male peers by about two full years of schooling.

In Bolivia and Guatemala, school attendance of indigenous people lags that of nonindigenous people both at early ages and in the teen years. At age 6, indigenous children in Bolivia are 12–15 percentage points less likely to attend school than nonindigenous children. Attendance rates for indigenous girls start to lag those of indigenous boys at age 9, with a more rapid decline after age 13. Patterns in Guatemala are not as clear, with noisier data reflecting a much smaller sample. Nonetheless, the data reveal that indigenous girls do not attend school at the same rates as their nonindigenous peers.

Patterns of school attainment in Bolivia and Guatemala are similar to patterns in Peru. Nonindigenous boys and girls have similar outcomes,

Figure 3.9 Average Years of Educational Attainment in
Bolivia, Guatemala, Mexico, and Peru, by Gender, Age, and
Per Capita Household Income Quintile, Circa 2003

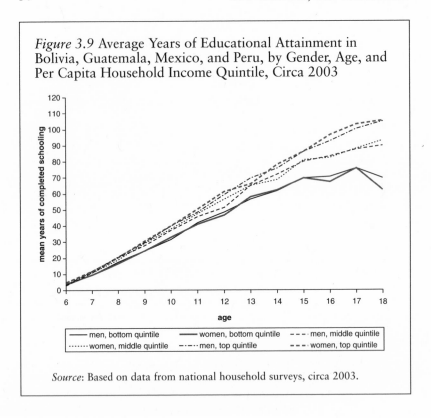

Source: Based on data from national household surveys, circa 2003.

followed by indigenous boys and then indigenous girls. The differences
are greatest after ages 13–15.

Although the three countries share some features in the patterns of
schooling attainment by gender and ethnicity, there is a striking difference in the levels of attainment. At age 15, indigenous girls have achieved
7.1 years of schooling in Peru, 6.1 years in Bolivia, and 4.6 years in
Guatemala.

Analysis of attendance and attainment for younger children reveals
that the largest gender differences in attendance occur among children
in the lowest income quintile. Although higher proportions of boys
than girls attend schools, boys nonetheless display lower attainment.
This result is consistent with the fact that repetition rates are higher
among boys.

Educational attainment of nonindigenous boys is similar to that of nonindigenous girls in Bolivia, Guatemala, and Peru. In contrast, attainment
of indigenous teenage girls lags behind that of indigenous teenage boys.

Notes

1. Monetary labor income generated by children is excluded when computing family income, in order to avoid problems with the causality relationship between income generation and schooling.

2. The number of years completed should not be confused with a measurement of number of years spent in the schooling system. The measure used is net of repetition.

References

Behrman, J., and A. Deolalikar. 1988. "Health and Nutrition." In *Handbook of Development Economics*, vol. 1, ed. H. Chenery and T. N. Srinivasan, 633–90. Amsterdam: North-Holland.

Behrman, R., S. Duryea, and M. Székely. 1999. "Schooling Investments and Macroeconomic Conditions: A Micro-Macro Investigation for Latin America and the Caribbean." Research Department Working Paper 407, Inter-American Development Bank, Washington, DC.

Blau, F. D., L. M. Kahn, and J. Waldfogel, 2000. "Understanding Young Women's Marriage Decisions: The Role of Labor and Marriage Market Conditions." *Industrial and Labor Relations Review* 53 (4): 624–47.

Cochrane, S. 1979. *Fertility and Education: What Do We Really Know?* Baltimore, MD: Johns Hopkins University Press.

Dollar, D., and R. Gatti. 1999. "Gender Inequality, Income, and Growth: Are Good Times Good for Women?" Gender and Development Working Paper Series 1, World Bank, Washington, DC. http://www.worldbank.org/gender/prr.

Duryea, D., S. Galiani, H. Ñopo, and C. Piras, 2007. "The Educational Gender Gap in Latin America and the Caribbean." RES Working Paper 4510, Inter-American Development Bank, Research Department, Washington, DC.

King, E. M., and M. A. Hill, eds. 1993. *Women's Education in Developing Countries*. Washington, DC: World Bank.

King, E. M., J. Peterson, S. M. Adioetomo, L. T. Domingo, and S. H. Syed. 1986. *Change in the Status of Women across Generations in Asia*. Santa Monica, CA: Rand Corporation.

Knodel, J., and G. Jones. 1996. "Does Promoting Girls' Schooling Miss the Mark?" *Population and Development Review* 22 (4): 683–702.

Marshall, J., and V. Calderón. 2005. "Social Exclusion in Education in Latin America and the Caribbean." Discussion draft, Inter-American Development Bank, Sustainable Development Department, Washington DC.

Parker, S., and C. Pederzini. 2000. "Gender Differences in Education in Mexico." World Bank Departmental Working Paper 21023, Washington, DC.

Psacharopoulos, G. 1994. "Returns to Investment in Education: A Global Update." *World Development* 22 (9): 1325–43.

Psacharopoulos, G., and Z. Tzannatos. 1992. "Latin American Women's Earnings and Participation in the Labor Force." Policy Research Working Paper 856, World Bank, Washington, DC.

Saardchom, N., and J. Lemaire. 2005. "Causes of Increasing Age at Marriage: An International Regression Study." *Marriage and Family Review* 3: 73–97.

Schultz, T. P. 1973. "A Preliminary Survey of Economic Analysis of Fertility." *American Economic Review* 63 (2): 77–78.

———. 1988. "Education Investments and Returns." In *Handbook of Development Economics*, vol. 1, ed. H. Chenery and T. N. Srinivasan, 543–630, Amsterdam: North-Holland.

———. 1993. "Economics of Women's Schooling." In *The Politics of Women's Education*, ed. J. K. Conway and S. C. Bourque, 237–44. Ann Arbor: University of Michigan Press.

Strauss, J., and D. Thomas. 1995. "Human Resources: Empirical Modeling of Household and Family Decisions." In *Handbook of Development Economics*, vol. 3A, ed. J. Behrman and T. N. Srinivasan, 1885–946. Amsterdam: Elsevier.

Part II

Gender Earnings Gaps

4

More Schooling, Lower Earnings: Women's Earnings in Latin America and the Caribbean

Gender earnings gaps in Latin America and the Caribbean were smaller than in other regions of the world until the late 1950s. The situation reversed after then (Frankema 2008).

Since the mid-1980s, the region has seen a steady increase in women's labor force participation. By the turn of the 21st century, 58 percent of women actively participated in the labor market.[1] Despite this improvement, in 2007, the World Economic Forum ranked Latin America and the Caribbean the third most unequal region (among nine) in economic participation of and opportunity for women (Hausmann, Tyson, and Zahidi 2007).[2]

This chapter presents nonparametric earnings gap decompositions in order to assess the extent to which observed gender earnings gaps correspond to gaps in individuals' demographic and job-related characteristics.[3] The analysis focuses on labor income earners ages 18–65 from a pooled data set of 18 countries representative of most of the working population in Latin America and the Caribbean; earnings are measured as hourly earnings in the main job.

This chapter was adapted from the following sources: "New Century, Old Disparities: Gender and Ethnic Wage Gaps in Latin America," Juan Pablo Atal, Hugo Ñopo, and Natalia Winder, RES Working Paper 4640, Inter-American Development Bank, 2009; Evolution of Gender Wage Gaps in Latin America at the Turn of the Twentieth Century: An Addendum to 'New Century, Old Disparities,' "Hugo Ñopo and Alejandro Hoyos, IZA Discussion Papers 5086, Institute for the Study of Labor, 2010.

Juan Pablo Atal is a graduate student in economics at the University of California, Berkeley, and Natalia Winder is a consultant at UNICEF, Division of Policy and Practice, New York. Alejandro Hoyos is a consultant at the Poverty Reduction and Economic Management Network (PREM) at the World Bank.

What Does the Literature Show?

The evidence suggests that women's insertion into the labor market has been facilitated by the region's economic growth, trade liberalization, rapid urbanization, and changes in fertility patterns (Psacharopoulos and Tzannatos 1992b; Cox and Roberts 1993). The increase in women's labor participation has been accompanied by a slow but steady rise in relative earnings for nearly two decades, allowing women in most countries to contribute about one-third of household income (Duryea, Edwards, and Ureta 2004). However, in most countries in the region, women are more likely than men to hold low-paid occupations (Márquez and Prada 2007), and gender earnings gaps in the region remain substantial.

Several authors have attempted to explain the sources of gender earnings differentials in the region, exploring issues such as differences in individual characteristics and human capital endowments (Atal, Ñopo, and Winder 2009); regulation (Lim 2002); fertility (Madrigal 2004; Urdinola and Wodon 2006; Cruces and Galiani 2007); and occupational segregation (Deutsch et al. 2004; Tenjo, Ribero, and Bernat 2006), among others.

The literature has also attempted to relate gender earnings gaps to differences in income-generating opportunities in urban and rural areas; however, no clear link can be found (Hertz et al. 2008). In an analysis of 15 countries in the region for which data were available for the late 1980s, Psacharopoulos and Tzannatos (1992a) show that human capital accounts for one-third of the earnings differential, leaving a large portion of the earnings gap unexplained. By the middle of the current decade, most countries in the region had closed the education attainment gender gap (see chapter 3 of this book; Hausmann, Tyson, and Zahidi 2007).

Some empirical research provides insights into the linkages between earnings differentials and differences in the types of jobs men and women hold. A review of 13 countries in the region finds that the gender earnings gap appears to be larger on average in the private sector than in the public sector (Panizza and Qiang 2005).

Researchers have also examined occupational segregation—the overrepresentation or underrepresentation of a group (women, men, youth, ethnic groups) in a specific activity—and its linkage with earnings differentials in the region. Most studies find that, in an effort to manage their housework and childcare responsibilities, women may permanently or temporarily withdraw from the labor market, choose occupations with flexible or fewer working hours (Tenjo, Ribero, and Bernat 2006), or invest less in education or on-the-job training, thereby limiting their work experience (Terrell 1992). As a result, women are concentrated in low-paid jobs and face high steeper barriers when attempting to reach higher-level (better-paid) positions.

These factors explain only part of the earnings gap in the region. In Costa Rica, Ecuador, and Uruguay, high and persistent levels of occupational segregation explain only a small portion of earnings differentials

(Deutsch et al. 2004). A comparative study of Brazil and Mexico shows that despite higher levels of gender occupational segregation in Mexico, gender earnings gaps are wider in Brazil (Salas and Leite 2007).

Women have an important presence in the region's informal sector. Some authors argue that this factor may provide an additional potential explanation for earnings disparities. Plausible explanations include the small impact of education on earnings in the informal sector and the greater importance of experience, where for the most part, men have an advantage over women (Freije 2009). Furthermore, although there may be no real difference in self-employment rates of men and women, there are considerable gender differences in quality, measured not only in terms of average earnings but also in work conditions and income security (Barrientos 2002).

Research has examined the role of regulation, such as maternity laws, gender quotas, and employer child care, as drivers of earnings gaps. Created to protect and provide flexibility for women in certain occupations, labor legislation in areas such as maternity leave and pregnancy protection increase women's nonsalary labor costs and may therefore increase earnings disparities. The empirical evidence in this regard is not clear (Angel-Urdinola and Wodon 2006). Other policies, such as access to affordable childcare and programs to prevent domestic violence, are correlated with increases in both women's labor force participation and earnings (Deutsch et al. 2004). Differentials may also correspond to women's roles in society, which, regardless of their skill levels or potential, leads them to choose low-skilled occupations in low-productive sectors (Contreras and Plaza 2004; Tenjo, Ribero, and Bernat 2006).

A review of the literature in Atal, Ñopo, and Winder (2009) provides a list of the studies on gender and ethnic earnings gaps for almost all Latin American countries. Most of the studies in that review use household surveys to disentangle the causes or components of the earnings gap.

How Do Male and Female Workers Differ?

Circa 2007, on average, men earn 10 percent more than women in the region. Men earn more than women at all ages; at every level of education; in all types of employment (self-employed, employers, and employees); and in both large and small firms. Only in rural areas do women earn on average the same as their male counterparts.

These earnings disparities are reported in the last two columns of table 4.1, where they are computed as multiples of average women's earnings. These disparities may reflect, to some extent, differences in observable individual characteristics.

Working women in the region have more years of schooling than men. They are nevertheless underrepresented in managerial positions

Table 4.1 Demographic and Job Characteristics and Relative Hourly Earnings of Men and Women in Latin America and the Caribbean, Circa 2007

	Composition (percent)		Relative earnings (base: average women's earnings = 100)	
	Men	Women	Men	Women
All	100.0	100.0	110.0	100.0
Personal characteristics				
Age	37.1	36.6		
18–24			79.6	74.9
25–34			106.6	100.9
35–44			122.5	108.7
45–54			127.2	111.3
55–65			113.0	97.8
Education level				
None or primary incomplete	20.9	15.9	73.1	71.1
Primary complete or secondary incomplete	44.5	37.6	95.3	76.0
Secondary complete or tertiary incomplete	29.1	38.0	141.7	118.1
Tertiary complete	5.5	8.5	202.0	178.9
Presence of children (12 years or younger in household)				
No	52.6	44.7	117.0	105.0
Yes	47.4	55.3	102.2	95.9
Presence of other household member with labor income				
No	39.8	23.6	108.8	102.0
Yes	60.2	76.4	110.8	99.4
Urban				
No	26.6	17.5	91.3	92.5
Yes	73.4	82.5	116.8	101.6
Job characteristics				
Type of employment				
Employer	4.9	2.3	195.3	180.1
Self-employed	28.0	26.2	95.9	88.8
Employee	67.1	71.5	109.6	101.5

(continued next page)

Table 4.1 (continued)

	Composition (percent)		Relative earnings (base: average women's earnings = 100)	
	Men	*Women*	*Men*	*Women*
Part time				
No	90.7	75.2	105.0	92.2
Yes	9.3	24.8	158.3	123.6
Formality				
No	56.4	55.9	95.8	86.8
Yes	43.6	44.1	128.4	116.7
Small firm (five workers or less)				
No	47.6	45.8	115.9	113.7
Yes	52.4	54.2	85.3	78.1
Occupation				
Professionals and technicians	9.6	15.1	208.7	182.2
Directors and upper management	3.3	2.7	212.5	176.7
Administrative personnel	5.0	10.5	134.0	107.7
Merchants and sellers	9.2	17.2	106.6	93.3
Service workers	11.8	32.5	93.4	70.9
Agricultural workers and similar	15.6	7.1	63.4	80.4
Nonagricultural blue-collars	32.0	9.4	95.6	70.4
Armed forces	0.8	0.1	105.6	116.2
Occupations not classified above	12.7	5.4	110.5	89.9
Economic sector				
Agriculture, hunting, forestry and fishing	18.1	3.8	59.1	54.0
Mining and quarrying	1.0	0.1	144.3	175.9
Manufacturing	16.7	15.3	115.5	85.4
Electricity, gas, and water supply	0.9	0.2	153.9	165.6

(continued next page)

Table 4.1 (continued)

	Composition (percent)		Relative earnings (base: average women's earnings = 100)	
	Men	Women	Men	Women
Construction	12.1	0.8	97.3	109.3
Wholesale and retail trade, and hotels and restaurants	21.0	27.9	106.6	88.8
Transport, storage	9.0	1.9	115.7	125.0
Financing, insurance, real estate, and business services	3.1	3.1	150.5	149.1
Community, social, and personal services	18.3	46.9	153.9	110.1

Source: Based on data from national household surveys from circa 2007.

and overrepresented in other occupations, such as service workers, merchants, administrative personnel, and professionals. Differences by economic sector are also apparent. Construction and agriculture are sectors dominated by men, whereas community, social, and personal services are dominated by women. Important gender differences are also evident in working hours: almost one-fourth of working women are part-time workers, compared with less than one-tenth of working men.[4]

This section assesses the role of individual differences in earnings gaps. It first provides decompositions of five sets of observable demographic characteristics as control variables. Each set adds a new characteristic to the previous set, in an order that first considers characteristic that are less likely to be endogenous to a model of earnings determination.

The full set of demographic control variables (in the order used in the matching exercise) are age, education, presence of children 12 or younger in the household (dummy), presence of other labor income earner in the household (dummy), and urban area (dummy). Country of residence is an implicit control variable in each specification, as only individuals within the same country are matched.

Table 4.2 shows the gender earnings gaps, the four components of its decomposition (for five different sets of controls), and the percentages of men and women belonging to the common support of observable characteristics (that is, people who were matched). Δ_M (Δ_F) is the portion of the earnings gap attributed to the existence of men (women) with combinations of characteristics that are not met by any women (men). Δ_X is the portion of the earnings gap attributed to differences in the observable characteristics of men and women. Δ_0 is the portion of the earnings

Table 4.2 Decomposition of Gender Earnings Gap in Latin America and the Caribbean after Controlling for Demographic Characteristics, Circa 2007 *(percent)*

	Age	+ Education	+ Presence of children in the household	+ Presence of other household member with labor income	+ Urban
Δ	10.0	10.0	10.0	10.0	10.0
Δ_0	8.9	17.2	17.4	17.9	18.8
Δ_M	0.0	0.1	0.2	0.2	−0.3
Δ_F	0.0	−0.0	−0.1	−0.4	−0.6
Δ_X	1.1	−7.2	−7.5	−7.8	−7.9
Percentage of men in common support	100.0	99.8	99.3	97.7	94.7
Percentage of women in common support	100.0	99.9	99.8	99.1	97.9

Source: Based on data from national household surveys from circa 2007.

Note: Δ_M (Δ_F) is the part of the earnings gap attributed to the existence of men (women) with combinations of characteristics that are not met by any women (men). Δ_X is the part of the earnings gap attributed to differences in the observable characteristics of men and women over the "common support." Δ_0 is the part of the earnings gap that cannot be attributed to differences in characteristics of the individuals. It is typically attributed to a combination of both unobservable characteristics and discrimination. The sum of these components equals the total earnings gap ($\Delta_M + \Delta_F + \Delta_X + \Delta_0 = \Delta$).

gap attributed to differences between men and women that cannot be explained by observable characteristics. The sum of Δ_X, Δ_M, Δ_F, and Δ_0 is equal to the total earnings gap (Δ).

More prime-age workers are men and, on average, male workers are older than female workers (probably because women retire earlier). However, after controlling only for age, most of the gender earnings gap remains unexplained (that is, most of Δ is captured by Δ_0): only 1 percentage point of the 10 percentage points in the gender earnings gap can be explained by the differences in age distributions between men and women in the labor market.

After controlling for education, the unexplained component of the gender earnings gap is larger than the original gap: if men and women had the same distribution of age and education in the labor market, the gender gap would increase from 10 percent to 17 percent of average women's earnings. This increase reflects higher educational achievement among women workers than among men, as shown in table 4.1. The unexplained component of the earnings gap is larger than the original gap after controlling for each subsequent set of controls, remaining almost constant after the addition of each characteristic.

The last two rows of table 4.2 show the percentages of matched men and women for each set of characteristics. These percentages are large even when controlling for the set of five characteristics, suggesting that the inclusion of more matching characteristics does not limit the explanatory capacity of the exercise. Differences in the "common support" do not play a major role in explaining the earnings gap, as confirmed by the small magnitude of both Δ_M and Δ_F.

Job characteristics can now be added. The new variables considered are type of employment (self-employed, employer, or employee); part-time work (a dummy equal to 1 for people working 35 hours or less a week); formality status (a dummy equal to 1 for people covered by social security obtained from their labor relationship); economic sector (nine categories of the International Standard Industrial Classification [ISIC] revision 2 at the one-digit level); occupation (nine categories of a slight modification of the International Standard Classification of Occupations [ISCO] system at the one-digit level); and small firm (dummy equal to 1 if firm has fewer than six workers).[5]

Because there was no strong a priori belief regarding which variable is "least endogenous" and some of the variables were strongly correlated, the variables were included in a way that differs from the previous analysis. The six job characteristics were added separately to the basic set of five sociodemographic matching variables reported in the last column of table 4.2. Including the variables in this way prevents conclusions from being drawn that are likely to depend on the order in which each variable is included. For ease of comparison, the first column of table 4.3 reproduces the last column of table 4.2.

Table 4.3 Decomposition of Gender Earnings Gap in Latin America and the Caribbean after Controlling for Demographic and Job Characteristics, Circa 2007 (percent)

	Demographic set	& Type of employment	& Part time	& Formality	& Sector	& Occupation	& Small firm	Full set
Δ	10.0	10.0	10.0	10.0	10.0	10.0	10.0	10.0
Δ_0	18.8	17.2	27.3	18.0	23.6	16.8	18.8	19.5
Δ_M	-0.3	1.1	-0.3	-0.1	-5.0	-0.8	-0.2	-2.0
Δ_F	-0.6	-1.2	-2.0	-1.0	-0.3	-1.1	-0.9	-2.9
Δ_X	-7.9	-7.1	-15.0	-6.8	-8.2	-4.9	-7.8	-4.5
Percentage of men in common support	94.7	87.3	91.3	90.8	64.3	73.0	90.8	27.3
Percentage of women in common support	97.9	95.1	93.5	96.4	88.0	86.8	96.3	44.7

Source: Based on data from national household surveys from circa 2007.

Note: Δ_M (Δ_F) is the part of the earnings gap attributed to the existence of men (women) with combinations of characteristics that are not met by any women (men). Δ_X is the part of the earnings gap attributed to differences in the observable characteristics of men and women over the "common support." Δ_0 is the part of the earnings gap that cannot be attributed to differences in characteristics of the individuals. It is typically attributed to a combination of both unobservable characteristics and discrimination. The sum of these components equals the total earnings gap ($\Delta_M + \Delta_F + \Delta_X + \Delta_0 = \Delta$).

As shown in table 4.3, none of the job characteristics is able to offset the increase in the unexplained gender earnings gap after controlling for education. The unexplained component of the gap is considerably larger than the original gap after the addition of every job characteristic independently (and also when they are added together). The unexplained gap widens substantially after controlling for economic sector, suggesting that gender segregation in economic sectors is not by itself the source of earnings differentials. The widening of the gap is driven mainly by the over-representation of men in agriculture, the sector with the lowest average earnings. The unexplained gap also widens substantially after controlling for part-time work, as women are overrepresented in part-time jobs, which have an hourly earnings premium over full-time jobs.

The four other job-related characteristics (type of employment, formality, occupation, and small firm size) reduce the unexplained component of earnings gaps after controlling for the five demographic characteristics, but only slightly. These findings challenge the popular belief that occupational segregation contributes to gender earnings gaps, reinforcing previous evidence on this issue (Barrientos 2002).

The last column of table 4.3, which shows the decomposition exercise after controlling for the full set of observable characteristics, suggests that the unexplained gender earnings gap in the region reaches 20 percent of average women's earnings. Indeed, the portion explained by gender differences in individual characteristics over the common support (Δ_x) is about −5 percent. Differences in the distribution of characteristics of men and women thus favor women because they share characteristics, such as higher educational levels, that are better rewarded in the labor market. Even though the common support is reduced after controlling for the full set of variables, the portion of the gap attributable to the uncommon support is small (in contrast to the results on ethnic earnings differences, presented in other chapters), indicating that barriers to access are not the most important factor explaining gender earnings gaps.

A country-by-country exploration of the gender earnings gap decompositions, reported in table 4.4, provides evidence of cross-country heterogeneity behind the averages reported in table 4.2. The table provides measures of the original gap and the unexplained component after controlling for three sets of controls: first, age and education; second, the whole set of demographic matching variables; and third, the whole set of demographic and job-related matching variables.

In 7 of the 18 countries examined, the original gender earnings gaps reported in table 4.4 are negative, reflecting higher average earnings for women than men. These results do not stand when comparing men and women with the same observable characteristics.

In the first specification, Δ_0 is statistically equal to zero in Bolivia and Guatemala and 29.7 percent in Brazil. The influence of controlling by education varies significantly from country to country. Whereas in Peru

Table 4.4 Original and Unexplained Components of Gender Earnings Gap in Latin America and the Caribbean by Country, Circa 2007 (*percent*)

Country	Δ	Age and education	+ Presence of children in the household, presence of other income earner in the household, and urban	+ Part-time, formality, occupation, economic sector, type of employment, and small firm
			Δ_0	
Argentina	0.5	14.2***	12.6***	10.8***
Bolivia	−5.5	−1.8	3.0	17.8
Brazil	20.5	29.7***	31.4***	26.4***
Chile	10.9	19.3***	18.6***	13.1***
Colombia	−0.9	7.1***	6.3***	7.3***
Costa Rica	−5.8	13.7***	13.6***	17.9***
Dominican Republic	−3.1	16.6***	17.3***	23.9***
Ecuador	−3.2	16.4***	13.6***	5.6
El Salvador	3.3	11.9***	16.0***	11.3***
Guatemala	−3.3	0.3	−0.7	17.7***
Honduras	5.6	16.3***	16.3***	24.2***
Mexico	2.6	7.8***	10.5***	15.3***
Nicaragua	1.5	20.3***	19.3***	28.4***
Panama	−8.6	13.6***	16.2***	10.4**
Peru	18.3	19.4***	25.9***	23.5***
Paraguay	6.2	16.0***	13.8***	6.9
Uruguay	5.7	26.3***	27.5***	23.4***
Venezuela, RB	0.4	13.9***	13.8***	12.3***
Latin America and the Caribbean	**10.0**	**17.2**	**18.8**	**19.5**

Source: Based on data from national household surveys from circa 2007.

Note: $**p < 0.05$, $***p < 0.01$. Δ is the total earnings gap. Δ_0 is the part of the gap attributed to differences between men and women that cannot be explained by observable characteristics.

the unexplained component of the gap is almost equal to the original gap, reflecting small educational differences by gender, in Argentina the unexplained component is almost 30 times the original gap. Gender differences in educational attainment for both countries are large, especially at the extremes of the distributions. At the lower extreme of educational distributions, the proportion of workers without education in Argentina is almost zero for both men and women; in Peru, the situation is unfavorable for women, as 7 percent of female workers but only 2 percent of male workers have no education. Among people with tertiary education, in Argentina, the educational gaps are wider: 40 percent of women and 25 percent of men have tertiary education. In Peru, 29 percent of women and 24 percent of men have tertiary education.

Figure 4.1 presents the four components of the earnings gap by country (sorted by the magnitude of the unexplained component) for the specification with the full set of control variables. Beyond the heterogeneity in the magnitudes of every component, interesting qualitative patterns arise. The portion of the gap attributable to differences in distributions of observable characteristics over the common support (Δ_X) is negative in every country, indicating that in every country in the region, women have combinations of characteristics (especially educational attainment) that are expected to yield higher labor market returns for them than for men.

Women's lower access to well-paid jobs or combinations of observable characteristics explain a substantial part of the earnings gap in Bolivia, Guatemala, Nicaragua, and Paraguay. At the other extreme, women's confinement to lower-paid segments of the labor market is prevalent in Argentina, Colombia, Costa Rica, Ecuador, El Salvador, Panama, and Peru. In the first group of countries, the evidence suggests that the problem of gender earnings gaps is linked to barriers in access to high-paying occupations (the "chief executive officer [CEO] effect"); in the second group of countries, earnings gaps seem to be linked to women's confinement to low-paying segments of the labor market (the "maid effect").

An advantage of the matching approach over traditional decomposition is that it is informative not only about the average unexplained gap but also about its distribution. Further evidence of the heterogeneity of the decomposition results appears when the unexplained component of the earnings gaps (after controlling for all demographic and job-related characteristics) is reported for different segments of the labor market (figure 4.2). Richer information about the nature of the unexplained gender earnings gaps emerges that can explain the problem and provide policy advice on how to address it.

The observations that emerge from the distribution of unexplained gender pay differentials include the following:

- *The unexplained gender earnings gap increases with age.* Although one possible (and optimistic) interpretation of this result is that

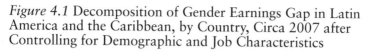

Figure 4.1 Decomposition of Gender Earnings Gap in Latin America and the Caribbean, by Country, Circa 2007 after Controlling for Demographic and Job Characteristics

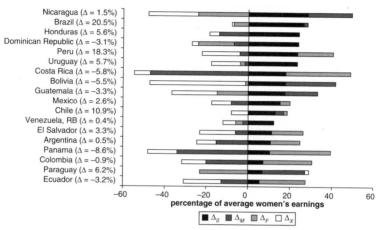

Source: Based on data from national household surveys from circa 2007.

Note: Δ_M (Δ_F) is the part of the earnings gap attributed to the existence of men (women) with combinations of characteristics that are not met by any women (men). Δ_X is the part of the earnings gap attributed to differences in the observable characteristics of men and women over the "common support." Δ_0 is the part of the earnings gap that cannot be attributed to differences in characteristics of the individuals. It is typically attributed to a combination of both unobservable characteristics and discrimination. The sum of these components equals the total earnings gap ($\Delta_M + \Delta_F + \Delta_X + \Delta_0 = \Delta$).

earnings gaps are narrowing over time, such an assertion must be made with caution, as this finding could also be driven by unobservable characteristics correlated with age. For instance, this result may reflect gender differences in labor experience, which could be exacerbated over time as women bear and raise children. Indeed, the unexplained component of the gender gap is slightly larger (although not statistically significant so) among workers with children.

• *The unexplained gender earnings gap is smaller among people with tertiary education.* One possible explanation is that more educated women fill positions in firms in which there is less room for discretionary earnings setting or other discriminatory behavior. This hypothesis is supported by the fact that the unexplained earnings gap

Figure 4.2 Confidence Intervals for Unexplained Gender
Earnings Gap in Latin America and the Caribbean, after
Controlling for Demographic and Job Characteristics,
Circa 2007
percentage of average women's earnings

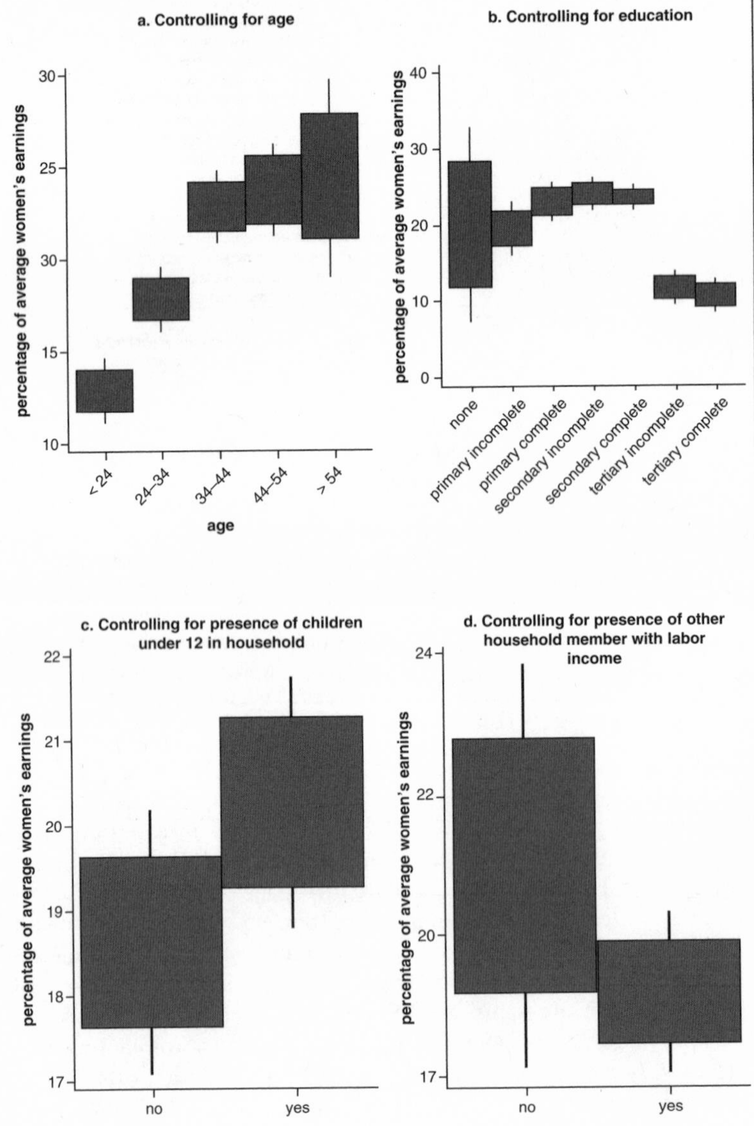

a. Controlling for age

b. Controlling for education

c. Controlling for presence of children
under 12 in household

d. Controlling for presence of other
household member with labor
income

(continued next page)

Figure 4.2 (continued)

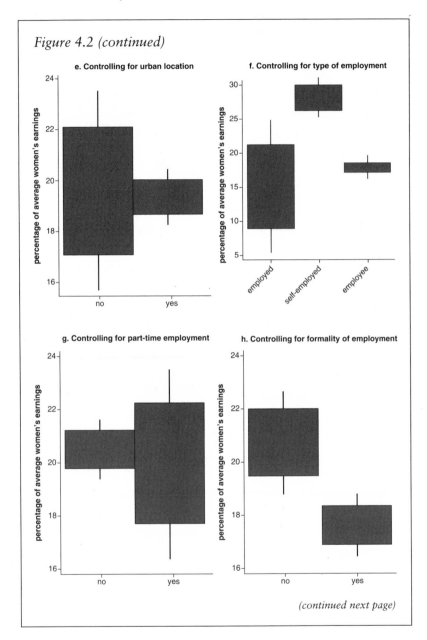

(continued next page)

Figure 4.2 (continued)

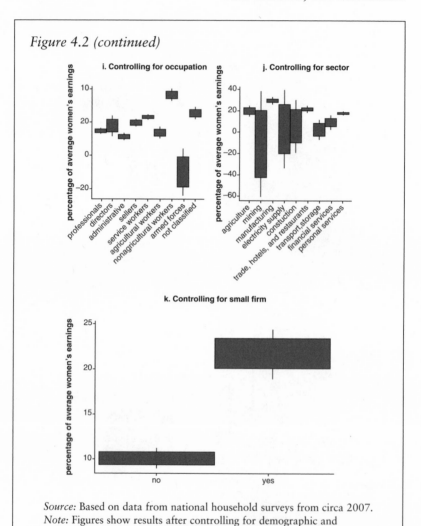

Source: Based on data from national household surveys from circa 2007.
Note: Figures show results after controlling for demographic and
job-related characteristics. Boxes show 90 percent confidence intervals for
unexplained earnings; whiskers show 99 percent confidence intervals.

is also smaller among formal workers and very high in small firms
(where there are fewer highly educated workers).
• *The unexplained gender earnings gap is larger among informal
workers and at small firms.* These findings reinforce the idea that
better-educated women are able to find niches within the labor market where there is less room for discriminatory behavior, whereas

women with lower education are confined to segments in which there is more room for discretionary earnings setting.

- *The unexplained gender earnings gap is larger among the self-employed.* This finding challenges the view that claims that gender earnings gaps reflect discrimination by employers. It does leave room for customer discrimination. Linked to this result, the unexplained gender earnings gap is also highly dispersed across employers, reflecting possible heterogeneities in entrepreneurial abilities and success.

- *The unexplained gender earnings gap is negative in the mining sector and the armed forces.* These professions and sectors are dominated by men: 0.77 percent of men but just 0.08 percent of women are employed in the armed forces, and 0.95 percent of men and just 0.14 percent of women work in mining. The few women who obtain a job in these environments dominated by men enjoy a considerable premium, however, on average earning more than their male counterparts. Presumably, selection plays an important role or the jobs women perform in these sectors differ substantially from the jobs men perform.

Figure 4.3 shows the magnitude of unexplained earnings gaps along percentiles of the earnings distribution. The earnings gap between the representative man and woman is calculated at each percentile of the distributions of earnings using the matched samples. Earnings differences are thus the differences that remain unexplained after controlling for observable characteristics.

The results depicted in figure 4.3 show larger unexplained earnings gaps at the lower end of the earnings distribution, followed by a sharp decrease after the 6th percentile, a somewhat flat or slightly increasing pattern in the middle, and a negative slope in the upper tail of the distribution (after the 80th percentile). The introduction of education as a matching variable increases the unexplained gender earnings gap, but it does not so do homogeneously along the distribution. The introduction of the presence of children and other income earners in the household leaves almost unchanged the magnitude of the unexplained gender earnings gaps for percentiles 40 and above but increases the magnitude by almost 10 percentage points for the lower percentiles (5–15).

One job characteristic—part-time work—is particularly important to highlight, because, as in the case of education, its inclusion increases the unexplained gender earnings gap. The increase is not homogenous—in fact, it is negligible until the 25th percentile of the earnings distribution, at which point it starts increasing. The inclusion of the part-time job variable causes an increase of 15 percentage points in the unexplained gap for the top 20 percentiles of the earnings distribution. The introduction of each of

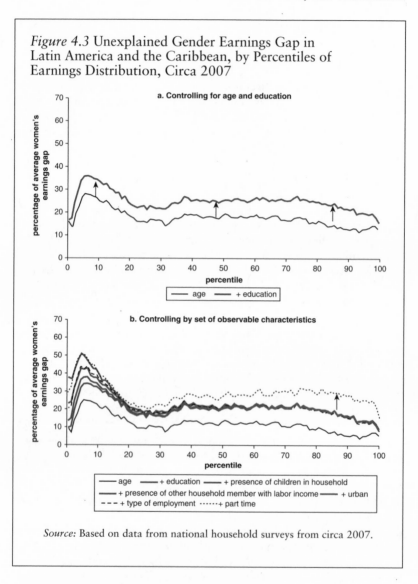

Figure 4.3 Unexplained Gender Earnings Gap in Latin America and the Caribbean, by Percentiles of Earnings Distribution, Circa 2007

a. Controlling for age and education

b. Controlling by set of observable characteristics

Source: Based on data from national household surveys from circa 2007.

the other labor characteristics reduces the unexplained component of the gap from the level it reaches when adding the part-time job variable.

When the complete set of job-related characteristics is included, the unexplained component of the gender gap increases among the lowest-earning individuals (percentiles 1–5), decreases among lower-earning individuals (percentiles 6–35), and increases for workers at the upper end of the distribution (percentiles 65 and above). This finding suggests important differences in the ways gender segmentation occurs in the labor market and the impacts of gender segmentation on labor earnings.

Linkages between Unexplained Gender Earnings Gaps and Macroeconomic, Social, and Governance Indicators

The gender earnings gaps that remain after controlling for differences in observable characteristics between men and women may reflect macroeconomic conditions. Economies may be shaped such that economic sectors that favor men are more developed than others, or the extent to which economies are open for trade with the rest of the world may favor the development of certain occupations that are dominated by men or by women.

Along similar lines, it can be argued that the way in which social investments are determined (in health and education, for instance) imposes certain conditions that favor the possibilities for high performance in the labor market differently for men and women. It could also be that the level of interpersonal trust and individuals' satisfaction with the performance of (political and market) institutions are linked to egalitarian attitudes and actions that operate in the labor market.

This section explores the possible linkages between these aggregate conditions and the unexplained gender earnings gaps from a cross-country perspective. It groups the aggregate variables considered for this exercise into four categories:

- macroeconomics and fundamentals (growth, gross domestic product [GDP] per capita, foreign investment, expenditure per capita, and so forth)
- sociodemographics and social spending (adolescent birth rate, life expectancy at birth, marital status, public spending on education, and so forth)
- employment (women's labor force participation, participation of women in industry, vulnerable employment on women, hiring and firing practices, and so forth)
- governance (interpersonal trust, satisfaction with local services, satisfaction with the market economy, percentage of female legislators, and so forth).

These variables were collected from the following sources: United Nations Children's Fund (UNICEF); the World Bank's World Development Indicators, Millennium Development Goals, Gender Statistics, and Health Nutrition Population Statistics; the Latin American Public Opinion Project's Americas Barometer; the Fraser Institute's Economic Freedom of the World; the World Economic Forum's Global Competitiveness Report; the Bertelsmann Foundation; and Latinobarómetro. From these data sources, only data that were available for at least 15 countries during the relevant period of analysis (circa 2007) were selected. Table 4.5 shows the variables, the years for which they were available, the number of countries for which data were available, the correlation coefficient between the variables and the unexplained gender earnings gap, and the data source.

Only a few variables show a statistically significant correlation with the unexplained gender earnings gaps: employee, industry, female (percent of women's employment); female legislators, senior officials, and managers (percent of total); and labor market liberalization index. The variables for which there is a significant correlation with the unexplained gender earnings gap are plotted in figures 4.4–4.6

Figure 4.4 reports the positive relationship between the earnings gap and the percentage of women employed in industry—a sector clearly dominated by men (there are 12 times more men than women in construction and 6 times more men than women in agriculture, for instance). The figure shows that 15 percent of employees in industry in Latin America and the Caribbean are women. Peru is an outlier (40 percent of employed women work in industry); for this reason, figure 4.4 includes two fitted lines, one including Peru and one without it. This figure suggests that economies with greater participation of women in sectors dominated by men have larger gender earnings disparities. This apparently paradoxical result is explored further in chapter 6, on Mexico, where, based on econometrics and a simple theoretical model linking segregation and earnings gaps, the result is substantiated. The finding raises some warnings about the apparent benefits of reducing occupational segregation.

The second statistically significant relationship among the variables explored also seems to be paradoxical. Figure 4.5 shows a positive relationship between the percentage of female legislators, senior officials, and managers and the size of the gender earnings gap. Countries in which women's visibility at top positions is higher tend to have larger unexplained gender earnings gaps in the aggregate. The same positive correlation holds for the subsample of highly educated people, although the correlation is no longer statistical significant (this result is not reported but available upon request). In countries in which women hold top positions, their status seems to be coming at the price of lower earnings. Women are thus breaking some "glass doors" (to get into selected high-profile positions) but still facing some "glass ceilings" (in the sense that they are not remunerated accordingly).

This result is similar to another finding reported in this book regarding women' entrance into flexible segments of the labor market at the price of lower earnings. Examining the same variables for European countries (not reported but available upon request to the author of this book) shows no

Table 4.5 Correlation between Gender Earnings Gap and Economic Indicators in Latin America and the Caribbean, Circa 2007

Variable	Years	Number of countries	Correlation coefficient	Source
Macroeconomics and fundamentals				
Domestic credit provided by banking sector (percentage of GDP)	2003–07	18	0.3	World Development Indicators
Exports of goods and services (constant 2000 U.S. dollars)	2003–07	18	0.1	World Development Indicators
Foreign direct investment, net inflows (percentage of GDP)	2003–07	18	0.2	World Development Indicators
GDP per capita growth (annual percentage)	2003–07	18	0.0	World Development Indicators
GDP per capita, (purchasing power parity) (constant 2005 international $)	2003–07	18	−0.2	World Development Indicators
Imports of goods and services (constant 2000 U.S. dollars)	2003–07	18	0.1	World Development Indicators
Industry, value added (percentage of GDP)	2003–07	18	−0.1	World Development Indicators
Sociodemographics and social spending				
Adolescent birth rate, number of births per 1,000 girls 15–19 years old	2000–08	18	0.1	UNICEF
Adolescent fertility rate (births per 1,000 women 15–19) years old	2003–07	18	0.2	Health, nutrition, and population statistics
Household final consumption expenditure per capita (constant 2000 U.S. dollars)	2003–07	18	−0.1	World Development Indicators

(continued next page)

Table 4.5 (continued)

Variable	Years	Number of countries	Correlation coefficient	Source
Fertility rate, total (births per woman)	2003–07	18	0.1	Health, nutrition, and population statistics
Life expectancy at birth, female (years)	2003–07	18	−0.2	Health, nutrition, and population statistics
Life expectancy at birth, male (years)	2003–07	18	−0.1	Health, nutrition, and population statistics
Population growth (annual percentage)	2003–07	18	−0.1	Health, nutrition, and population statistics
Public spending on education, total (percentage of government expenditure)	1983–87	18	−0.4	World Development Indicators
Survival to age 65, female (percentage of cohort)	2003–07	18	−0.3	Health, nutrition, and population statistics
Survival to age 65, male (percentage of cohort)	2003–07	18	−0.2	Health, nutrition, and population statistics
Employment				
Employees, agriculture, female (percentage of female employment)	2003–07	17	0.1	Gender statistics

Variable	Years	Number of countries	Correlation coefficient	Source
Employees, agriculture, male (percentage of male employment)	2003–07	17	0.3	Gender statistics
Employees, industry, female (percentage of female employment)	2003–07	17	0.5*	Gender statistics
Employees, industry, male (percentage of male employment)	2003–07	17	0.1	Gender statistics
Employees, services, female (percentage of female employment)	2003–07	17	-0.4	Gender statistics
Employees, services, male (percentage of male employment)	2003–07	17	-0.4	Gender statistics
Employment to population ratio, 15+, female (percentage)	2003–07	18	-0.2	Millenium Development Goals
Employment to population ratio, 15+, male (percentage)	2003–07	18	0.2	Millenium Development Goals
Flexibility of earnings determination	2009–10	18	-0.1	Global Competitiveness Report
Hiring and firing practices	2009–10	18	0.2	Global Competitiveness Report
Labor force participation rate, female (percentage of female population 15-64)	2003–07	18	0.2	Gender statistics
Labor force participation rate, male (percentage of male population 15-64)	2003–07	18	0.2	Gender statistics
Labor market liberalization index	2007	18	0.4*	Economic Freedom of the World

(continued next page)

Table 4.5 *(continued)*

Variable	Years	Number of countries	Correlation coefficient	Source
Governance				
Interpersonal trust	2008–09	18	-0.1	Americas Barometer
Satisfaction with local services	2008–09	18	-0.2	Americas Barometer
Trust in political parties	2008–09	18	0.2	Americas Barometer
Female legislators, senior officials, and managers (percentage of total)	2003–07	16	0.4*	World Development Indicators
Political transformation (Bertelsmann transformation index)	2008	18	0.2	Bertelsmann Foundation
Proportion of seats held by women in national parliaments (percent)	2003–07	18	0.1	World Development Indicators
Public institutions index	2009–10	18	0.1	Global Competitiveness Report
Satisfaction with democracy	2009	18	0.1	Latinobarómetro
Satisfaction with market economy	2009	18	0.1	Latinobarómetro
Strength of legal rights index (0 = weak to 10 = strong)	2003–07	17	0.1	World Development Indicators

Sources: UNICEF; World Bank's World Development Indicators, Millennium Development Goals, gender statistics, and health, nutrition, and population statistics; Latin American Public Opinion Project's Americas Barometer; Fraser Institute's Economic Freedom of the World; World Economic Forum's Global Competitiveness Report; Bertelsmann Foundation; Latinobarómetro; and calculations based on Inter–American Development Bank's harmonized household surveys from circa 2007.

Note: * $p < 0.10$.

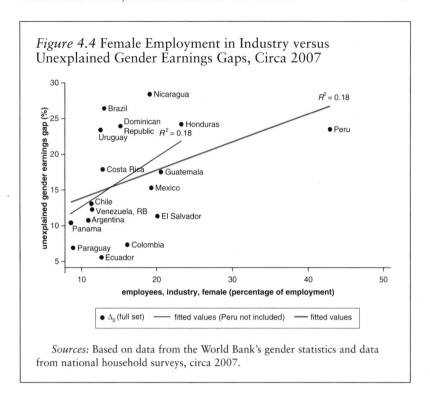

Figure 4.4 Female Employment in Industry versus Unexplained Gender Earnings Gaps, Circa 2007

Sources: Based on data from the World Bank's gender statistics and data from national household surveys, circa 2007.

correlation between women's participation in top positions and the gender earnings gap.

The third positive correlation is between labor market liberalization and the unexplained gender earnings gap (Figure 4.6). Countries in which workers have less job security, allowing more room for earnings negotiation, tend to have larger gender earnings disparities. This correlation may be linked to the tendency of women to be less willing to negotiate, in labor markets and out of them (Babcock and Laschever 2003).

These findings are merely correlations; there is no attempt to attribute causality. Nonetheless, it is noteworthy that among more than 100 aggregate variables explored, only three showed statistically significant correlations with the unexplained gender earnings gap (and two of them showed apparently paradoxical results, although one of the apparent paradoxes is disentangled in chapter 6). This finding may suggest that the problem of gender earnings disparities is microeconomic rather than macroeconomic, probably linked more closely to the persistence of cultural biases in favor of men's role in society and women's lack of empowerment and less linked to GDP growth or the trade balance. The reasons behind the correlations,

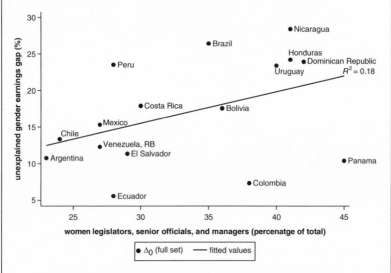

Figure 4.5 Female Legislators, Senior Officials, and Managers versus Unexplained Gender Earnings Gaps, Circa 2007

Sources: Based on data from the World Bank's World Development Indicators and data from national household surveys, circa 2007.

Note: Legislators, senior officials, and managers corresponds to the ISCO-88, major group 1: legislators and senior officials (government), corporate managers, and general managers (private sector).

however, are not entirely known. More research is needed to investigate these linkages.

How Did Differences between Male and Female Workers Change between Circa 1992 and Circa 2007?

The figures presented up to this point describe gender earnings disparities at a point in time, circa 2007. Do the results for circa 2007 represent a change since circa 1992?

The rest of this chapter analyzes the evolution of gender earnings gaps in the same 18 countries between 1992 and 2007. It compares two data points, without making inferences about trajectories of the variables under analysis during the period. Metaphorically, this section compares two

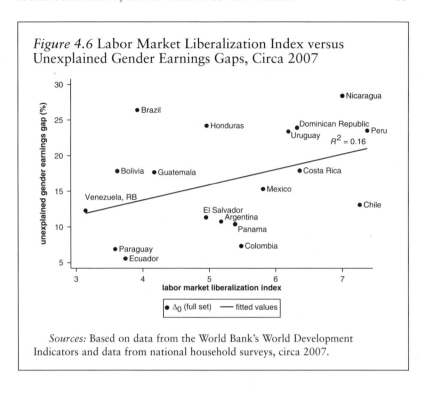

Figure 4.6 Labor Market Liberalization Index versus Unexplained Gender Earnings Gaps, Circa 2007

Sources: Based on data from the World Bank's World Development Indicators and data from national household surveys, circa 2007.

photographs; it does not show the film of what happened between them. The approach is the same as that described in chapter 2.

The Evolution of the Earnings Gap at the Turn of the 20th Century

Table 4.6 shows relative labor earnings for men and women in circa 1992 and 2007. Earnings are normalized so that average women's earnings are equal to 100 for both years. Average men's earnings can be read directly as the gender earnings gap, which declined from 16.3 to 8.9 percent of average women's earnings between 1992 and 2007.

Earning patterns are remarkably similar across years. Working youth show the lowest earnings; as individuals age, earnings rise up to a mature age, at which point they drop slightly. There is also a clear pattern of earnings progression along the educational ladder. The presence of children (in this analysis: six years old and younger) in the household is linked to lower labor earnings; the presence of other labor income earners at home seems to be linked to no significant earnings differences. For both women

Table 4.6 Relative Hourly Earnings for Men and Women in Latin America and the Caribbean by Demographic and Job Characteristics, Circa 1992 and 2007

	Circa 1992 (base: average women's earnings = 100)		*Circa 2007* (base: average women's earnings = 100)	
	Men	*Women*	*Men*	*Women*
All	116.3	100.0	108.8	100.0
Personal characteristics				
Age				
15–24	78.4	72.6	71.1	69.1
25–34	121.0	110.5	106.0	101.0
35–44	139.2	115.9	121.0	109.2
45–54	134.4	105.9	132.5	114.1
55–64	113.4	86.6	119.0	104.7
Education level				
None	62.0	52.6	55.8	52.3
Incomplete primary	90.7	65.1	74.0	61.2
Primary complete	104.8	80.6	84.1	67.3
Secondary incomplete	106.4	83.6	87.9	73.0
Secondary complete	148.0	124.2	116.2	90.7
Tertiary incomplete	193.8	157.4	156.7	132.2
Tertiary complete	271.6	214.9	242.6	203.6
Presence of children (6 years or younger in the household)				
No	119.4	102.3	110.9	101.5
Yes	100.2	82.6	87.0	79.2
Presence of other household member with labor income				
No	124.4	107.8	109.8	103.9
Yes	111.1	98.1	108.3	98.9
Urban				
No	78.4	66.1	71.7	69.2
Yes	130.4	107.2	117.0	103.8

(continued next page)

Table 4.6 (continued)

	Circa 1992 (base: average women's earnings = 100)		Circa 2007 (base: average women's earnings = 100)	
	Men	Women	Men	Women
Job characteristics				
Type of employment				
Employer	197.8	181.9	195.9	187.9
Employee	113.6	103.7	107.4	102.4
Self-employed	104.5	83.1	92.2	81.5
Time worked				
Part time	148.3	121.1	130.4	114.9
Full time	120.8	102.3	111.3	101.2
Over time	97.0	61.1	93.5	69.7

Source: Based on data from national household surveys from circa 1992 and circa 2007.

and men, hourly labor earnings are significantly higher in urban areas, for both employers and part-time workers.

Not all observable characteristics used in the analysis for circa 2007 alone can be used here, because some of them are not available for some countries in their surveys circa 1992. This is particularly the case for some variables related to individuals' jobs. Nonetheless, most of the variables are available and comparable. Table 4.7 shows the distribution of observable individual and job characteristics for men and women for each period.

These descriptive statistics show demographic changes among the working population. In both periods, the percentages of men 55–64 years are higher than the percentage of women, although there was an increase for both women and men. Workers are staying in the labor market longer, but gender differences in retirement age remain.

The gender gap in educational attainment widened during this 15-year span. In circa 1992, 16 percent of women and just 11 percent of men had (complete or incomplete) tertiary levels of education. By circa 2007, the percentages had increased for both, but the increase was greater for women: 26 percent of women and 17 percent of men had attained at least some tertiary education.

Another characteristic that changed during this period is fertility. The percentages of women and men who live with children at home fell by almost half. By circa 2007, only about 7 percent of the working population had a child six or under at home.

Table 4.7 Demographic and Job Characteristics of
Men and Women in Latin America and the Caribbean,
Circa 1992 and 2007
(*percent*)

	Circa 1992		Circa 2007	
	Men	*Women*	*Men*	*Women*
Personal characteristics				
Age				
15–24	24.1	26.0	20.1	18.7
25–34	29.5	30.4	27.3	28.1
35–44	23.7	24.7	24.4	26.4
45–54	14.5	13.2	18.5	19.0
55–64	8.2	5.8	9.8	7.9
Education				
None	8.0	7.7	4.1	3.4
Incomplete primary	37.3	31.1	24.7	18.7
Primary complete	14.4	12.1	14.4	12.1
Secondary incomplete	16.6	15.0	20.0	17.3
Secondary complete	13.1	17.8	19.6	22.6
Tertiary incomplete	4.5	6.6	7.1	10.4
Tertiary complete	6.2	9.8	10.2	15.7
Presence of children (6 years or younger in the household)				
No	84.1	88.6	91.2	93.2
Yes	16.0	11.4	8.9	6.8
Presence of other household member with labor income				
No	39.4	19.6	34.6	21.3
Yes	60.6	80.4	65.5	78.8
Urban				
No	27.1	17.6	18.1	11.1
Yes	72.9	82.5	81.9	88.9
Job characteristics				
Type of employment				
Employer	6.0	2.2	5.6	2.9
Employee	68.38	71.90	70.65	73.80

(*continued next page*)

Table 4.7 (continued)

	Circa 1992		Circa 2007	
	Men	*Women*	*Men*	*Women*
Self-employed	25.61	25.94	23.71	23.32
Time worked				
Part time	11.29	31.41	13.54	32.20
Full time	56.89	48.60	57.78	50.08
Over time	31.83	19.98	28.68	17.71

Source: Based on data from national household surveys from circa 1992 and circa 2007.

Another demographic change is marital and cohabitation arrangements. The percentage of men who live with another labor income earner at home increased 5 percentage points between circa 1992 and 2007, and the percentage of women dropped 2 percentage points. Both demographic changes are symptomatic of a process of changes in household and gender dynamics that societies (and labor markets) in the region have been experiencing.

The data also show that the region continued to urbanize. The percentages of urban workers increased about 8 percentage points during this 15-year span. During this period, there was also a slight decrease in self-employment and overtime work and a slight increase in part-time work for both women and men.[6]

Table 4.8 shows the decomposition exercise for the two periods for various sets of observable characteristics: the overall earnings gap dropped from 16.3 percent of average women's earnings to 8.9 percent during this 15-year span. The components of the gender earnings gap attributable to the segregation of men or women to certain segments of the labor market in which there are no peers of the opposite sex is almost zero: Δ_M and Δ_F are different from zero with statistical significance (at the 99 percent level) only when all controls are included in period 1 (circa 1992). In some other circumstances, Δ_M is statistically significant; in even fewer circumstances, Δ_F is statistically different from zero. In addition, the measure of the common supports increases for both men and women in period 2 (circa 2007). Although this change is probably linked to the larger sample sizes in period 2, it may also be indicative of a reduction in gender differences in observable characteristics.

The results suggest progress in reducing the access barriers of women and men to all segments of the labor market. More still needs to be done to reduce remaining gender pay differentials, however.

Unexplained gender earnings gaps increased between circa 1992 and 2007, particularly after adding education (which increases the unexplained

Table 4.8 Decomposition of Gender Earnings Gap in Latin America and the Caribbean after Controlling for Demographic and Job Characteristics, Circa 1992 and 2007 (percent)

	Age	+ Education	+ Presence of children in the household	+ Presence of other household member with labor income	+ Urban	+ Type of employment	+ Time worked
Period							
Period 1 (circa 1992)							
Δ	16.3	16.3	16.3	16.3	16.3	16.3	16.3
Δ_0	13.4	25.2	25.4	24.9	25.0	24.0	33.7
Δ_M	0.0	0.4	0.5	0.8	0.1	2.2	1.3
Δ_F	0.0	-0.1	0.1	-0.1	0.1	0.3	-1.4
Δ_X	2.9	-9.2	-9.7	-8.4	-8.8	-10.2	-17.2
percentage of men in common support	100.0	99.5	98.2	93.4	89.3	79.6	65.6
percentage of women in common support	100.0	99.9	99.5	98.9	97.4	92.8	80.7

Period 2 (circa 2007)

Δ	8.8	8.8	8.8	8.8	8.8	8.8
Δ_0	9.7	22.2	22.2	21.8	22.6	20.8	29.6
Δ_M	0.0	0.1	0.1	-0.3	-0.9	-0.3	-2.1
Δ_F	0.0	0.1	0.1	0.1	0.2	0.3	0.4
Δ_X	-0.9	-13.4	-13.4	-12.9	-13.1	-12.0	-19.1
percentage of men in common support	100.0	99.9	99.2	97.4	95.3	89.6	79.4
percentage of women in common support	100.0	100.0	99.7	99.4	98.8	96.4	89.1

Source: Based on data from national household surveys from circa 1992 and 2007.

gap to 12 percentage points in both periods) and time worked (which increases the unexplained gap 3–4 percentage points in both periods). The other observable characteristics do not greatly change the unexplained earnings gap. The unexplained gender earnings gaps move in the same direction in the two periods when adding control characteristics, suggesting that the role of observable characteristics in explaining gender earnings gaps is qualitatively similar during both periods.

Figure 4.7 reports confidence intervals for the unexplained gender earnings gaps for various combinations of matching variables during circa 1992 and circa 2007 (the sequence follows the same pattern as in table 4.8). It shows decreasing unexplained earnings gaps for all controls included. In addition, the confidence intervals for circa 1992 do not intercept with the corresponding confidence intervals for circa 2007 in any of the pairs of unexplained earnings gaps shown. As a result, the reduction

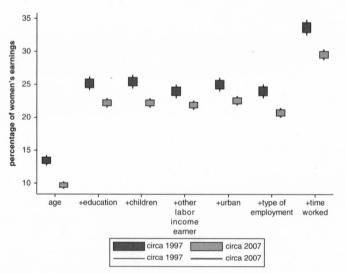

Figure 4.7 Confidence Intervals for Unexplained Gender Earnings Gap in Latin America and the Caribbean after Controlling for Demographic and Job Characteristics, Circa 1992 and 2007

Source: Based on data from national household surveys from circa 1992 and 2007.

Note: Figures show results after controlling for demographic and job related characteristics. Boxes show 90 percent confidence intervals for unexplained earnings; whiskers show 99 percent confidence intervals.

in unexplained earnings gaps is statistically significant and robust to different specifications.

There are two important increases in the unexplained components of the gender earnings gaps, both statistically significant for both periods of analysis. The first occurs after adding education. No characteristic added after education can offset the fact that the education control results in larger unexplained gender earnings gaps. In fact, the addition of a last characteristic, time worked, increases the unexplained components of the gaps in both periods.[7]

The declines in the unexplained components of the earnings gaps between circa 1992 and 2007 may reflect the general trend of narrowing gaps for all segments of the labor market. It could also be the result of changes over time in the distribution of individuals' observable characteristics, which change the composition of the labor market. If it were the case that women moved to segments of the market with less (more) evidence of unexplained earnings gaps during this 15-year span, one would expect a reduction (increase) in earnings gaps like the one shown in figure 4.7.

A "matching-after-matching" exercise is conducted to disentangle the effects of general trends versus changes in the composition of the labor market. Using the matching approach, each matched set (in a given year of data) corresponds to a hypothetical world in which men and women have the same distribution of observable characteristics. Performing a matching between women circa 1992 and women circa 2007 would preserve the distribution of men's characteristics (which, by construction, are the same as those of women for each corresponding year).

Three sets of individuals are generated in matching the two sets of data with the methodology described in chapter 2. In this matching after matching exercise, the distributions of observable characteristics in the set of matched individuals will be the same between men and women and the same between circa 1992 and 2007. The increase in the unexplained gender earnings gap that remains in the matched set of matched individuals corresponds to a counterfactual situation in which there is no change over time in the distribution of observable characteristics (or no change in the composition of the labor market).

The results of this exercise are reported in table 4.9. In all cases, the first stage of matching is performed with all of the observable characteristics shown in figure 4.7. The matching after matching exercise is then performed with each observable characteristic, one at a time. The results show that in the hypothetical situation of no changes over time in the distribution of characteristics, the decline in unexplained gender earnings gaps would have been even greater than what was observed. This narrowing is more pronounced when using age and education independently and even more pronounced when using the whole set of observable characteristics.

Figure 4.8 compares unexplained gaps along the earnings percentiles for the two periods. The comparison is made for four sets of matching

Table 4.9 Decomposition of Changes in Unexplained Gender
Earnings Gap in Latin America and the Caribbean
between Circa 1992 and 2007
(percent)

Characteristics	Counterfactual change if no change in observable characteristics	Part of the change attributed to changes in observable characteristics
Age	−7.1	3.1
Education	−7.3	3.3
Presence of children in the household	−4.6	0.5
Presence of other household member with labor income	−4.2	0.1
Urban	−5.4	1.3
Type of employment	−4.2	0.1
Time worked	−4.6	0.5
Full set	−12.1	7.9

Source: Based on data from national household surveys from circa 1992 and
circa 2007.

variables (only the results for the full set of variables are reported; for a full
set of graphs, see Ñopo and Hoyos 2010). The results indicate that most of
the reduction in the average unexplained gender earnings gap in the region
occurred at the extremes of the earnings distribution. The unexplained gender
earnings gaps at the middle of the distribution (percentiles 35–60) remained
almost unchanged. The gaps at the bottom of the distribution narrowed by
about 10 percentage points (at the 5th percentile of the distributions of earnings, for instance, unexplained gender gaps declined from 38–48 percent to
28–38 percent) The gaps at the top of the distribution narrowed by 3–9 percentage points (at the 90th percentile of the distribution, for instance, the
unexplained gender gaps declined from 10–42 percent to 7–33 percent).

The U-shape of the curve of unexplained gender earnings gap with
respect to the percentiles of the earnings distributions that was evident in
circa 1992 smoothed in circa 2007. Nonetheless, there is still a pattern
of larger unexplained earnings gaps at the bottom of the distributions of
earnings. The correlation between gender earnings gaps and poverty or
low income generation remains prevalent in the region.

Having explored changes over time in the patterns of unexplained gender
earnings gaps across the earnings distributions, the analysis turns next to

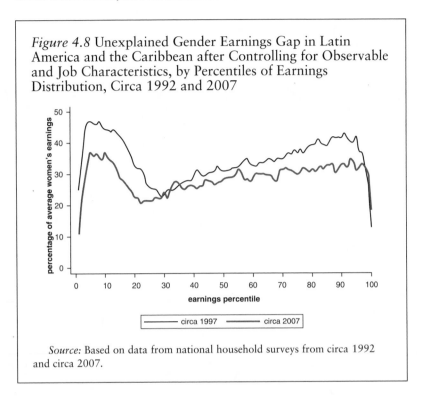

Figure 4.8 Unexplained Gender Earnings Gap in Latin America and the Caribbean after Controlling for Observable and Job Characteristics, by Percentiles of Earnings Distribution, Circa 1992 and 2007

Source: Based on data from national household surveys from circa 1992 and circa 2007.

an exploration of unexplained gender earnings gaps for different segments of the labor market (for graphs reporting the results, see Ñopo and Hoyos (2010). Segments of the labor market for which the unexplained gender earnings gaps are larger (or smaller) are similar in both periods. The unexplained gender earnings gaps decreased for all age groups, especially people 25–44 years old. Regarding education, the earnings gaps increased for workers in the middle of the distribution and decreased for workers at the extremes, especially for workers with no education. The confidence interval for unexplained earnings gaps fell from 40–49 percent to 13–21 percent. The unexplained gaps also narrowed among people who live with children under six, live in rural areas, are self-employed, and work part time.

A Cohort Approach to Understanding Unexplained Changes in Gender Pay Differences

Until now, results for the evolution of the gap were presented in a format as close as possible to the results for the analysis of circa 2007 alone. However, with data for two points in time, it is possible to analyze in greater depth some of the assertions made earlier.

In particular, the unexplained gender earnings gap was shown to increase with age. It was argued that this result implied either a narrowing of the gender earnings gap over time or a correlation between this gap and unobservable characteristics, such as labor experience or the bearing and raising of children. To determine which explanation is more accurate, the rest of this chapter is dedicated to detecting changes in earnings gaps over time through a cohort analysis. The analysis examines gender earnings gaps among individuals who were age 15–29, 30–44, and 45–59 in 1992.[8]

Figure 4.9 shows the results for the analysis after controlling for the full set of observable characteristics. The results show that the unexplained gender earnings gaps for the two older cohorts decreased as individuals aged. For the youngest cohort, the gap increased. For this cohort, the secular trend of reduction of gender earnings disparities was outweighed by the increase in gender earnings gaps workers faced as they entered adulthood.

The increases in unexplained gender earnings gaps shown for the three cohorts are disaggregated for different segments of the market in table 4.10. The analysis corresponds to a pseudo-panel analysis, in the sense that the same individuals are not followed in both periods; instead, the same segments of the labor market are compared in periods 1 and 2.

The results suggest differences across the life cycle. In the youngest cohort, the largest increases in the unexplained earnings gaps occurred among workers who completed primary and secondary education; for the other two cohorts, the largest increases occurred among the least educated workers. For the oldest cohort, the unexplained earnings gaps fell among the least educated individuals, which may suggest that the earnings penalty faced by women with little education declines with maturity (and perhaps experience).

Among workers with children in the household, the largest increases in unexplained gender gaps occurred in the two youngest cohorts and the oldest cohort. For workers with children at home, the unexplained gender earnings gaps narrowed over time for all three cohorts.

Regarding the presence of other income generators at home, the data show no differences for the two oldest cohorts. The narrowing in gender earnings gaps was similar for workers with and without other labor income earners at home. For the youngest cohort, however, the largest increase in the gap occurred among workers who lived with another income generator. For workers with no other labor income earner at home, the unexplained gender earnings gap narrowed for all cohorts: women who had no other option than generating income to maintain their households were successful at reducing their gender earnings disparities.

The reductions in unexplained earnings gaps also occurred among all cohorts in rural areas. It changed substantially among employers as well, increasing for the two youngest cohorts and falling for the oldest one.

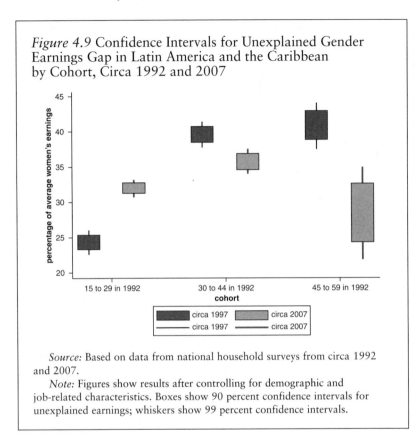

Figure 4.9 Confidence Intervals for Unexplained Gender Earnings Gap in Latin America and the Caribbean by Cohort, Circa 1992 and 2007

Source: Based on data from national household surveys from circa 1992 and 2007.

Note: Figures show results after controlling for demographic and job-related characteristics. Boxes show 90 percent confidence intervals for unexplained earnings; whiskers show 99 percent confidence intervals.

To what extent do the reported changes correspond to changes in the earnings gap within segments of the labor market, and to what extent do they correspond to changes in the composition of those segments?

The same "matching after matching" exercised shown in table 4.9 was conducted within the cohorts in this pseudo-panel to answer this question (for more detailed results, see Ñopo and Hoyos 2010). The evidence points to the same results, which attribute a small role to the composition of the labor market. Most of the changes during this period can be attributed to changes within the segments of the labor market. Table 4.10 identifies the segments of the labor market within which most of the reductions in gender earnings gaps occurred.

The cross-country heterogeneity in unexplained gender gaps shown earlier can be seen in terms of the evolution of these differences. Figure 4.10 shows confidence intervals for the original earnings gap and the unexplained component of the gender earnings gaps by country, after controlling for the full set of observable characteristics. The original earnings

Table 4.10 Unexplained Gender Earnings Gap in Latin America and the Caribbean by Cohort and Demographic and Job Characteristics, Circa 2007
(*percent*)

	Age		
Characteristics	15–29 in 1992	30–44 in 1992	45–59 in 1992
Overall	7.6	–3.8	–12.4
Education			
None	8.9	–51.6	–7.2
Primary incomplete	–4.1	–17.4	–43.1
Primary complete	19.5	0.4	19.8
Secondary incomplete	12.8	12.6	–15.9
Secondary complete	22.5	5.8	–1.1
Tertiary incomplete	11.6	-0.6	18.1
Tertiary complete	–1.4	–2.4	–4.3
Presence of children (6 years or younger in household)			
No	9.01	–4.4	–12.6
Yes	–10.3	–14.1	–3.4
Presence of other household member with labor income			
No	–3.2	–3.9	–10.3
Yes	9.1	–3.8	–13.2
Urban			
No	–1.8	–16.7	–23.5
Yes	8.1	–3.5	–12.1
Type of employment			
Employer	21.5	5.8	–46.0
Employee	7.5	–1.8	–12.7
Self-employed	5.4	–11.1	–6.0
Time worked			
Part time	5.9	–7.9	–8.9
Full time	8.2	–2.9	–15.5
Over time	4.1	–2.0	–15.1

Source: Based on data from national household surveys from circa 2007.

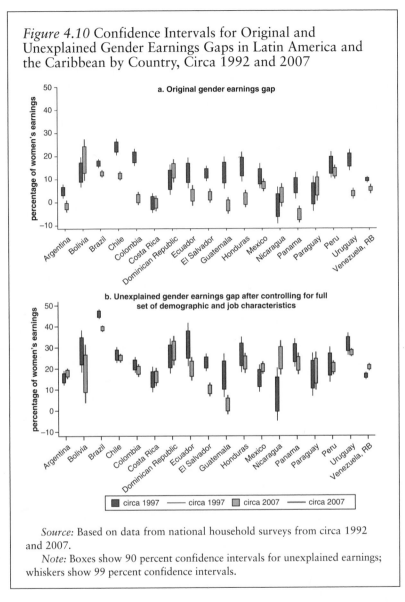

Figure 4.10 Confidence Intervals for Original and
Unexplained Gender Earnings Gaps in Latin America and
the Caribbean by Country, Circa 1992 and 2007

a. Original gender earnings gap

b. Unexplained gender earnings gap after controlling for full
set of demographic and job characteristics

■ circa 1997   —— circa 1997   ▢ circa 2007   —— circa 2007

Source: Based on data from national household surveys from circa 1992
and 2007.
   Note: Boxes show 90 percent confidence intervals for unexplained earnings;
whiskers show 99 percent confidence intervals.

gap peaks in Chile in period 1 (circa 1992) and Bolivia in period 2 (circa
2007). However, these measures of earnings gaps incorporate differences
in observable characteristics. Regarding unexplained gender earnings gaps,
the most salient result, consistent with the results reported for circa 2007
alone, is that Brazil shows the largest gap across both periods, although the

gap decreased. Brazil, El Salvador, and Guatemala show the largest drops in unexplained gender earnings gaps. In contrast to the regional trend of declining unexplained earnings gaps, these gaps increased in Nicaragua and República Bolivariana de Venezuela between circa 1992 and 2007. To a lesser extent (and one that is not statistically significant), the gaps also widened in Argentina and Mexico.

It is precisely this cross-country heterogeneity that motivates the studies included in this book. Chapters 5 (on Peru) and 6 (on Mexico) examine countries that have not achieved gender educational parity. The next six chapters examine countries and regions that have achieved parity: Chile (chapter 7), Colombia (chapter 8), Brazil (chapter 9), Ecuador (chapter 10), Central America (chapter 11) and the Caribbean (chapter 12).

Notes

1. Among working women, almost 10 percent worked in the agriculture sector, 14 percent in industry, and 76 percent in the service sectors circa 2006. The percentage of women in services is significantly higher than in other regions of the world. Women's unemployment rate in Latin America and the Caribbean was about 10 percent (ILO 2007).

2. This ranking is based on an index that includes earnings disparities and other variables. The index also includes differences in labor participation and access to certain type of occupations (legislators, senior officials, and managers, and professional and technical workers). For more details, see Hausmann, Tyson, and Zahidi (2007).

3. For a description of the methodology used in this chapter, see chapter 2.

4. Part-time workers are people who work 35 hours or less a week at their main occupation.

5. In the Dominican Republic, workers are considered formal if they report having a contract. Firm size is not used as a control variable in Brazil, because it was not possible to construct the "small firm" variable there.

6. Time worked is divided in three categories: part time (less than 35 hours a week), full time (35–48 hours a week), and overtime (more than 48 hours a week).

7. The cross-country heterogeneity reported for circa 2007 alone is also evident in these data. For an analysis of the unexplained component of the gender earnings gaps by country, see Ñopo and Hoyos (2010).

8. The Dominican Republic and Guatemala were dropped from this part of the analysis, because data for the 15-year span were not available.

References

Angel-Urdinola, D., and Q. Wodon. 2006. "The Gender Wage Gap and Poverty in Colombia." *Labour* 20 (4): 721–39.

Atal, J. P., H. Ñopo, and N. Winder, 2009. "New Century, Old Disparities: Gender and Ethnic Earnings Gaps in Latin America." RES Working Paper 4640, Research Department, Inter-American Development Bank, Washington, DC.

Babcock, L. and S. Laschever. 2003. *Women Don't Ask: Negotiation and the Gender Divide*. Princeton, NJ: Princeton University Press.

Barrientos, A. 2002. "Women, Informal Employment and Social Protection in Latin America." IDPM Discussion Paper 30557, Institute for Development Policy and Management, University of Manchester, United Kingdom.

Contreras, D., and G. Plaza. 2004. "Participación femenina en el mercado laboral chileno¿cuánto importan los factores culturales?" Universidad de Chile, Santiago. http://.estudiosdeltrabajo.cl2Fwp-content2Fuploads2F20092F122F-factores-culturales-en-participacion-laboral-femenina-d-contreras-g-plaza.pdf&ei=SSA8T5GMOcHd0QH3iKiqCw&usg=AFQjCNFQqH1vr79I69Uyrd KzBPNwhn5PXg&sig2=Tl5wueYQWxtana-oGtfNRA.

Cox, A., and J. Roberts. 1993. "Macroeconomic Influences on Female Labor Force Participation: The Latin American Evidence." *Estudios de Economía* 20: 87–106.

Cruces, G., and S. Galiani. 2007. "Fertility and Female Labor Supply in Latin America: New Causal Evidence." *Labour Economics* 14 (3): 565–73.

Deutsch, R., A. Morrison, H. Ñopo, and C. Piras. 2004. "Working within Confines: Occupational Segregation by Gender in Costa Rica, Ecuador, and Uruguay." In *Women at Work: Challenges for Latin America*, ed. C. Piras, 187–226. Washington, DC: Inter-American Development Bank.

Duryea, S., A. C. Edwards, and M. Ureta. 2004. "Women in the LAC Labor Market: The Remarkable 1990s." In *Women at Work: Challenges for Latin America*, ed. C. Piras, 27–60. Washington, DC: Inter-American Development Bank.

Frankema, E. 2008. "Wage Gaps in Twentieth Century Latin America: Persistent Inequality or Distributional Change." Utrecht University, the Netherlands.

Freije, S. 2009. "Informal Employment in Latin America and the Caribbean: Causes, Consequences, and Policy Recommendations." Inter-American Development Bank, Washington, DC.

Hausmann, R., L. D. Tyson, and S. Zahidi, eds. 2007. *The Global Gender Gap 2007*. Davos, Switzerland: World Economic Forum.

Hertz, T., P. Winters, A. Paula de la O, E. J. Quiñones, B. Davis, and A. Zezza. 2008. "Wage Inequality in International Perspective: Effects of Location, Sector, and Gender." ESA Working Paper 8/08, Food and Agriculture Organization of the United Nations, Agricultural and Development Economics Division (ESA), Rome. ftp://ftp.fao.org/docrep/fao/011/ak230e/ak230e00.pdf.

ILO (International Labour Organization). 2007. *Modelo de tendencias mundiales del empleo*. Geneva: International Labour Organization.

Lim, L. L. 2002. "Female Labour Force Participation." International Labour Organization, Gender Promotion Programme (GENPROM), Geneva. http://www.un.org/esa/population/publications/completingfertility/RevisedLIMpaper.PDF.

Madrigal Correa, A. L. 2004. "La evolución de la participación laboral de la mujer en México: el efecto del tamaño de la familia 1970–2000." Master's thesis, Centro de Investigaciónes y Docencia Económicas, Mexico City.

Márquez, G., and M. F. Prada. 2007. "Bad Jobs, Low Productivity, and Exclusion." Inter-American Development Bank, Research Department, Washington, DC.

Ñopo, H. 2008. "Matching as a Tool to Decompose Wage Gaps." *Review of Economics and Statistics* 90 (2): 290–99.

Ñopo, H., and A. Hoyos. 2010. "Evolution of Gender Wage Gaps in Latin America at the Turn of the Twentieth Century: An Addendum to 'New Century, Old Disparities.'" IZA Discussion Paper 5086, Institute for the Study of Labor, Bonn, Germany.

Panizza, U., and C. Z.-W. Qiang. 2005. "Public-Private Wage Differential and Gender Gap in Latin America: Spoiled Bureaucrats and Exploited Women?" *Journal of Socio–Economics* 34 (6): 810–33.

Psacharopoulos, G., and Z. Tzannatos, eds. 1992a. *Case Studies on Women's Employment and Pay in Latin America*. Washington, DC: World Bank.

———. 1992b. "Latin American Women's Earnings and Participation in the Labor Force." World Bank Policy Research Working Paper 856, Washington, DC.

Salas, C., and M. Leite. 2007. "Segregación sectorial por género: una comparación Brasil-México." Cadernos PROLAM/USP. Ano 7 - vol.

Tenjo, J., R. Ribero, and L. Bernat. 2006 "Evolución de las diferencias salariales de género en seis países de América Latina." In *Mujeres y trabajo en América Latina*, ed. C. Piras, 149–98. Washington, DC: Inter-American Development Bank.

Terrell, K. 1992. "Female-Male Earnings Differentials and Occupational Structure." *International Labor Review* 131 (4–5): 387–98.

Urdinola, A. D. F., and Q. Wodon. 2006. "The Gender Wage Gap and Poverty in Colombia." *Labour* 20 (4): 721–39.

5

The Mostly Unexplained Gender Earnings Gap: Peru 1997–2009

Gender disparities in the Peruvian labor market are pronounced. There are substantial gaps in participation and employment rates, occupations, and hourly and monthly earnings. Peru has high occupational segregation (Blau and Ferber 1992), and a sizable share of jobs tend to fail at least one of the formality conditions (formal contract or access to insurance). Formality affects men and women differently: 55 percent of men and 65 percent of women have jobs in the informal sector. Gender gaps are also associated with differences in observable characteristics of the working population, such as age, schooling, marital status, and household responsibilities.

Peru experienced labor market reforms during the early 1990s.[1] These reforms included dramatic reductions in firing costs, linked to reductions in formality, and a subsequent increase in turnover rates, as a result of shorter durations of both employment and unemployment (Saavedra 2000; Saavedra and Torero 2000). These reforms may have influenced women's participation in labor markets, but the theoretical literature has no clear predictions as to how these kind of changes in employment dynamics affect earnings differentials.

In addition to gender differences in labor market outcomes, there are also gender disparities in individual characteristics. Men in Peru tend to have more years of education than women and longer tenure in higher-paying occupations.

This chapter was adapted from "The Gender Wage Gap in Peru 1986–2000: Evidence from a Matching Comparisons Approach," Hugo Ñopo, *Economica*, La Plata, vol. L, 1–2, 2004.

The extent to which these differences in observable characteristics account for gaps in labor market outcomes is a longstanding question. This chapter analyzes both the evolution of the gender earnings gap between 1997 and 2009 and the role of individual characteristics in explaining earnings gaps during this period. The results suggest a steady reduction in gender differences in participation and employment rates, accompanied by cyclical evolution of the gender gap in hourly earnings.

The analysis in this chapter is based on 1997–2009 data from the Encuesta Nacional de Hogares (ENAHO), Peru's national household survey, conducted by the National Institute of Statistics and Informatics (INEI). As the main objective of this chapter is to estimate and explain gender earnings gaps, only the working population ages 16–75 is examined.

How Do Male and Female Workers Differ?

It can be argued that the gender earnings gap simply reflects gender differences in some observable characteristics of the individuals that are determinants of earnings. To some extent, this is a valid argument, as there are gender differences in age, education, occupational experience, and occupations, among other characteristics rewarded in labor markets. However, these differences only partially explain the earnings gap. The purpose of this chapter is to measure the extent to which differences in characteristics explain differences in pay in Peru.[2]

On average during 1997–2009, working men in Peru were 0.65 years older than working women. This result contrasts with figures for the Peruvian population as a whole, in which the average age is slightly higher for women than for men. The difference in the average age among workers may reflect women's earlier entrance into or earlier retirement from the labor market. Either circumstance is expected to have a negative impact on earnings. Early entry into the labor market may imply fewer years of schooling; early retirement implies shorter tenure.

There are also significant differences between men and women in educational attainment (table 5.1). Although the proportion of working men and women that completed high school or have some years of university is fairly similar, there are important differences in all other educational levels. Women with university degrees represent a larger proportion of the labor force than men with the same educational level, even though, on average, working women attain fewer years of education than working men in most years of the sample. Women at the other extreme of the educational ladder also participate more in the Peruvian labor market than men at that educational level. As a result, working women are concentrated at the extremes of the educational distribution.

Table 5.1 Demographic and Job Characteristics and Relative
Earnings of Men and Women in Peru's Labor Force, 1997–2009

	Composition (percent)		Relative earnings (average women's earnings for each year = 100)	
	Women	Men	Women	Men
Personal characteristics				
Age				
16–24	20.8	20.3	76.2	85.9
25–34	27.5	26.5	109.2	113.6
35–44	23.5	22.3	117.2	139.0
45–54	15.6	16.4	107.1	150.1
55–65	12.5	14.5	78.3	127.6
Education				
None	9.1	3.7	35.0	40.9
Primary incomplete	9.5	9.5	51.9	57.7
Primary complete	13.5	16.3	63.6	72.3
Secondary incomplete	12.8	16.7	74.5	91.3
Secondary complete	26.3	29.0	88.9	110.1
Tertiary incomplete	8.2	8.2	128.5	158.3
Tertiary complete	20.6	16.6	193.2	257.6
Urban				
No	22.8	32.2	46.7	62.6
Yes	77.2	67.8	115.7	149.7
Job characteristics				
Part-time work				
No	66.0	77.6	82.4	103.8
Yes	34.0	22.4	134.2	183.5
Small firm				
No	31.3	37.6	148.3	160.0
Yes	68.7	62.4	78.0	98.6
Occupation				
Professionals and technicians	16.9	14.6	211.9	265.9

(continued next page)

Table 5.1 (continued)

| | Composition (percent) | | Relative earnings (average women's earnings for each year = 100) | |
	Women	Men	Women	Men
Directors and upper management	0.5	0.8	315.3	552.8
Administrative personnel	6.7	3.9	145.3	177.8
Merchants and sellers	27.9	10.3	80.5	111.9
Service workers	22.0	9.9	72.4	90.3
Agricultural workers and similar	13.9	30.3	42.8	60.1
Nonagricultural blue-collars	12.2	30.2	70.8	108.6
Armed forces	0.0	0.2	107.6	90.3
Economic Sector				
Agriculture, hunting, forestry, and fishing	14.1	31.0	44.4	62.3
Mining and quarrying	1.2	1.8	102.8	175.3
Manufacturing	11.0	11.7	87.0	139.7
Electricity, gas, and water supply	0.1	1.2	201.1	128.9
Construction	1.0	7.3	154.9	137.2
Wholesale and retail trade and hotels and restaurants	36.6	16.7	86.1	125.0
Transport, storage	2.7	10.2	141.1	124.7
Financing, insurance, real estate, and business services	4.2	5.4	215.8	236.8
Community, social, and personal services	29.1	14.7	126.4	169.6

Source: Based on 1997–2009 data from ENAHO.

Figure 5.1 shows average years of education of the labor force. The education gap favors working men for most of the period. However, the gap has been almost zero since 2006, and the figure for 2009 shows a gap in favor of women. These figures lie in contrast with figures for the Peruvian population as a whole, where a gender education gap remains. The finding may reveal that women in the labor force have more human capital than the average Peruvian woman, reflecting selection into the labor market.

Figure 5.2 reveals the evolution of the gender composition of the labor force by educational level. It shows that the gap between men and women at each educational level decreased throughout the period. Women's participation was greatest at the extremes of the educational ladder.

There are gender differences in human capital accumulation, probably the observable characteristic most rewarded in the labor market. However, this difference narrowed over the period.

This relationship partially explains the gender earnings gap and its evolution. Figure 5.3 shows average hourly earnings gaps as multiples of women's average hourly earnings. It shows that the gender earnings gap fluctuated around an average value of 21 percent (that is, men earned an average of 21 percent more per hour than women). However, there are significant fluctuations around this average measure, and there are two years in the sample (2007 and 2009) when men reportedly earned less than women (the earnings gap was negative).

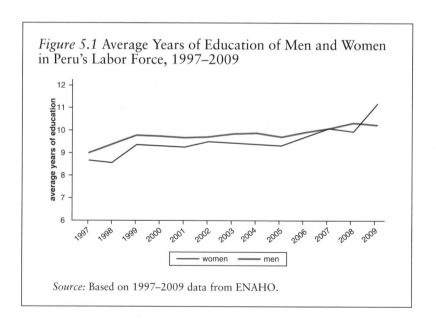

Figure 5.1 Average Years of Education of Men and Women in Peru's Labor Force, 1997–2009

Source: Based on 1997–2009 data from ENAHO.

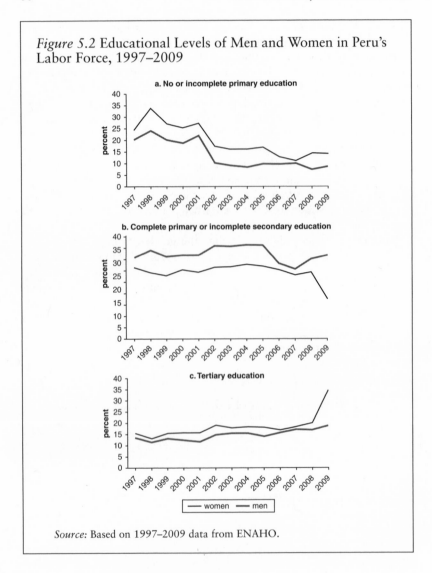

Figure 5.2 Educational Levels of Men and Women in Peru's Labor Force, 1997–2009

Source: Based on 1997–2009 data from ENAHO.

The measures of the gap (multiples of average hourly earnings for women) are crude data, as they consider all men and women regardless of differences in observable characteristics or whether it is possible to compare them. If variation in these gender differences in average hourly earnings according to individual characteristics is explored, the results displayed in table 5.1 are obtained.

The gender earnings gap tends to increase at about age 30, reaching a peak at age 45–54. It increases monotonically with educational attainment.

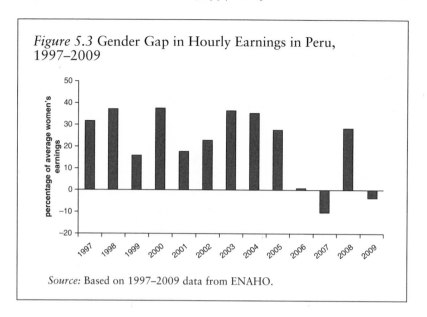

Figure 5.3 Gender Gap in Hourly Earnings in Peru, 1997–2009

Source: Based on 1997–2009 data from ENAHO.

The largest gap occurs among people with university degrees. The gap is larger in urban than in rural areas and for people who work part time. It is largest in the best rewarded occupations, directors and upper-level managers.

The Role of Individual Characteristics in Explaining the Gender Earnings Gap

Figure 5.4 presents the earnings gap in relative terms (as a multiple of women's earnings) and decomposes it into the four components introduced in chapter 2. The height of each bar is proportional to the earnings gap in each year. The height of each component is proportional to the value of the component; a component with a negative value is illustrated below the zero line. The first set of decompositions was calculated using a combination of explanatory variables, such as age, education, marital status, and residence in an urban area.

The results show that most of the earnings gap remains unexplained after including these controls, as the unexplained gender earnings gap (Δ_0)—the portion of the gap attributed to differences between men and women that cannot be explained by observable characteristics—is large in all years. Δ_X is the portion of the gap due to differences in characteristics between men and women in the "common support." It is negative except in 1998, when it is positive and particularly large. When negative, this

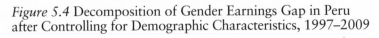

Figure 5.4 Decomposition of Gender Earnings Gap in Peru after Controlling for Demographic Characteristics, 1997–2009

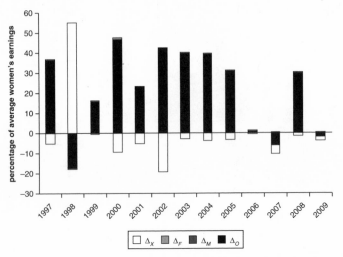

Source: Based on 1997–2009 data from ENAHO.

Note: Δ_M (Δ_F) is the part of the earnings gap attributed to the existence of men (women) with combinations of characteristics that are not met by any women (men). Δ_X is the part of the earnings gap attributed to differences in the observable characteristics of men and women over the "common support." Δ_0 is the part of the earnings gap that cannot be attributed to differences in characteristics of the individuals. It is typically attributed to a combination of both unobservable characteristics and discrimination. The sum of these components equals the total earnings gap ($\Delta_M + \Delta_F + \Delta_X + \Delta_0 = \Delta$).

component indicates that matched women exhibit a distribution of characteristics that is better rewarded by the labor market than the distribution of characteristics exhibited by men. This is the case for education, for example. Within the working population, a larger percentage of women than men hold university degrees. In 1998, when the Δ_X component is positive, two events come into play. Both the gap in average years of education between men and women and the share of working women with no education are largest in 1998.

The other components—the portions of the earnings gap attributable to the nonoverlapping supports of women (Δ_F) and men (Δ_M)—are fairly close to zero in all years analyzed. Δ_F, however, is positive in most years, indicating that unmatched women earn less than matched ones. Δ_M is negative, implying that unmatched men earn less than matched men.

In general, the average components of the earnings gap for the whole period point to an insignificant role of Δ_M, Δ_F, and Δ_X in explaining the earnings gap. For the whole period, the average value of these components is zero. In contrast, Δ_0 has an average value (21.3) that is almost equal to the entire gender earnings gap (21.5). The demographic characteristics considered as controls thus cannot account for gender differences in pay.

The decompositions in figure 5.5 use different combinations of age, education, economic sector, occupation, and firm size (a dichotomous variable equal to one for firms with five workers or less) as controls.

After controlling for these job characteristics, the average unexplained gender earnings gap is about 23.1 percent—slightly higher than the average

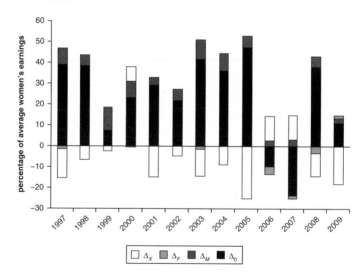

Figure 5.5 Decomposition of Gender Earnings Gap in Peru after Controlling for Demographic and Job Characteristics, 1997–2009

Source: Based on 1997–2009 data from ENAHO.

Note: Δ_M (Δ_F) is the part of the earnings gap attributed to the existence of men (women) with combinations of characteristics that are not met by any women (men). Δ_X is the part of the earnings gap attributed to differences in the observable characteristics of men and women over the "common support." Δ_0 is the part of the earnings gap that cannot be attributed to differences in characteristics of the individuals. It is typically attributed to a combination of both unobservable characteristics and discrimination. The sum of these components equals the total earnings gap ($\Delta_M + \Delta_F + \Delta_X + \Delta_0 = \Delta$).

total gap when these variables are not considered. The results show that most of the earnings gap remains unexplained even after including the complete set of controls. The role of the other three components play in the decomposition is also similar to the roles explained earlier. In most years, Δ_X is negative and Δ_F close to zero. However, there is a change in Δ_M, which becomes larger and is positive in all years, meaning that when controlling for job characteristics, men matched with women tend to earn lower earnings than unmatched men.

The components Δ_0 and Δ_M explain more than 80 percent of the earnings gap during all years when using the full set of observable characteristics. These components may be regarded as noisy discrimination measures or unexplained differences. The first of them is determined in the labor market, while the second is outside of it (in the acquisition of particular characteristics). Whereas discrimination measures are linked to differences in pay, unexplained differences are presumably linked to differences in access to particular combinations of characteristics that are rewarded in the labor market.

Table 5.2 shows descriptive statistics for women in and out of the common support. Just 1 percent of working women exhibit combinations of age, education, location (urban or rural), and marital status that cannot be matched by any men in the sample; 0.2 percent of working men report combinations of these characteristics that cannot be matched by any women in the sample. The percentage of unmatched individuals grows when more characteristics are included: 3 percent of working women and 11 percent of working men exhibit combinations of age, education, economic sector, occupation, and firm size that cannot be matched by any individual of the opposite sex in the sample.

Unmatched men and women are older than matched men and women when controlling by both sets of characteristics explored. Unmatched women are concentrated in the lowest educational levels, whereas unmatched men are frequently found among workers with some high school or university education. Most unmatched women are service workers, whereas most unmatched men are agricultural or blue collar workers. Most of the matched working population is concentrated in wholesale and retail trade; the hotel and restaurant sector; and community, social, and personal services. This pattern may reflect women's concentration in services.

Exploring the Unexplained Component of the Gender Earnings Gap

This section analyzes the distribution of unexplained gender differences in earnings obtained from the matching process by comparing the distribution of earnings for women with the counterfactual distribution

Table 5.2 Demographic and Job Characteristics of Matched and Unmatched Samples of Men and Women in Peru's Labor Force, 1997–2009 (percent)

Characteristics	Age, education, marital status, and urban area			Age, education, firm size, occupation, and economic sector		
	Matched women and men	Unmatched men	Unmatched women	Matched women and men	Unmatched men	Unmatched women
Average hourly earnings (constant 1994 Peruvian soles)		2.6	2.4		4.8	5.5
Average age	37.1	42.8	59.6	36.90	43.5	43.6
Average years of schooling	9.6	5.4	9.8	9.58	8.8	10.3
Education level						
No education or primary incomplete	18.2	59.0	21.5	18.20	29.6	12.9
Primary incomplete or secondary complete	26.4	12.8	34.2	26.50	19.2	33.9
Secondary complete or tertiary incomplete	34.7	16.9	28.4	34.70	29.7	34.4
Tertiary complete	20.7	11.2	15.9	20.60	21.5	18.8

(continued next page)

Table 5.2 *(continued)*

Characteristics	Age, education, marital status, and urban area			Age, education, firm size, occupation, and economic sector		
	Matched women and men	Unmatched men	Unmatched women	Matched women and men	Unmatched men	Unmatched women
Marital status						
Single	30.4	9.1	32.0			
Married	51.0	2.8	29.5			
Divorced	12.3	39.7	26.8			
Widower	6.3	48.5	11.7			
Living in urban area	77.4	60.5	24.7			
Working in small firm				68.9	60.6	42.2
Occupation						
Professionals and technicians				16.9	14.9	16.9
Directors and upper management				0.4	4.1	4.2
Administrative personnel				6.2	22.6	5.8
Merchants and sellers				28.4	8.9	4.2
Service workers				21.5	35.7	11.7
Agricultural workers and similar				14.3	0.5	2.4
Nonagricultural blue-collars				12.2	13.2	53.6

Table 5.2 (continued)

Characteristics	Age, education, marital status, and urban area			Age, education, firm size, occupation, and economic sector		
	Matched women and men	Unmatched men	Unmatched women	Matched women and men	Unmatched men	Unmatched women
Armed forces				0.0	0.1	1.2
Economic sector						
Agriculture, hunting, forestry, and fishing				14.4	3.1	7.2
Mining and quarrying				0.9	10.2	5.7
Manufacturing				10.8	15.4	8.8
Electricity, gas, and water supply				0.1	1.5	9.4
Construction				0.9	4.7	16.1
Wholesale and retail trade and hotels and restaurants				37.0	25.0	15.7
Transport, storage				2.5	9.8	17.7
Financing, insurance, real estate, and business services				4.0	10.6	9.3
Community, social, and personal services				29.3	19.8	10.2

Source: Based on 1997–2009 data from ENAHO.
Note: Blank cells indicate that the variable is not being controlled for.

of earnings for men when they are resampled to mimic the distribution of women's characteristics. Figure 5.6 shows the relative earnings gap as a percentage of women's earnings for each percentile of the earnings distribution. The gap exhibits a slight *U*-shape when controlling for both demographic and job characteristics. When controlling only for demographic characteristics, an increase in the gap is observed after including the control dummy for urban area, indicating that the unexplained earnings gap is greater in urban areas across the distribution of earnings. The gap reaches a maximum for people in the 20th percentile of the earnings distribution, after which it monotonically decreases until the 80th percentile before reaching another peak at the 95th percentile. Men in the 20th percentile earn on average 60 percent more than women; men in the top percentiles earn on average 25 percent more than women. When introducing job market controls (see figure 5.7), the gap again shows a slight *U*-shape, but this time the gender differences at the lowest percentiles of the earnings distribution are larger.

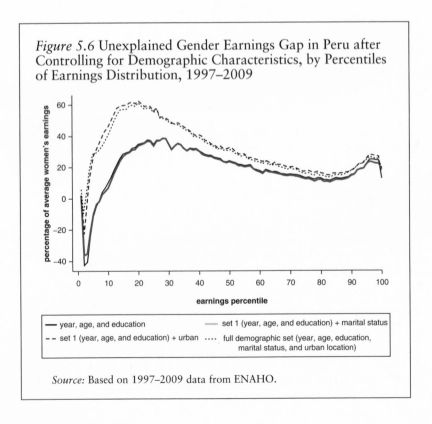

Figure 5.6 Unexplained Gender Earnings Gap in Peru after Controlling for Demographic Characteristics, by Percentiles of Earnings Distribution, 1997–2009

Source: Based on 1997–2009 data from ENAHO.

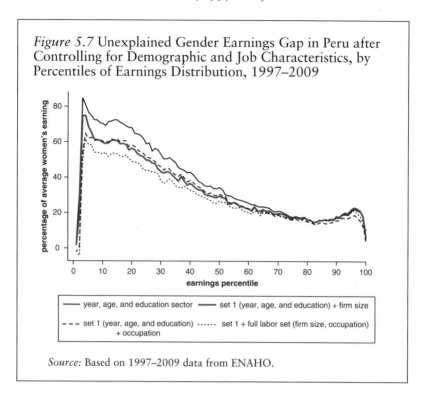

Figure 5.7 Unexplained Gender Earnings Gap in Peru after Controlling for Demographic and Job Characteristics, by Percentiles of Earnings Distribution, 1997–2009

Source: Based on 1997–2009 data from ENAHO.

The distribution of unexplained gender earnings differences can also be analyzed by computing confidence intervals (figures 5.8 and 5.9). The extremes of the boxes correspond to a 90 percent confidence interval for the average unexplained differences in pay; the extremes of the whiskers correspond to a 99 percent confidence interval. The figures show no evidence of a monotonic decrease in earnings differences when controlling for either demographic or job characteristics. The unexplained hourly gender earnings gap reached its lowest levels in 1999, 2006, and 2007; it attained peaks in 2000 and 2005, evolving in a way that seems correlated with the cycle of the Peruvian economy.

Changes in Women's Participation and Unemployment Rates

The measure of gender differences shown in the previous section was earnings. This section examines changes in women's participation and unemployment rates.

Figure 5.8 Confidence Intervals for Unexplained Gender
Earnings Gap in Peru after Controlling for Demographic
Characteristics, 1997–2009

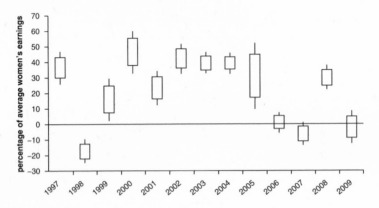

Source: Based on 1997–2009 data from ENAHO.
Note: Boxes show 90 percent confidence intervals for unexplained earnings;
whiskers show 99 percent confidence intervals.

Figure 5.9 Confidence Intervals for Unexplained
Gender Earnings Gap in Peru after Controlling for
Demographic and Job Characteristics, 1997–2009

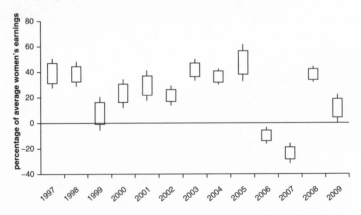

Source: Based on 1997–2009 data from ENAHO.
Note: Boxes show 90 percent confidence intervals for unexplained earnings;
whiskers show 99 percent confidence intervals.

The gender gap in participation decreased over the period, as a result of both a slight decrease in men's participation and a larger increase in women's participation (figure 5.10). In 1997, 64 percent of women were participating in the labor market; by 2009, this proportion reached 71 percent. The proportion for men was 85 percent in 1997 and 2009, with slight changes during the period.

Gender differences in unemployment rates decreased between 1997 and 2009 (figure 5.11). The unemployment rate among men fell from 3.5 percent to 3.0 percent; the unemployment rate among women rose and fell over the period, declining from 3.5 percent to 2.5 percent over the period as a whole.

There are also differences in the number of hours worked. On average, over the whole period, men worked 45 hours a week and women worked 40 hours, an 11 percent difference. These differences decreased between 1986 and 2000. Whereas men worked 15 percent more hours than women in 1997, they worked 11 percent more hours than women during 2005. The difference decreased to almost zero in 2006 and 2007 before increasing again in 2008 and 2009.

Both participation and unemployment rates show the significant presence of women in the Peruvian labor market. In fact, women's participation force was the second highest in the region in the early 1990s and the

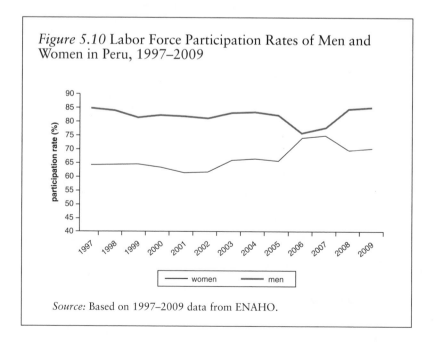

Figure 5.10 Labor Force Participation Rates of Men and Women in Peru, 1997–2009

Source: Based on 1997–2009 data from ENAHO.

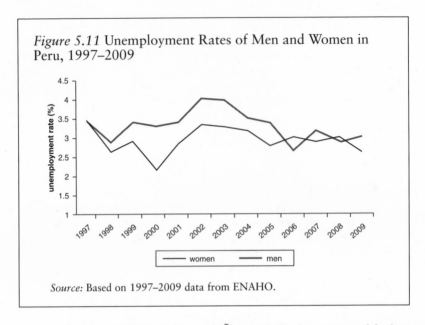

Figure 5.11 Unemployment Rates of Men and Women in Peru, 1997–2009

Source: Based on 1997–2009 data from ENAHO.

highest in the mid-2000s (Elías and Ñopo 2010). In contrast, Mexico, analyzed in the next chapter, experienced the lowest women's participation rates in the region.

Notes

1. The two waves of reform occurred in 1991 and 1995.
2. For a description of the methodology used in this chapter, see chapter 2.

References

Blau, F., and M. Ferber. 1992. *The Economics of Women, Men, and Work*, 2nd ed. Englewood Cliffs, NJ: Prentice-Hall.

Elías, J., and H. Ñopo. 2010. "The Increase in Female Labor Force Participation in Latin America 1990–2004: Decomposing the Changes." Inter-American Development Bank, Research Department, Washington, DC.

Saavedra, J. 2000. "La flexibilización del mercado laboral." In *La reforma incompleta: rescatando los noventa*, ed. R. Abusada, 379–428. Lima: Universidad del Pacífico.

Saavedra, J., and M. Torero. 2000. "Labor Market Reforms and Their Impact on Formal Labor Demand and Job Market Turnover: The Case of Peru." Research Network Working Paper R-394, Inter-American Development Bank, Washington, DC. http://pws.iadb.org/res/laresnetwork/files/pr111 finaldraft.pdf.

6

Is Gender Segregation in the Workplace Responsible for Earnings Gaps? Mexico 1994–2004

Low women's labor force participation rates by women make Mexico an interesting country to analyze. Mexico had the lowest women's participation rate in Latin America by the early 1990s, at 37 percent. Since then, it has experienced important changes in the labor market from a gender perspective. The increase in the labor market participation rate of women has been the largest in a region where the women's participation rate has increased substantially. Nonetheless, women's labor participation in Mexico is still below the Latin American average and gender segregation in the workplace is still pervasive (Elías and Ñopo 2010).

This chapter links the gender pay differential and labor market segregation. It explores the linkages between gender differences in observable human capital characteristics, (occupational and hierarchical) segregation, and earnings. The data are drawn from the National Survey of Urban Employment (Encuesta Nacional de Empleo Urbano [ENEU]), Mexico's national urban employment survey.[1] These quarterly data cover the period from the third quarter of 1994 to the fourth quarter of 2004.

This chapter was adapted from the following sources: "Gender Segregation in the Workplace and Wage Gaps: Evidence from Urban Mexico 1994–2004," Sebastián Calónico and Hugo Ñopo, Research Department Working Paper 636, Inter-American Development Bank, Washington, DC; and Sebastián Calónico and Hugo Ñopo, "Gender Segregation in the Workplace and Wage Gaps: Evidence from Urban Mexico 1994–2004," in *Occupational and Residential Segregation* (*Research on Economic Inequality, Volume 17*), ed. Yves Flückiger, Sean F. Reardon, and Jacques Silber, (Emerald Group Publishing Limited), 245–70.

Sebastián Calónico is a graduate student in economics at the University of Michigan, Ann Arbor.

What Does the Literature Show?

Gender pay differentials in Mexico have been documented from various perspectives (Sánchez 1998; Pagan and Sánchez 2000; López Acevedo 2003; Chinhui and Airola 2005). Brown, Pagan, and Rodriguez-Oreggia (1999) study the effect of occupational attainment on the increase in gender earnings differentials between 1987 and 1993. Using data from the ENEU, they find that the decline in gender differences in occupational attainment somewhat attenuated the increase in the gender earnings differential. They also find important roles for labor supply decisions (hours of work per week) and changes in the regional structure of earnings.

This finding contrasts with the results of Parker (1999), who examines the gender earnings gap in rural areas of Mexico between 1986 and 1992 by looking at skill levels within groups of occupations. She finds that earnings differentials among labor income earners were low and remained roughly constant throughout the period, although they varied widely across occupations. She finds the largest earnings gaps in managerial positions (in both the private and public sectors) and the smallest among public service workers and administrative positions.

Rendón (2003) analyzes gender differences in employment, segregation, and earnings. She documents that, in spite of the large increase in women's labor force participation in recent decades, there is still a large concentration of women in certain activities. She documents an increase in segregation by productive sectors from 1990 to 2000. However, she suggests that there are reasons to believe that such segregation should decline in the future, because women tend first to enter activities more populated by other women before entering activities that are more gender neutral. She also provides estimates for the high degree of hierarchical (vertical) segregation (the holding of higher-ranking positions by men). When analyzing the evolution of the gender earnings gap, she argues that the observed reduction can be explained by an increase in women's working hours.

Rendón and Maldonado (2004) study the relationship between domestic work, occupational segregation, and the gender earnings gap in Mexico. Their motivation is the large increase observed in women's labor force participation, which reflects both cultural factors and changes in the country's occupational and productive structure (namely, the increase in the relative importance of professionals, office workers, and salespeople). However, this increase in participation did not imply that conditions faced by men and women equalized. Occupational segregation and earnings gaps are still notable, partly because of the number of hours worked, and they vary substantially across sectors and occupations.

Colmenares (2006) analyzes occupational segregation by gender and its relation with earnings difference in the industry sector. She finds variability across regions in gender occupational segregation.

Measuring Occupational and Hierarchical Segregation

In this chapter, occupational and hierarchical (vertical) segregation by gender are measured using the Duncan index (Duncan and Duncan 1955). The occupational index shows the percentage of men (women) that would need to switch from jobs that are dominated by men (women) to jobs that are dominated by women (men) in order to achieve a labor force with no segregation. The hierarchical index shows the percentage of women that would need to be promoted to better labor positions in order to eliminate segregation.

The index ranges from zero to one, with a higher index representing greater segregation. The occupational index is computed using disaggregated information on seven occupations at the one-digit level (professionals and technicians, managers, administrative personnel, salespeople, workers in the service sector, workers in agricultural activities, and workers in industrial activities).[2]

The Duncan index of hierarchical segregation uses hierarchical categories instead of occupations. The ENEU survey includes five hierarchical categories (managers, independent workers, piece-rate or commission workers, fixed-salary workers, and members of a cooperative). Table 6.1 reports average measures of occupational and hierarchical segregation for various segments of the market for the period under analysis.

Table 6.1 Average Duncan Index of Occupational and Hierarchical Segregation in Mexico, by Demographic and Job Characteristics, 1994–2004

Characteristics	Occupational segregation	Hierarchical segregation
Years of schooling		
0	0.40	0.11
1–6	0.39	0.10
7–12	0.33	0.10
13 or more	0.24	0.14
Age		
15–24	0.31	0.09
25–49	0.34	0.10
50–64	0.33	0.09

(continued next page)

Table 6.1 (continued)

Characteristics	Occupational segregation	Hierarchical segregation
Marital status		
Single (never married)	0.29	0.11
Married	0.34	0.09
Separated	0.30	0.12
Firm size (number of workers)		
1–5	0.49	0.19
5–50	0.30	0.09
50+	0.28	0.01
Management		
Private	0.34	0.10
Public	0.33	0.01
Economic sector		
Agriculture	0.31	0.25
Extraction and electricity	0.57	0.02
Manufacturing	0.05	0.07
Construction	0.81	0.29
Commerce	0.18	0.11
Communications and transports	0.70	0.50
Services	0.31	0.19
Public administration and defense	0.40	0.00
All	0.33	0.09
In 1994: III quarter	0.35	0.11
In 2004: IV quarter	0.33	0.08

Source: Based on data from 1994 to 2004 ENEU.

Occupational segregation by gender in Mexico, as in most labor markets, is less pronounced among people with more years of schooling. Interestingly, however, hierarchical segregation is more pronounced among people with more years of schooling. Although younger workers display lower levels of occupational segregation, hierarchical segregation appears to remain constant over the life cycle. Occupational segregation is lower among single (including both never-married and separated) individuals than among married people; the opposite is true for hierarchical segregation. Both types of segregation are significantly more pronounced in smaller firms.

Although the Mexican public sector exhibits almost no hierarchical segregation, it displays levels of occupational segregation similar to those in the private sector. The ENEU records eight firm activities (agriculture, extraction and electricity, manufacturing, construction, commerce, communications and transport, services, and public administration and defense). The rankings of sectors according to occupational and hierarchical segregation show some differences across these sectors. The greatest occupational segregation by gender is found in construction firms, followed by communications and transport; the lowest is found in manufacturing. The greatest hierarchical segregation by gender is among people who work in communications and transport; the lowest is in public administration and defense.

Overall, occupational segregation is substantially greater than hierarchical segregation. Both have been decreasing, albeit slightly. During the 10-year span analyzed, occupational segregation dropped 2 percentage points (from 0.35 to 0.33), and hierarchical segregation dropped 3 percentage points (from 0.11 to 0.08).

The Role of Individual Characteristics in Explaining the Earnings Gap

To some extent, gender differences in individual characteristics that are important for the labor market can explain gender differences in occupations and hierarchies. It could be the case that gender disparities in education, for example, which are still prevalent in Mexican labor markets, somehow determine occupational and hierarchical sorting by gender.

The extent to which this argument is valid is evaluated here by analyzing three counterfactual situations, in which, first, there are no gender differences in age, schooling, or marital status; second, there are no gender differences in hierarchies; and third, there are no gender differences in age, schooling, marital status, or hierarchies. The evolution of occupational segregation in each of these situations is explored by comparing the original Duncan index with the index that would prevail in each hypothetical counterfactual situation (figure 6.1). The counterfactual situations are generated with the same matching approach used to decompose earnings gaps, illustrating the versatility of the matching approach.[3]

The results suggest that eliminating all gender differences in age, schooling, and marital status in the labor market would have reduced occupational segregation by 2–3 percentage points for the period 1994–2004. Eliminating gender differences in hierarchies would have reduced occupational segregation by about 1 percentage point. Eliminating both

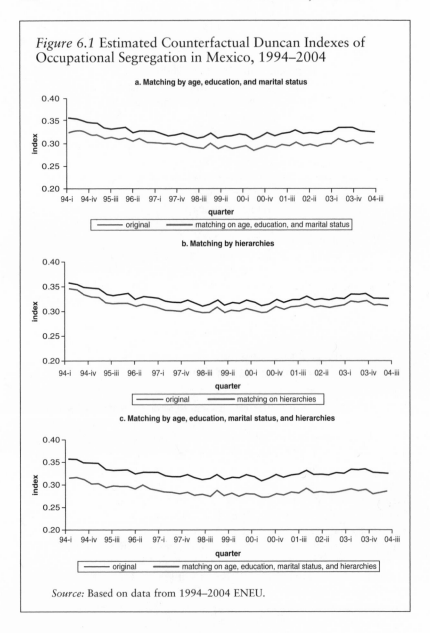

Figure 6.1 Estimated Counterfactual Duncan Indexes of Occupational Segregation in Mexico, 1994–2004

a. Matching by age, education, and marital status

b. Matching by hierarchies

c. Matching by age, education, marital status, and hierarchies

Source: Based on data from 1994–2004 ENEU.

sets of differences would have reduced the Duncan index by about 4 percentage points. The differences between the counterfactual and the actual indexes are roughly constant over the period.

The same exercise is conducted to analyze the evolution of hierarchical segregation. In this case, the first counterfactual situation is one in which there are no gender differences in age, schooling, or marital status; the second is one in which gender differences in occupations are eliminated; and the third is one in which there are no gender differences in age, schooling, marital status, or occupations (figure 6.2).

The results suggest that the impact of the observable characteristics on the reduction in hierarchical segregation is greater than the impact of occupational segregation (especially when taking account of the fact that the original levels of hierarchical segregation are lower than the levels of occupational segregation). The role of occupations decreases in importance during the later portion of the period under analysis. The hypothetical situation in which working men and women have the same age, schooling, and marital status leads to a hierarchical segregation that would have been lower by 1 percentage point than the one actually observed between 1994 and 2004. Eliminating occupational segregation would have reduced hierarchical segregation by as much as 6–7 percentage points in the mid-1990s and about 3 percent in 2004. The combined effect of eliminating occupational segregation and gender differences in individual characteristics (age, schooling, and marital status) would have reduced hierarchical segregation by 7–8 percentage points in the mid-1990s and by 4 percentage points in 2004.

These results indicate that individual characteristics play a (somewhat small) role in determining gender segregation in the Mexican labor market. Occupational and hierarchical segregation are linked, in the sense that a reduction in one leads to a reduction in the other.

The counterfactual analysis seeks to answer the questions "by how much would the gender earnings gap change if (occupational or hierarchical) segregation were reduced to zero?" and "by how much would the gender earnings gap change if gender differences in observable characteristics were reduced to zero?" To answer these questions, the analysis matched men and women based on first, age, schooling, and marital status; second, hierarchies; and third, occupations.

The gender earnings gap shows a decreasing trend during most of the period under analysis, interrupted by only two years of increase (Figure 6.3). By the mid-1990s, on average, men earned about 18 percent more than women per hour worked. This gap declined to almost 12 percent by 2004.

The role of age, schooling, and marital status in explaining gender differences in earnings changed as well. During the mid-1990s, these characteristics explained almost half of the earnings gap. After 2002, they seem to play almost no role in determining gender differences in pay.

During the late 1990s, a hypothetical world in which there was no hierarchical segregation but everything else remained the same would have shown gender earnings gaps similar to those in a hypothetical world in which there were no gender differences in age, schooling, or marital status in the labor market. Later, the hypothetical gender earnings gap without hierarchical segregation becomes somewhat smaller than the hypothetical

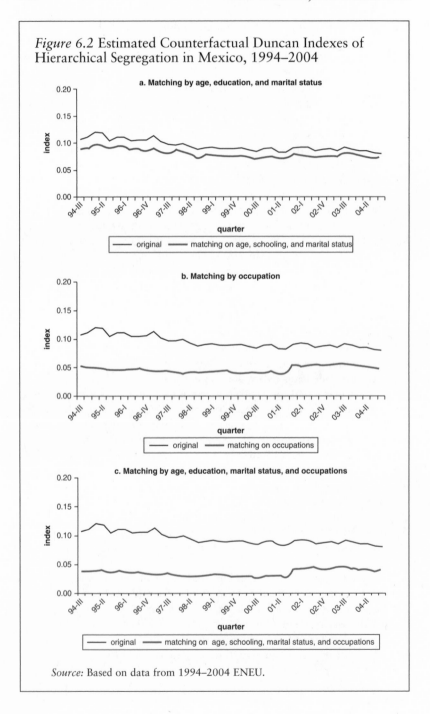

Figure 6.2 Estimated Counterfactual Duncan Indexes of Hierarchical Segregation in Mexico, 1994–2004

Source: Based on data from 1994–2004 ENEU.

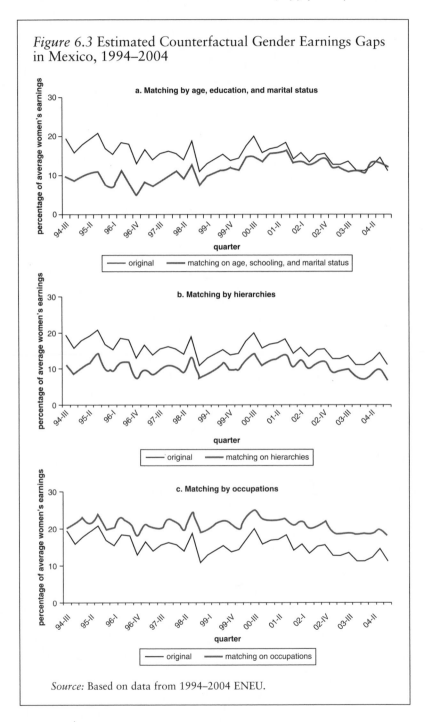

Figure 6.3 Estimated Counterfactual Gender Earnings Gaps in Mexico, 1994–2004

Source: Based on data from 1994–2004 ENEU.

gender earnings gap without age, gender, and marital status differences. For 2000–04, the average gender earnings gap was about 14 percent; in the hypothetical world with no hierarchical segregation, that gap would have reached only 10 percent.

The hypothetical world in which there is no occupational segregation shows results that are somewhat surprising, as the earnings gap exceeds the one actually observed. Moreover, the difference between the hypothetical and the actual gap increases over time, mainly during the 1990s, so that by 2004 the earnings gap would have been 3 percentage points larger than the gap at the beginning of the period.

Why is it that a reduction in hierarchical segregation would lead to a reduction of earnings gaps but a reduction in occupational segregation would not? What forces were behind this development, and how did they evolve during the period of analysis? To approach these questions, one would like to know how the earnings gap changes when occupational segregation varies. Analyzing this question requires defining occupations dominated by men and women and studying the earnings structure in each type of occupations.

Mathematically, the element of interest is $\partial G/\partial D$, the rate at which the earnings gap (G) varies for infinitesimal changes in occupational segregation (D). This element has two components $(W_{MM} - W_{MF})$ and $(W_{FM} - W_{FF})$. (For a demonstration of this result and the theoretical framework behind it, see Calónico and Ñopo 2008.) These components can be interpreted as two different gaps. The first is the earnings gap for men—the difference between the average earnings for men in occupations dominated by men and the average earnings for men in occupations dominated by women. The second is the gap for women: the difference between the average earnings for women in occupations dominated by men and the average earnings for women in occupations dominated by women.

Male and female dominance were defined on the basis of the gender composition in each occupation over the period under analysis. Three out of seven occupations at the one-digit level (managers, workers in agricultural activities, and workers in industrial activities) were considered dominated by men. The other four (professionals and technicians, administrative personnel, salespersons, and workers in the service sector) were considered dominated by women.

The upper panel of Figure 6.4 shows the estimation of $\partial G/\partial D$ and its components. Both components, and hence $\partial G/\partial D$, are negative for the whole period under analysis—that is, average earnings of men and women in occupations dominated by women were higher than average earnings of men and women in occupations dominated by men. Hence, it is not surprising to observe that a reduction in gender occupational segregation would lead to an increase in gender earnings gaps in Mexico.

The difference between the actual earnings gap and the hypothetical earnings gap without occupational segregation increased during the period

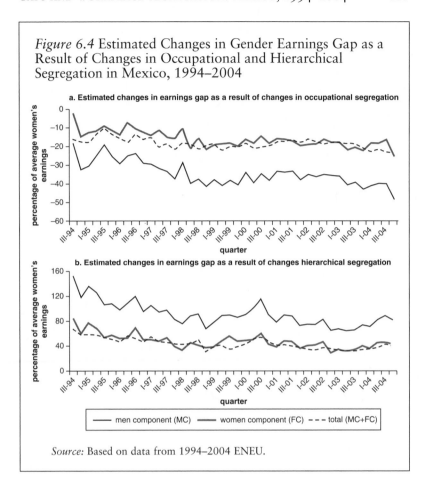

Figure 6.4 Estimated Changes in Gender Earnings Gap as a Result of Changes in Occupational and Hierarchical Segregation in Mexico, 1994–2004

Source: Based on data from 1994–2004 ENEU.

of analysis. This result is observed in the estimation of $\partial G/\partial D$, which was more negative in the later years of the analysis. A more than proportional decrease in earnings in occupations dominated by men guides this increasing difference.

The analogous exercise was performed with hierarchies instead of occupations (panel b in Figure 6.4). For this purpose, three of the five hierarchical categories (managers, piece-rate or by commission workers, and members of cooperatives) were considered dominated by men, and two categories (independent workers and fixed-salaried workers) were considered dominated by women. In contrast to the results for occupations, these results indicate that reductions in hierarchical segregation are expected to be linked to reductions in the earnings gap. This finding is in line with the results reported earlier in this chapter.

Hence, although hierarchical segregation by gender has been substantially lower than occupational segregation during the last two decades, the two types of segregation have had highly dissimilar impacts on earnings. Eliminating hierarchical segregation would reduce the observed gender earnings gap by about 5 percentage points, whereas eliminating occupational segregation would increase it by about 6 percentage points. A reduction in gender differences in age, schooling, and marital status would have a greater impact on the reduction of observed occupational segregation than on hierarchical segregation. A reduction in occupational segregation would have a significant impact on the reduction of hierarchical segregation, although the reverse may not necessarily be true. The results also suggest that gender equalization of human capital characteristics would help reduce not only gender earnings gaps but also both hierarchical and occupational segregation.

The next four chapters analyze what happened in countries in which this equalization occurred. As in all Latin American countries, women's labor participation in these countries increased in the past two decades. However, the ranking of these countries varied. In Chile (chapter 7), women's labor participation has been below the Latin American average since the early 1990s. In Colombia (chapter 8), women's labor force participation has been about average for the region since the early 1990s. Brazil (chapter 9) and Ecuador (chapter 10) are among the top five Latin American countries based on women's labor participation in both the early 1990s and the 2000s.

Notes

1. At the end of 2001, the Encuesta Nacional de Empleo (ENE) replaced the ENEU, extending coverage to the entire country. The analysis here is restricted to the urban subsample of the ENE, however, which is comparable to the ENEU sample. At the beginning of the period under consideration, the cities included in the sample represented about 40 percent of Mexico's working population. During the 10-year span examined in this chapter, coverage increased to 60 percent (48 cities).

2. Computation at the two-digit level, which includes 18 occupations, yields results that are qualitatively similar (albeit somewhat stronger). These computations are available from the authors upon request. For a discussion of the influence of the number of categories on the computation of the Duncan index, see Anker (1998).

3. For a description of the matching methodology, see chapter 2.

References

Anker, R. 1998. *Gender and Jobs: Sex Segregation of Occupations in the World.* Geneva: International Labor Organization.

Brown, C., J. Pagan, and E. Rodriguez-Oreggia. 1999. "Occupational Attainment and Gender Earnings Differentials in Mexico." *Industrial and Labor Relations Review* 53 (1): 123–35.

Calónico, S., and H. Ñopo. 2008. "Gender Segregation in the Workplace and Wage Gaps: Evidence from Urban Mexico, 1994–2004." Research Department Working Paper 636, Inter-American Development Bank, Washington, DC.

Calónico, S., and H. Ñopo. 2009. "Gender Segregation in the Workplace and Wage Gaps: Evidence from Urban Mexico 1994–2004." In *Occupational and Residential Segregation (Research on Economic Inequality, Volume 17)*, ed. Yves Flückiger, Sean F. Reardon, and Jacques Silber, 245–70. Bingley, U.K.: Emerald Group Publishing Limited.

Chinhui, J., and J. Airola. 2005. "Wage Inequality in Post-Reform Mexico." Working Paper 2005–01, Department of Economics, University of Houston, Houston, TX.

Colmenares, G. 2006. "Segregación en el empleo por sexo: salario y ocupación en los modelos de industrialización de las regiones centro-occidente y fronteriza." *Frontera Norte* 18 (35): 87–110.

Duncan, O. D., and B. Duncan. 1955. "A Methodological Analysis of Segregation Indexes." *American Sociological Review* 20 (2): 210–17.

Elias, J., and H. Ñopo. 2010. "The Increase in Women Labor Force Participation in Latin America 1990–2004: Decomposing the Changes." Report, Inter-American Development Bank, Washington, DC.

López Acevedo, G. 2003. "Wages and Productivity in Mexican Manufacturing." Policy Research Working Paper 2964, World Bank, Washington, DC.

Pagan, J., and S. Sánchez. 2000. "Gender Differences in Labor Market Decisions: Evidence from Rural Mexico." *Economic Development and Cultural Change* 48 (3): 619–37.

Parker, S. 1999. "Niveles salariales de hombres y mujeres: diferencias por ocupación en las áreas urbanas de México." In *México diverso y desigual: enfoques sociodemográficos*, coord. B. F. Campos, 373–90. Serie Investigación Demográfica en México 4, Colegio de México/Sociedad Mexicana de Demografía, Mexico City.

Rendón, T. 2003. "Empleo, segregación y salarios por género." In *La situación del trabajo en México*, ed. E. de la Garza and C. Salas, 129–50. Mexico City: Plaza y Valdés.

Rendón, T., and V. M. Maldonado. 2004. *Vínculos entre trabajo doméstico, segregación ocupacional y diferencias de ingreso por sexo, en el México actual.* Instituto de Estudios del Trabajo, Mexico City.

Sánchez, S. 1998. "Gender Earnings Differentials in the Microenterprise Sector: Evidence from Rural and Urban Mexico." Report, World Bank, Latin America and the Caribbean Region, Finance, Private Sector, and Infrastructure Sector Unit, Washington, DC.

7

Low Participation by Women, Heavy Overtime by Men: Chile 1992–2009

Despite major advances in the education of women in Chile's labor force relative to men, gender differences in earnings remain. This chapter explores the relatively low remuneration of women's human capital.

All of the statistics and estimations presented in this chapter are based on the CASEN, the official household survey of Chile conducted by the Ministry of Social Development, (earlier named, Ministry of Planning and Cooperation [MIDEPLAN]) since 1987. The survey covers Chile's entire population, in both urban and rural areas.

The period under analysis runs from 1992 to 2009. As the main objective of this chapter is to estimate and explain gender earnings gaps in Chile, the population under consideration is all employed men and women 16–75 years old. Selection issues are ignored; earnings are measured as hourly earnings.

What Does the Literature Show?

The literature on the Chilean gender earnings gap is not new. The first studies on the topic include work by Paredes (1982) and Paredes and Riveros (1994). Performing Blinder-Oaxaca decompositions for the period 1958–90 in the metropolitan area of Santiago, they provide evidence of

This chapter was adapted from the following sources: "The Gender Wage Gap in Chile 1992–2003 from a Matching Comparisons Perspective," Hugo Ñopo, IZA Discussion Paper 2698, Institute for the Study of Labor, 2007; "The Gender Wage Gap in Chile 1992–2003 from a Matching Comparisons Perspective," Hugo Ñopo, RES Working Paper 4463, Inter-American Development Bank, 2007.

unexplained gender earnings differences, which they find correlated with the business cycle.

Along similar lines, both methodologically and with respect to the data set utilized, Contreras and Puentes (2000) study the evolution of the gender gap for the period 1958–96 in Greater Santiago, reaching similar conclusions. Their evidence suggests that unexplained differences in earnings decreased from the 1960s to the 1980s, before this trend was reversed in the 1990s. Additionally, they find that these unexplained gender differences in pay are largely a result of the underpayment of women rather than the overpayment of men.

Montenegro and Paredes (1999) introduce a quantile regressions approach to the analysis, complementing the Blinder-Oaxaca decompositions with a deeper exploration of the distribution of unexplained pay differences. Using the same data set as the previous studies for the period 1960–98, they find systematic gender differences in returns to education and experience along the conditional earnings distribution. Returns to education are higher for women in lower quantiles and lower for women in upper quantiles. The authors do not find a systematic pattern in the level of unexplained differences in pay over time except for the last decade, when, despite a tighter labor market, they observe an increase in the gender earnings differential. They show that the gender earnings gap is much larger in the upper quantiles and report that although the gender earnings gap was falling in Chile, the unexplained component of it was increasing. This result is consistent with the findings of García, Hernández, and López (2001).

Montenegro (2001) analyzes gender differentials in returns to education, returns to experience, and earnings. Using quantile regressions with Blinder-Oaxaca decompositions and micro data from Chile's National Socioeconomic Characterization Survey (Encuesta de Caracterización Socioeconómico Nacional [CASEN]), which are nationally and regionally representative for the period 1990–98, he finds systematic gender differences in returns to education and experience along the conditional earnings distribution. The results show that returns to education are significantly different for men and women by quintiles, although returns to education at the median produce very similar results for men and women, implying that an ordinary least squares mean estimate will not detect the richness of these gender differences. The results for returns to years of experience show that in the lower quantiles, men and women have similar rates of return, whereas in the upper quintiles men tend to have higher rates of return. Montenegro also finds evidence that the unexplained earnings differential is larger in the upper quintiles of the conditional earnings distribution. In particular, he shows that the unexplained earnings gap steadily increases from 10 percent to 40 percent when moving from the lower to the upper part of the conditional earnings distribution.

Bravo, Sanhueza, and Urzúa (2008) use the Chilean Social Protection Survey 2002 (SPS02), which includes information on variables that determine social security participation in Chile. They focus their attention on individuals age 28–40 at the time of the survey, who have most likely completed their last level of schooling and studied under the same education system (which changed radically in 1980 in Chile). Their study uses traditional linear and nonlinear models of earnings differentials with selection correction (Heckman 1979). The authors find that gender earnings gaps are about 23 percent of women's earnings and grow to 29 percent after correcting for selection. They also find that the gender gap is larger (36–38 percent of women's earnings) among university graduates, regardless of their experience. All other labor market characteristics explored show no significant gender difference among university graduates. The largest gender gaps in weekly hours worked, unemployment, and experience are found among less educated groups.

Using the same database, Perticará (2007) estimates gender earnings differentials with a sensitivity analysis that explores the earnings gap obtained from ordinary least squares estimations for different levels of actual experience. The information in the data set allows the construction of a variable for actual experience that takes into account the fact that patterns of experience differ for men and women, because women are out of the labor market for longer periods than men. As a result, although average years of work after school (potential experience) are similar for both men and women, average actual experience is 16.7 years for men and 9.3 years for women, and women's experience is more volatile. Gender differences in experience are smaller among the more educated. Perticará finds that the inclusion of variables measuring actual experience reduces the gender earnings gap about 50 percent, but when controlling for selection bias, the unexplained component of the gender earnings gap increases.

Perticará and Bueno (2008) explore the gender earnings gap and its relation to years of actual experience. Based on a detailed sensitivity analysis with ordinary least squares estimations, instrumental variables, and selection correction, they find that gender earnings gaps are negative for all variables analyzed and that gaps are larger after controlling for actual experience only. Recent actual experience yields higher labor market returns, which may help explain the increase in real earnings from 2002 to 2006. The different estimation approaches presented reveal the importance of correcting for endogeneity and selection problems. When not correcting for the endogeneity of the variables for educational attainment and work experience, the effect of education on earnings differentials is overestimated and the effect of experience underestimated. Perticará and Bueno calculate earnings differentials across occupations after correcting for labor market selection. They observe larger gender earnings gaps among blue-collar workers and salespeople and smaller gaps among professionals and administrative personnel.

Using the CASEN survey, García (2000) studies the labor market participation of women and the gender earnings gap for the period 1990–98.

She observes that the participation of women in the labor market increased across income quintiles: 24 percent of the women in the bottom income quintile and 42 percent of women in the top quintile work. The gender earnings gap also varies across income quintiles, from 43 percent in the bottom quintile to 59 percent in the top quintile. García finds similar results when analyzing the gender earnings gap for different sectors and types of job. As the difference in earnings for men and women remained stable over the period, she concludes that there is evidence that underpayment of women is a persistent phenomenon in Chile.

Perticará and Astudillo (2008) use quantile regression techniques and the decomposition technique suggested by Mata and Machado (2005) to evaluate the unexplained component of the gender earnings gaps along the conditional earnings distribution after controlling for actual experience. They find that the portion of the gender earnings gap explained by characteristics is small and not statistically significant until the 50th percentile, where it becomes positive and thus favors women, growing monotonically until it reaches 7 percent in the 90th percentile. At the top of the distribution, women compensate for "discrimination" with attributes that are better rewarded in the labor markets.

How Do Male and Female Workers Differ?

When trying to explain differences in earnings between men and women, one can attribute them to some observable individual characteristics that determine earnings. Doing so would be a valid argument in cases where differences in age, education, occupational experience, and occupation, among other characteristics, exist. The purpose of this chapter is to measure the extent to which these differences in characteristics explain differences in pay between men and women in Chile.[1] Exploring some descriptive statistics by gender elucidates this notion. This section explores the main characteristics of working men and women, including education, labor market participation, unemployment rates, average working hours, and hourly earnings.

Differences in Education

Female workers in Chile have higher levels of education than men (figure 7.1). On average, women have one more year of schooling than men in Chile. In 1992, on average, women had 10.2 years of education and men had 9.1 years. In 2009, the average was 12.0 years of schooling for women and 11.2 years for men. The observed increase in average years of schooling during this period was slightly greater for men than for women: between 1992 and 2009, average years of education increased 18.5 percent for women and 22.8 percent for men. As a result, the schooling gender gap narrowed slightly during the 1990s and 2000s, although it still favors women.

The educational gender gap in Chile is evident in both rural and urban areas. Over the 1992–2009 period, the average number of years of schooling for all workers was 7.5 years in rural areas and 11.1 years in urban areas. The average increased in both areas. Large differences are observed in years of schooling of working men and women in rural areas, where women have on average 1.6 years of education more than men. In urban areas, this difference is 0.5 year.

The share of less educated workers decreased sharply between 1992 and 2009, and the share of workers with university education rose. In 2009, 11.2 percent of working people had no education or had not completed primary school. This proportion was 25.2 percent in 1992. Over the same period, the share of working people who completed university rose from 8.0 percent to 14.6 percent (figure 7.2). Both men and women saw important improvements over the period, during which the difference in favor of female workers remained almost constant.

The percentage of the working population with university education is lower in rural areas (2.2 percent) than in urban areas (10.8 percent). This difference widened during the period of analysis. Gender differences persisted over the whole period, and the difference in the percentage of

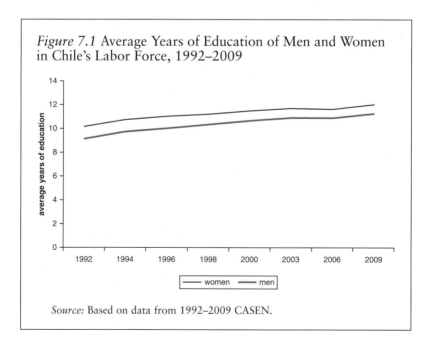

Figure 7.1 Average Years of Education of Men and Women in Chile's Labor Force, 1992–2009

Source: Based on data from 1992–2009 CASEN.

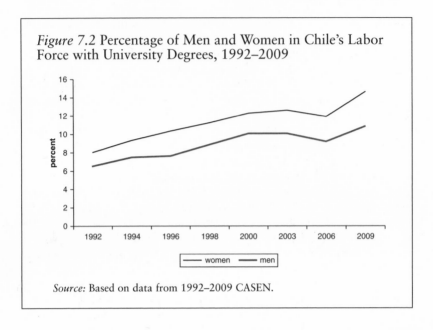

Figure 7.2 Percentage of Men and Women in Chile's Labor Force with University Degrees, 1992–2009

Source: Based on data from 1992–2009 CASEN.

men and women with at least a university degree grew. The gap widened more quickly in rural areas, although it is larger in urban areas.

Figure 7.3 presents the percentage of employed men and women with less than high school education. It shows evidence of both a general improvement in education and a gender gap in favor of women. About 80 percent of employed men and women in rural areas have not completed high school; in urban areas, this percentage falls to 42 percent.

Differences in Labor Force Participation, Unemployment, and Hours Worked

The Chilean labor market has several particularities. Two striking stylized facts are low female labor force participation and the high number of hours of work, especially among men.

Figure 7.4 shows the evolution of participation rates for men and women. The evidence indicates that the gender gap in participation narrowed during the last decade, as a result of both a decrease in male participation and an increase in female participation. In 1992, only 25 percent of women participated in the labor market; by 2009, this proportion reached 33 percent.

Accompanying this increase in participation, Chile experienced an increase in unemployment, particularly in 1998, when the unemployment

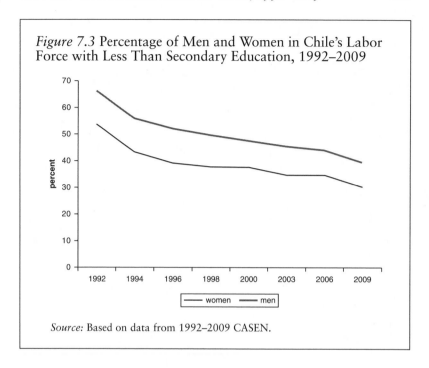

Figure 7.3 Percentage of Men and Women in Chile's Labor Force with Less Than Secondary Education, 1992–2009

Source: Based on data from 1992–2009 CASEN.

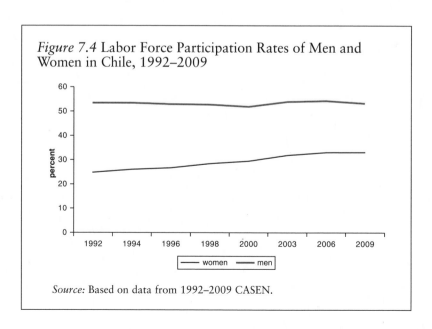

Figure 7.4 Labor Force Participation Rates of Men and Women in Chile, 1992–2009

Source: Based on data from 1992–2009 CASEN.

rate jumped from 2.3 percent to 4.0 percent, affecting men and women equally (figure 7.5). Overall, gender differences in unemployment did not change much from the beginning to the end of the period, although they increased between 1996 and 2000 and decreased between 2000 and 2006, when unemployment and the difference between men and women increased again.

Gender differences in unemployment rates are evident by level of educational attainment as well (figure 7.6). Less educated people in Chile, especially women, display higher unemployment rates. Among less educated people, the increase in unemployment in 1998 (with respect to 1996) was similar for men and women. For university graduates, however, the change in unemployment disproportionately affected women, unemployment of whom more than doubled between 1996 and 1998.

The evolution of the gender composition of the labor force by occupations shows a slight reduction in the gap among merchants and workers in the service and agricultural sectors. Another stylized fact to highlight is the apparent lack of a gap among managers. Women's participation in the labor force is concentrated in the service sector (about 45 percent of working women are employed as service workers, merchants, or salespeople). In contrast, about 60 percent of men are blue-collar or agricultural workers.

An important variable to take into account when analyzing earnings gaps is occupational experience. Traditionally, studies have used a

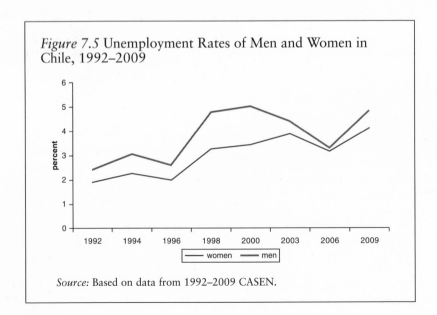

Figure 7.5 Unemployment Rates of Men and Women in Chile, 1992–2009

Source: Based on data from 1992–2009 CASEN.

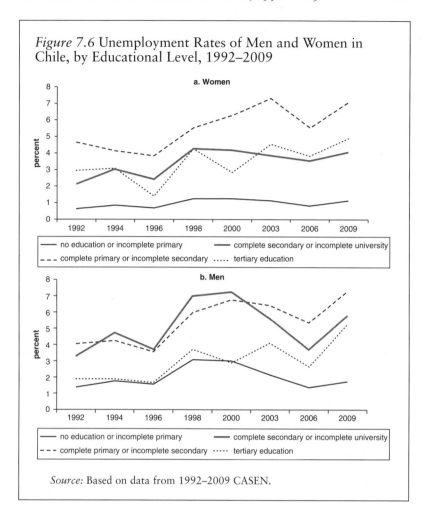

Figure 7.6 Unemployment Rates of Men and Women in Chile, by Educational Level, 1992–2009

Source: Based on data from 1992–2009 CASEN.

proxy—potential experience—computed as a linear combination of age and schooling. The evidence suggests that this approach tends to produce biased estimates of the gender gap (see Weichselbaumer and Winter-Ebmer 2003). The CASEN data provide a rare opportunity to use occupational experience, at least for the last four years under analysis (figure 7.7). Average years at the same occupation remained fairly constant over 2000–09, but gender differences grew in the last year and favored men during the whole period.

Figure 7.8 presents the average number of hours of work per week by gender. Working hours increased from 49.5 hours per week in 1992 to 51.6 in 1998, decreasing after that to 43.6 in 2009. The peak—observed in 1998, when men worked an average of 53.4 hours a week—can be

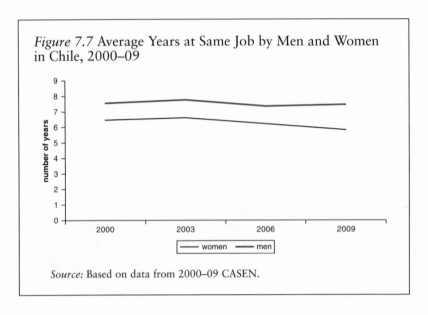

Figure 7.7 Average Years at Same Job by Men and Women in Chile, 2000–09

Source: Based on data from 2000–09 CASEN.

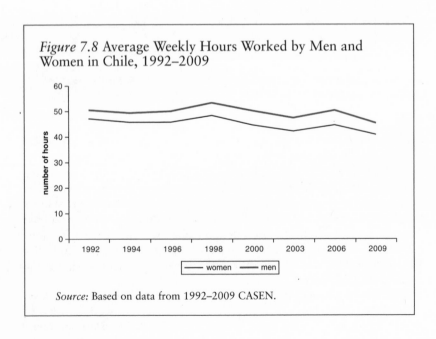

Figure 7.8 Average Weekly Hours Worked by Men and Women in Chile, 1992–2009

Source: Based on data from 1992–2009 CASEN.

linked to the recession of 1998 (and the corresponding increase in unemployment). The gender gap in hours of work was about 3.5 hours at the beginning of the 1990s; it increased until 2006, reaching 5.9 hours, before decreasing to 4.4 hours in 2009. However, there was an overall increase in the gap during the period of analysis. Working hours is one of the few individual characteristics for which the gender gap widened during the decade.

Workers with less education used to devote more hours to the labor market than skilled workers (figure 7.9). However, this gap, which was wide in the early 1990s, narrowed until 2003, as hours worked fell for all levels of skill but especially for less skilled workers. In 2009, a typical highly educated Chilean worked one hour less than in 1990, but a typical unskilled worker worked nearly five hours less than in the early 1990s. The differences in the hours of work by workers of different education levels started to narrow in 1998 and had almost disappeared by 2003. At the beginning of the decade, the difference in the number of hours worked by educational level was larger for women than for men; by 2009, such differences had become almost negligible for both men and women. However, by 2009, the average hours of work of employed men and women seem to be independent of educational level.

Differences in Earnings

Working women in Chile have more schooling than men, in both rural and urban areas. As education is an important determinant of earnings, it would be expected that women would have higher earnings than men. In fact, the statistics show the opposite result.

During the 1990s, the Chilean economy performed better than that of all other countries in the region. Average annual gross domestic product growth was 6.3 percent, and the rate of inflation was the lowest in four decades. As a result, earnings increased considerably since 1996, even in 1998, when the economy suffered a slowdown. Between 1990 and 2009, average real hourly earnings (deflated by the consumer price index) increased 51 percent (54 percent for men, 51 percent for women).

Figure 7.10 shows the average hourly earnings gap as a multiple of average hourly earnings of women. The gap between men and women reached the widest level of the decade in 2000, when men earned on average 35 percent more than women. The gender earnings gap ranged from 25 percent at the beginning of the decade to 35 percent in 2000, when it started decreasing, reaching 15 percent of women's earnings in 2006. The period ended with an increase in the gap, which rose to 30 percent in 2009. The gender gap in hourly earnings is substantially higher in urban than in rural areas.

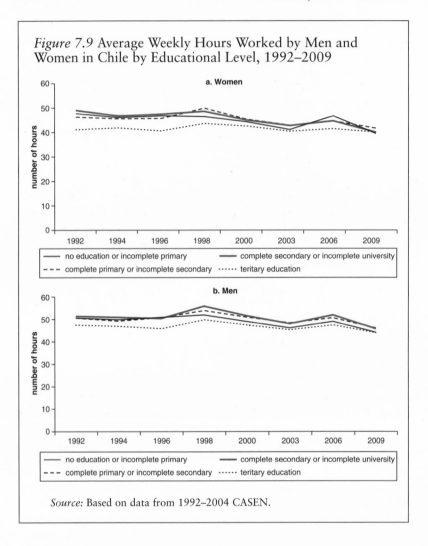

Figure 7.9 Average Weekly Hours Worked by Men and Women in Chile by Educational Level, 1992–2009

Source: Based on data from 1992–2004 CASEN.

The Role of Individual Characteristics in Explaining the Gender Earnings Gap

The gender earnings gap reported in Figure 7.10 does not take account of the fact that men and women differ in observable characteristics that the labor market rewards. It is important to measure the extent to which gender differences in observable human capital characteristics explain the gender earnings gap and the extent to which gender differences remain unexplained. Doing so involves decomposing the gender earnings gap.

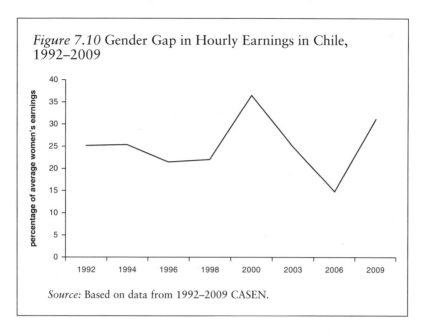

Figure 7.10 Gender Gap in Hourly Earnings in Chile, 1992–2009

Source: Based on data from 1992–2009 CASEN.

In this section, men and women are matched on the basis of five combinations of observable characteristics. The first set considers age, marital status, and years of schooling. The second set adds a variable that captures whether the worker works full time or part time. The third set replaces full-time and part-time status with occupational category (which aggregates occupations at the one-digit level). The fourth set simultaneously considers all the variables considered in the three previous sets. The fifth set adds years of occupational experience to the set of variables in the fourth set.

Table 7.1 reports the average statistics for men and women in and out of the "common support" for each set of matching characteristics. In general, unmatched men and women are older than their matched counterparts. In contrast, average years of education are higher in matched groups than in unmatched ones (except in the set of controls that includes occupational experience). Most of the men and women in the common support are (formally or informally) married. This is also the case for male workers outside the common support. In contrast, most unmatched women are separated or widows. Most of the matched men and women (about 30 percent) are service workers. A smaller percentage of men and women in the common support work as directors or managers relative to men and women outside the common support.

On average, matched men and women work more hours than unmatched workers, and the difference is larger for women. When average years at the

Table 7.1 Demographic and Job Characteristics of Matched and Unmatched Samples of Men and Women in Chile's Labor Force, 1992–2009 *(percent)*

Characteristics	Age, education, marital status, and occupation			Age, education, marital status, time worked, and occupation			Age, education, marital status, and years at the same job		
	Matched sample	Unmatched women	Unmatched men	Matched sample	Unmatched women	Unmatched men	Matched sample	Unmatched women	Unmatched men
Average age	37.7	48.9	48.0	37.5	47.3	49.3	36.8	46.0	46.5
Average years of schooling	11.3	10.8	10.8	11.4	10.2	10.3	11.7	11.8	10.5
Marital status									
Single	35.0	20.6	17.9	35.4	19.7	20.1	34.0	31.0	15.7
Married	51.1	2.9	62.8	51.8	12.3	60.7	57.8	28.0	74.0
Divorced	11.2	26.5	11.5	10.5	33.0	11.3	7.5	28.7	7.8
Widower	2.8	50.0	7.8	2.3	34.9	7.9	0.8	12.3	2.5
Education level									
No education or primary incomplete	16.6	17.5	20.4	16.4	22.6	23.1	12.5	15.4	23.5
Primary incomplete or secondary incomplete	21.2	31.8	21.0	21.1	30.1	23.5	20.4	23.0	30.7
Secondary incomplete or tertiary incomplete	50.7	36.3	41.3	51.0	36.2	37.4	55.9	43.0	32.6
Tertiary complete	11.5	14.3	17.2	11.6	11.1	16.0	11.3	18.6	13.2

Table 7.1 (continued)

Characteristics	Age, education, marital status, and occupation			Age, education, marital status, time worked, and occupation			Age, education, marital status, and years at the same job		
	Matched sample	Unmatched women	Unmatched men	Matched sample	Unmatched women	Unmatched men	Matched sample	Unmatched women	Unmatched men
Occupation									
Professionals and technicians	22.2	13.8	8.4	22.4	12.7	10.0			
Directors and upper management	5.0	12.9	6.9	4.9	10.4	9.0			
Administrative personnel	14.9	20.6	6.8	15.0	15.3	6.3			
Merchants and sellers	12.6	18.7	4.7	12.5	18.0	5.5			
Service workers	30.7	28.0	2.9	30.3	37.3	4.1			
Agricultural workers and similar	5.1	1.1	11.7	5.2	1.3	12.5			
Nonagricultural blue-collars	9.5	3.3	21.2	9.7	4.2	28.1			
Armed forces	0.0	0.4	33.5	0.0	0.2	21.9			
Average hours of work				45.3	32.3	42.8			
Average Years at the same job							4.8	11.2	13.7

Source: Based on data from 1992–2009 CASEN.
Note: Blank cells indicate that a variable is not being controlled for.

same job are used as a control for the matching, men and women in the common support remain at the same job for 4.8 years on average, whereas women out of the common support stay 11.2 years and men 13.7 years.

Figures 7.11 and 7.12 report the earnings gap decompositions in which some empirical regularities arise.

First, the differences in observable characteristics (Δ_X), and to some extent the component of the earnings gap that reflects the fact that women achieve certain combinations of characteristics that men do not (Δ_F), are negative. This result reflects the fact that human capital characteristics, especially education, are better rewarded for women than for men in Chile.

Second, the component of the gap that reflects the fact that men achieve certain combinations of characteristics that women do not (Δ_M) is generally

Figure 7.11 Decomposition of Gender Earnings Gap in Chile after Controlling for Demographic and Job Characteristics, 1992–2009

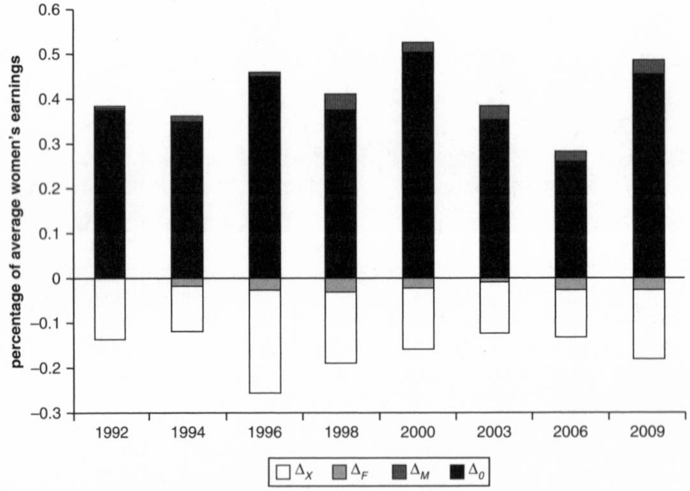

Source: Based on data from 1992–2009 CASEN.

Note: Δ_M (Δ_F) is the part of the earnings gap attributed to the existence of men (women) with combinations of characteristics that are not met by any women (men). Δ_X is the part of the earnings gap attributed to differences in the observable characteristics of men and women over the "common support." Δ_0 is the part of the earnings gap that cannot be attributed to differences in characteristics of the individuals. It is typically attributed to a combination of both unobservable characteristics and discrimination. The sum of these components equals the total earnings gap ($\Delta_M + \Delta_F + \Delta_X + \Delta_0 = \Delta$).

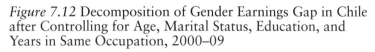

Figure 7.12 Decomposition of Gender Earnings Gap in Chile after Controlling for Age, Marital Status, Education, and Years in Same Occupation, 2000–09

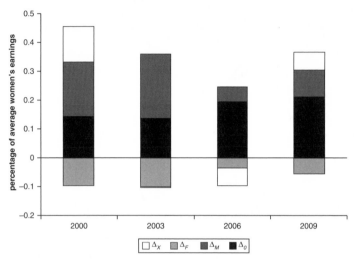

Source: Based on data from 2000–09 CASEN.

Note: Δ_M (Δ_F) is the part of the earnings gap attributed to the existence of men (women) with combinations of characteristics that are not met by any women (men). Δ_X is the part of the earnings gap attributed to differences in the observable characteristics of men and women over the "common support." Δ_0 is the part of the earnings gap that cannot be attributed to differences in characteristics of the individuals. It is typically attributed to a combination of both unobservable characteristics and discrimination. The sum of these components equals the total earnings gap ($\Delta_M + \Delta_F + \Delta_X + \Delta_0 = \Delta$).

positive, suggesting the existence of a sort of glass ceiling effect—that is, there are men with combinations of observable characteristics for which there are no comparable women, and these men have earnings that are on average higher than those in the rest of the economy.

Third, the component that remains unexplained by observable characteristics (Δ_0)—the component that cannot be attributed to differences in observable characteristics between men and women—is slightly larger than the original measure of gender earnings gaps (measured before matching). This is equivalent to saying that the measure of the gender earnings gap that remains unexplained after a Blinder-Oaxaca decomposition is larger than the original measure of the earnings gap, as reported in the literature on gender gaps in Chile summarized at the beginning of this chapter.

Exploring the Unexplained Component of the Gender Earnings Gap

Figure 7.13 presents confidence intervals for Δ_0, the component that measures the extent to which the gender earnings gap cannot be explained by observable individual characteristics. The extremes of the boxes represent confidence intervals at the 90 percent level; the extremes of the whiskers represent confidence intervals at the 99 percent level. The confidence intervals obtained from the last set of matching characteristics are larger than all others, because of the smaller number of matched men and women that corresponds to this large number of matching variables. This combination of individual characteristics best controls for gender differences (the unexplained component is the smallest of all combinations). However, it is so restrictive that it imposes a cost in terms of standard errors.

The next set of figures report on the distribution of the unexplained component. Figure 7.14 shows the distribution for the whole period, 1992–2009, using four sets of matching characteristics of the unexplained differences in earnings by percentiles of the earnings distribution. The results suggest that the unexplained component is larger among people in the highest percentiles of the earnings distribution. At the bottom of the earnings distribution, men earn an unexplained premium of 10–20 percent over comparable women; at the top of the distribution, this premium increases to 40–80 percent, depending on the set of matching characteristics.

This result differs from all previous results for the rest of Latin America and the Caribbean, where earnings gaps are larger for the poorest segments of the income distribution. In Chile alone, for all controls used, the gender earnings gap and its unexplained component is largest among the richest income quintile. This component increases more for the rich with each characteristic added to the controls, especially when time worked is added.

Analysis of the distribution of the unexplained component of the gender earnings gap by other observable characteristics shows that the largest and most disperse measures are among people with more education. The largest and most dispersed gap is among managers and, to a lesser extent, professionals.

There is some evidence of larger and more dispersed gaps among older individuals for almost all combinations of control characteristics, except for the one that includes on-the-job experience, for which larger and more dispersed gaps are found among middle-age individuals. By marital status, the largest gaps are found among married people. When experience (measured as years working at the same job) is introduced, however, all groups seem to have similar unexplained gaps, although the gaps are more dispersed among people who are separated. The unexplained earnings gap

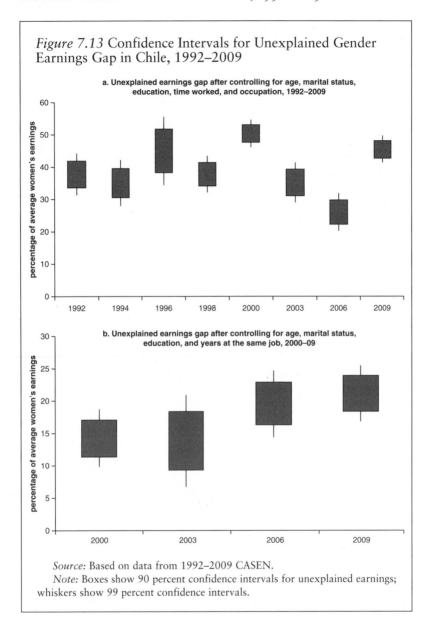

Figure 7.13 Confidence Intervals for Unexplained Gender Earnings Gap in Chile, 1992–2009

a. Unexplained earnings gap after controlling for age, marital status, education, time worked, and occupation, 1992–2009

b. Unexplained earnings gap after controlling for age, marital status, education, and years at the same job, 2000–09

Source: Based on data from 1992–2009 CASEN.

Note: Boxes show 90 percent confidence intervals for unexplained earnings; whiskers show 99 percent confidence intervals.

is substantially larger and more dispersed among people who work less than 20 hours per week than among the rest of the labor market.

The evidence of unexplained gaps by geographic location is mixed. When experience is not taken into account, the unexplained gap is larger

Figure 7.14 Unexplained Gender Earnings Gap in Chile, by
Percentiles of Earnings Distribution, 1992–2009

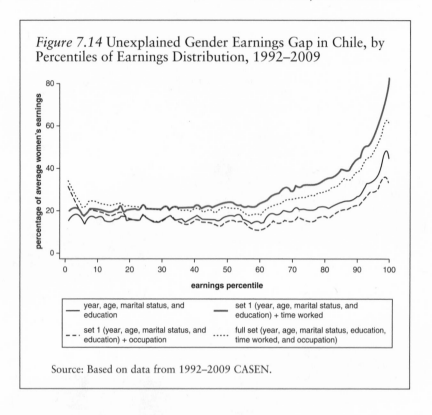

Source: Based on data from 1992–2009 CASEN.

in Santiago than in the rest of the country. But when experience is considered as one of the matching variables, the unexplained gap in the provinces is larger (and more disperse) than the gap in Santiago.

These results indicate that the earnings gender gap is proportionately larger among highly paid people, people with university education, directors, older workers, married workers, and part-time workers. There is no clear evidence that the unexplained gender earnings gap is higher in Santiago than in the rest of the country.

The results suggest the existence of a glass ceiling effect in Chile. There are particular combinations of experience, age, marital status, and education for which it is not possible to make gender comparisons. Married, older men (in their 50s and 60s) with more than 10 years of occupational experience are more likely to have no female counterparts actively working in the Chilean labor market. These men are more likely to work in managerial occupations and earn hourly earnings that are substantially higher than the national average. This segment of the labor force may account for 5–8 percentage points of the gender earnings gap in Chile.

Occupational experience seems to play an important role in explaining gender earnings gaps in Chile. Unfortunately, this variable is not available for all the years under consideration. For the years for which data are available, there are important differences in favor of men: men average eight years of occupational experience, whereas women average just six. These differences account for a large part of the earnings gap. If public policies in Chile led to increased occupational experience for women, there are good reasons to think that the gender earnings gap would narrow.

The next chapter examines the gender earnings gap in a country that has passed laws in this direction. Legislation in Colombia helps prevent women from dropping out of the labor market when they give birth and begin to raise their children. Such legislation may provide disincentives to hire them but can encourage women to stay longer in their jobs.

Note

1. For a description of the methodology used in this chapter, see chapter 2.

References

Bravo, D., C. Sanhueza, and S. Urzúa. 2008. "An Experimental Study of Labor Market Discrimination: Gender, Social Class, and Neighborhood in Chile." Research Network Working Paper R–541, Inter-American Development Bank, Washington, DC.

Contreras, D., and Puentes, E. 2000. "Is Gender Earnings Discrimination Decreasing in Chile? Thirty Years of 'Robust' Evidence." Department of Economics, University of Chile, Santiago.

García Durán, B. 2000. "Diagnóstico de la disciminación salarial de la mujer en el mercado laboral chileno." Ph.D. diss., Universidad de Chile, Santiago.

García, J., P. J. Hernández, and A. López. 2001. "How Wide Is the Gap? An Investigation of Gender Wage Differences Using Quantile Regression." *Empirical Economics* 26 (1): 149–67.

Heckman, J. 1979. "Sample Selection Bias as a Specification Error." *Econometrica* 47(1): 153–61.

Mata, J., and J. A. F. Machado. 2005. "Counterfactual Decomposition of Changes in Wage Distributions Using Quantile Regression." *Journal of Applied Econometrics* 20 (4): 445–65.

Montenegro, C. 2001. "Wage Distribution in Chile: Does Gender Matter? A Quantile Regression Approach." Policy Research Report on Gender and Development Working Paper 20, Development Research Group/Poverty Reduction and Economic Management Network, World Bank, Washington, DC.

Montenegro, C., and R. Paredes. 1999. "Gender Wage Gap and Discrimination: A Long Term View Using Quantile Regression." World Bank, Washington, DC, and University of Chile, Santiago. http://www.ricardoparedes.cl/paperweb/Montenegro_Paredes.PDF.

Paredes, R. 1982. "Diferencias de ingreso entre hombres y mujeres en el gran Santiago 1969 y 1981." *Estudios de Economía* 18: 99–121.

Paredes, R., and L. Riveros. 1994. "Gender Wage Gaps in Chile. A Long Term View: 1958–1990." *Estudios de Economía* 21(Número especial): 211–30.

Perticará, M. 2007. "Brechas salariales por género en Chile: un análisis de sensibilidad." ILADES–Georgetown University Working Paper inv195, Latin American Institute of Doctrine and Social Studies (ILADES), Universidad Alberto Hurtado, Santiago, and Georgetown University, Washington, DC.

Perticará, M., and A. Astudillo. 2008. "¿Qué tan alta puede ser la brecha de salarios en CHILE? Investigando diferencias salariales entre hombres y mujeres a partir de regresiones de cuantiles." ILADES–Georgetown University Working Paper inv211, Latin American Institute of Doctrine and Social Studies (ILADES), Universidad Alberto Hurtado, Santiago, and Georgetown University, Washington, DC.

Perticará, M., and I. Bueno. 2008. "Entendiendo las brechas salariales por genero en Chile." ILADES–Georgetown University Working Papers inv212, Latin American Institute of Doctrine and Social Studies (ILADES), Universidad Alberto Hurtado, Santiago, and Georgetown University, Washington, DC.

Puentes, E., and D. Contreras. 2000, "Is the Gender Wage Discrimination Decreasing in Chile? Thirty Years of 'Robust' Evidence." Latin American and Caribbean Economic Association, Chile.

Weichselbaumer, D., and R. Winter-Ebmer. 2003. "A Meta-Analysis of the International Gender Wage Gap." IZA Discussion Paper 906, Institute for the Study of Labor, Bonn, Germany.

8

The Resilient Earnings Gap: Colombia 1994–2006

Colombia's labor market experienced important changes during the last three decades. Despite strong improvement in the labor market characteristics of women and the legal framework to promote equality, however, the gender earnings gap changed little between 1994 and 2006. Moreover, the unemployment rate among women over the past two decades has consistently been about 5 percentage points higher than the rate for men (Sabogal 2009).

This chapter estimates the gender earnings gap between 1994 and 2006—a period that includes booms and recessions—and decomposes it using the methodology described in chapter 2. The data are drawn from quarterly household surveys conducted by the Colombian National Statistical Agency. Up to 2000, every other year the survey included an extensive labor market module in its second quarter release. This module included information on labor earnings, social security coverage, and firm size, among other areas. Since 2000, the extensive labor module has been included annually. This chapter analyzes all data from 1994 to 2006. As a result, 10 shifts of the survey for the period under analysis are included.

The evolution of hourly earnings for women and men during this period can be divided into three qualitatively different periods. During the first period, 1994–98, earnings grew, but with marked fluctuations. This period is characterized by a slowdown in overall economic activity. During the second period, 2000–01, earnings fell more than 10 percent, and the economy suffered a steep economic decline. During the third period, 2002–06, real

This chapter was adapted from "The Persistent Gender Earnings Gap in Colombia, 1994–2006," Alejandro Hoyos, Hugo Ñopo, and Ximena Peña, IZA Discussion Paper 5073, Institute for the Study of Labor, 2010.

Alejandro Hoyos is a consultant at the Poverty Reduction and Economic Management Network (PREM) at the World Bank. Ximena Peña is assistant professor of economics at the Universidad de los Andes, Bogota.

earnings and gross domestic product grew. The analysis of the evolution of earnings gaps is based on pooled datasets that include all available surveys in each period. The analysis is restricted to the 10 largest metropolitan areas in Colombia (Barranquilla, Bucaramanga, Bogotá, Manizales, Medellín, Cali, Pasto, Villavicencio, Pereira, and Cúcuta). Within these cities, the sample includes only people 18–65 years old who reported positive earnings and who worked 10–84 hours a week. The sample excludes people on whom information regarding their observable characteristics was missing. For each year and gender, the top 1 percent of the earnings distributions was dropped, because these data likely represented measurement error outliers for the variable of interest.

What Does the Literature Show?

Several studies measure the average gender earnings gap in Colombia (Tenjo 1993; Tenjo, Ribero, and Bernat 2006). Their findings identify a substantial gender earnings gap, which is explained largely by differences in the rewards to labor market characteristics rather than gender differences in characteristics.

Abadía (2005) tries to determine whether statistical discrimination can explain gender pay disparities in Colombia.[1] She argues that if firms do not apply statistical discrimination, the gender earnings gap will not change with experience, whereas if they do, the gap will depend less on easily observable characteristics (such as gender and education). Based on such intuition, she finds evidence of statistical discrimination against women in the private sector but not in the public sector.

In response to the possible discrimination against women in the labor market, Colombia has issued labor regulations favoring women. Angel–Urdinola and Wodon (2006) document the long–term increase in the gender earnings gap in the years following the issuing of Law 50 of 1990, which ensures that pregnant women cannot be fired and gives them 12 weeks of paid leave following childbirth. The law raised the cost to firms of employing women.

Sabogal (2009) finds that the gender earnings gap is procyclical for workers 25–55 years old. Three mechanisms contribute to the procyclicality of the gap: the additional worker effect, which leads to an increase in the labor supply from a nonworking household member when another member becomes unemployed; changes in the composition of the formal and informal worker forces; and changes in the sectoral composition of the labor force.

Although gender earnings gaps in Colombia appeared to start diminishing in 2000, no major advances have been made in reducing discrimination (Bernat 2007). Studies that go beyond the analysis confined to averages and analyze gender earnings gaps along the distributions of earnings or its conditional distribution yield other interesting finding on the persistence of differences between men and women in the Colombian labor market. Bernat (2007) explores the distribution of the gender gap, using discrimination curves for 2000, 2003, and 2006. She reports that the percentage of women discriminated against actually increased throughout the period of analysis. Her results also suggest the existence of a glass ceiling (barriers that prevent women from reaching the top of the earnings distribution) for professional women.

Fernández (2006) also finds evidence of glass ceilings for women in Colombia's urban labor market, where the gap favoring men reaches 25 percent of hourly earnings at the top of the income distribution. Using the urban subsamples of the 1997 and 2003 Living Standards Measurement Survey, she reports no statistically significant gender differences in earnings along the distribution of income.

The behavior along the whole distribution portrays interesting variations in addition to the glass ceiling effect. At the bottom 3 percent of the distribution, the earnings gap favors men; in percentiles 4–85, the earnings gap favors women. Using quantile regression analysis, Fernández reports that the gap largely reflects differences in rewards rather than observable characteristics. Badel and Peña (2009) use the Colombian household surveys to measure the gender earnings gap for people 25–55 years old in the country's seven main cities in 1986, 1996, and 2006. They use quantile regression techniques to examine the degree to which differences in the distribution of observable characteristics explain the gender earnings gap. The gender earnings gap for their sample is always positive, significant, and U–shaped with respect to earnings: women's earnings fall farther below men's at the extremes of the distribution and are closer to men's earnings around the middle of the distribution. The authors account for selection, as self–selection of women into work is important. They find that more able women self–select into work. If all women worked, the observed gender earnings gap would be 50 percent higher than it is.

How Do Male and Female Workers Differ?

Table 8.1 reports normalized relative earnings by different sets of observable individual characteristics (the data are normalized to make average women's earnings equal to 100 at each period). The gender earnings gap was higher during the earlier period (reaching almost 18 percent of average women's earnings) and similar in the intermediate and later period (at almost 14 percent).

Some gender differences are worth noting over the life cycle. Men reach their earnings peak at 45–54 during all three periods under analysis.

Table 8.1 Relative Hourly Earnings of Men and Women in Colombia, 1994–2006

Characteristics	1994–98 (Base: average women's earnings for each year = 100)		2000–01 (Base: average women's earnings for each year = 100)		2002–06 (Base: average women's earnings for each year = 100)	
	Women	Men	Women	Men	Women	Men
All	100.0	118.3	100.0	113.8	100.0	113.5
Age						
18–24	76.2***	79.4	74.1***	76.3	72.4	72.9
25–34†	102.2	114.0	102.3	109.6	101.3	109.2
35–44†	113.1	134.1	108.8	127.1	107.0	126.4
45–54†	106.3	143.6	112.7	135.7	114.7	131.8
55–65†	89.9	130.7	91.5	124.6	95.0	129.6
Education						
None or primary incomplete†	50.4	68.4	48.6	61.8	45.5	56.9
Primary complete or secondary incomplete†	66.4	85.7	62.6	78.7	58.4	71.4
Secondary complete or tertiary incomplete†	109.6	124.2	103.1	116.3	92.8	107.0
Tertiary complete†	223.5	291.8	244.1	286.3	229.4	277.3
Presence of children (6 years or younger in household)						
No†	100.9	120.4	102.6	115.6	101.4	115.5
Yes†	97.0	113.3	90.5	108.7	94.3	107.2

Table 8.1 (continued)

Characteristics	1994–98 (Base: average women's earnings for each year = 100)		2000–01 (Base: average women's earnings for each year = 100)		2002–06 (Base: average women's earnings for each year = 100)	
	Women	Men	Women	Men	Women	Men
Marital status						
Cohabiting†	81.2	94.7	79.2	90.9	81.5	88.7
Married†	124.6	144.6	126.4	142.2	129.7	147.9
Widowed, divorced or separated†	88.4	113.3	90.8	106.7	91.1	107.9
Single (never married)†	95.0	101.4	97.6	101.9	95.0	98.6
Presence of other household member with labor income						
No	94.7	113.1	101.0	113.8	103.5	113.2
Yes	101.4	121.2	99.6	113.7	98.8	113.7
Type of employment						
Employer	157.6***	192.1	185.6	186.3	177.4***	202.6
Self-employed†	82.3	105.6	71.8	88.2	74.9	89.8
Private employee†	98.8	106.4	105.4	109.0	107.5	105.9
Public employee	178.8**	183.9	218.0	216.4	233.2	230.4
Domestic servants†	40.2	54.3	46.9	67.2	45.0	64.6

(continued next page)

Table 8.1 (continued)

Characteristics	1994–98 (Base: average women's earnings for each year = 100)		2000–01 (Base: average women's earnings for each year = 100)		2002–06 (Base: average women's earnings for each year = 100)	
	Women	Men	Women	Men	Women	Men
Time worked						
Part time†	129.5	165.8	112.7	155.9	104.6	147.7
Full time†	105.0	126.4	113.3	130.0	115.8	131.4
Over time†	67.1	96.3	67.8	87.1	70.2	89.1
Formality						
No†	73.4	94.6	67.3	81.3	63.3	77.0
Yes†	119.2	139.2	129.3	145.6	130.1	142.6
Small firm						
No	121.2***	131.3	134.1***	139.9	135.7*	136.9
Yes†	75.4	102.9	69.1	90.0	67.3	88.8
Economic sector						
Primary	113.5***	140.8	93.2***	115.1	123.5	128.2
Secondary†	88.3	103.5	91.2	101.4	90.4	98.6
Tertiary†	103.5	125.8	102.4	119.3	102.3	120.5
Occupation						
White collar†	128.4	162.4	134.6	156.8	137.5	159.7
Blue collar†	66.3	89.2	65.4	84.6	62.7	80.5

Source: Based on data from 1994–2006 household surveys conducted by the Colombian National Statistical Agency.
Note: * $p < 0.1$, ** $p < 0.05$, *** $p < 0.01$. † indicates that the earnings differences between men and women are statistically different at the 99 percent level in all three periods.

In contrast, women's earnings profile over the life cycle changed slightly during the period. In the earliest period, their earnings peaked at 35–44. For the two later periods, the peaks were achieved at 45–54. This change may reflect a secular trend in which women are remaining longer in the labor market, maintaining their productive cycles and avoiding early retirement.

Regarding education, men earn more than women in all education categories in all three periods. Individuals living in households with children younger than six tend to earn less than individuals living in households with no children. This difference remained constant over the period of analysis. The presence of other income earners in the household does not seem to play an important role in earnings differentials.

Married people earn more than unmarried people. Never–married people earn almost the same as people who live together, but people living together outside of a formal marriage persistently earn the lowest earning. Gender earnings gaps are more pronounced among people cohabiting than among people who never married. The largest earnings gaps are among people who are widowed, divorced, or separated.

Not surprisingly, in the private sector, employers earn much more than employees, who earn more than the self-employed, who earn more than domestic servants. An unexpected result is that public employees are at the top of average earnings by type of employment. Part-time workers (people who work less than 35 hours a week) earn much more per hour than people working full time, who in turn earn more per hour than people working overtime (more than 48 hours a week). Informal workers earn less than their formal counterparts, and people working at small firms (five workers or less) earn less than people working at larger firms. Services (business and social) and construction are among the highest-paid economic sectors, especially for women. At the other extreme, household and personal services was the lowest-paid sector during the whole period of analysis, for both men and women. White-collar workers earn more than blue-collar workers.

Table 8.2 describes the differences in observable characteristics between men and women for the three periods under study. Working men are slightly older than working women. However, both women and men are staying longer in the labor market, creating an older labor force, especially for women. The percentage of workers with secondary and tertiary education increased in each subperiod.

Although the majority of working men live in households with children six or under, the prevalence of children decreased over the period of study, and gender differences narrowed. In line with the findings by Amador and Bernal (2009), important changes took place in patterns of family formation and dissolution in Colombia, similar to changes that have occurred in the rest of the region. The percentages of cohabiting people increased for men and women (although cohabitation is more common among men).

Table 8.2 Demographic and Job Characteristics of Men and Women in Colombia's Labor Force, 1994–2006
(percent)

Characteristics	1994–98		2000–01		2002–06	
	Women	*Men*	*Women*	*Men*	*Women*	*Men*
Real hourly earnings (1998 Colombian pesos)	2,225	2,632	1,948	2,217	1,998	2,269
Personal characteristics						
Age						
18–24	19.8	18.6	18.4	17.5	17.2	16.6
25–34	36.0	33.8	32.2	32.2	30.5	30.6
35–44	27.4	25.5	29.3	27.2	29.0	26.7
45–54	12.4	14.6	14.8	15.7	17.7	18.0
55–65	4.4	7.5	5.2	7.4	5.7	8.2
Education						
None or primary incomplete	11.6	12.2	10.4	11.4	8.8	9.5
Primary complete or secondary incomplete	38.5	45.9	37.9	41.0	32.6	35.8
Secondary complete or tertiary incomplete	37.7	30.9	38.9	36.3	42.0	40.6

Table 8.2 (continued)

Characteristics	1994–98		2000–01		2002–06	
	Women	*Men*	*Women*	*Men*	*Women*	*Men*
Tertiary complete	12.2	11.1	12.7	11.2	16.5	14.1
Presence of children (6 years or younger in the household)	22.7	29.6	21.3	26.6	19.2	23.5
Marital Status						
Cohabiting	15.2	24.5	18.9	29.3	19.8	29.8
Married	28.5	41.6	25.9	36.7	24.6	34.9
Widowed, divorced, or separated	20.6	4.6	23.4	6.7	22.3	7.0
Single (never married)	35.6	29.3	31.8	27.4	33.3	28.3
Presence of other household member with labor income	79.5	64.5	73.3	62.1	73.5	63.8
Job characteristics						
Type of employment						
Employer	3.3	7.1	2.6	5.6	2.8	5.9
Self-employed	22.0	26.4	27.3	32.6	26.9	30.9

(continued next page)

145

Table 8.2 (continued)

Characteristics	1994–98		2000–01		2002–06	
	Women	Men	Women	Men	Women	Men
Private employee	54.8	58.4	49.7	54.6	50.8	57.0
Public employee	10.5	7.9	8.0	6.8	6.1	5.7
Domestic servants	9.4	0.2	12.4	0.4	13.4	0.5
Time worked						
Part time	16.5	6.9	21.6	10.5	20.6	8.9
Full time	59.6	57.2	49.5	45.2	49.9	45.4
Overtime	23.9	35.9	29.0	44.2	29.6	45.7
Small firm (five workers or less)	46.3	45.8	52.5	52.3	52.2	48.7
Formality	58.1	53.1	52.8	50.4	54.9	55.7
Economic sector						
Primary	0.8	1.8	0.9	2.0	0.8	2.1
Secondary	23.5	35.0	20.9	30.5	20.4	32.5
Tertiary	75.7	63.2	78.3	67.5	78.8	65.4
Occupation						
White collar	54.2	39.8	50.0	40.4	49.8	41.7
Blue collar	45.8	60.2	50.0	59.6	50.2	58.3

Source: Based on data from 1994–2006 household surveys conducted by the Colombian National Statistical Agency.

About two out of three men and less than half of working women in Colombia are married (either formally or informally).

Working women are more likely than working men to live in households in which other members earn labor income. The presence of other income earners at home did not change for men between 1994 and 2006 but changed slightly for women. The percentage of women who share the breadwinning responsibilities in their household dropped almost 5 percentage points during the period of analysis, reflecting the increase in the number of households headed by women that Colombia and the region have experienced in recent years.

Very few workers are employers, and about two–thirds of employers are men. The share of self-employment increased at the expense of the share of employees. The percentage of men working overtime increased, such that in the last period, almost half of men reported working more than 48 hours a week. For women, the data show both an increase in overtime and an increase in part-time work (at the expense of full–time work). About half of workers (both men and women) are formal employees at small firms. The transportation sector increased its share of employment among men. The prevalence of white-collar workers decreased slightly among women and increased among men.

The Role of Individual Characteristics in Explaining the Gender Earnings Gap

Table 8.3 decomposes the earnings gap for the three subperiods.[2] Each column adds a demographic variable to the set in the previous one. The full set of demographic control variables, in the order included in the matching exercise, is as follows: year, urban area, age, education, presence of children in the household, marital status, and presence of other labour income earner in the household.

The first panel in Table 8.3 shows that during 1994–98, men earned 18.3 percent more than women (as a percentage of average women's earnings). Year, city, and age group account for just 0.1 percentage points of average women's earnings; the rest of the gap remains unexplained.

Adding education increases the unexplained earnings gap (Δ_0)—the part of the gap attributed to differences between men and women that cannot be explained by observable characteristics that—slightly, reflecting women's higher education attainment. The component that reflects the fact that men achieve certain combinations of characteristics that women do not (Δ_M) reaches almost 2 percent; this percentage remains after the addition of other demographic characteristics. The addition of the other demographic characteristics slightly reduces the unexplained component of the earnings gap and Δ_M but increases Δ_F, the component that captures the lack of matchable women.

Table 8.3 Decomposition of Gender Earnings Gap in Colombia after Controlling for Demographic Characteristics, 1994–2006
(percent)

	Year, metropolitan area, and age	+ Education	+ Presence of children in the household	+ Marital status	+ Presence of other household member with labor income
1994–98					
Δ	18.3	18.3	18.3	18.3	18.3
Δ_O	18.2	19.9	19.4	17.5	18.5
Δ_M	0.0	1.8	2.5	1.6	0.7
Δ_F	0.0	-0.1	-0.4	0.8	1.7
Δ_X	0.1	-3.3	-3.3	-1.6	-2.6
Percentage of men in common support	99.8	97.4	93.0	76.5	57.6
Percentage of women in common support	100.0	99.3	97.5	78.4	68.3

Table 8.3 (continued)

	Year, metropolitan area, and age	+ Education	+ Presence of children in the household	+ Marital status	+ Presence of other household member with labor income
2000–01					
Δ	13.8	13.8	13.8	13.8	13.8
Δ_0	13.0	15.4	15.8	13.8	14.5
Δ_M	0.0	2.4	3.8	5.1	4.9
Δ_F	0.0	-0.7	-1.2	-2.3	-2.0
Δ_X	0.7	-3.4	-4.7	-2.7	-3.6
Percentage of men in common support	99.9	96.9	92.3	73.6	55.9
Percentage of women in common support	100.0	98.7	96.1	74.1	61.2

(continued next page)

Table 8.3 (continued)

	Year, metropolitan area, and age	+ Education	+ Presence of children in the household	+ Marital status	+ Presence of other household member with labor income
2002–06					
Δ	13.5	13.5	13.5	13.5	13.5
Δ_0	13.9	17.5	17.4	16.1	15.1
Δ_M	0.0	1.1	1.5	1.3	1.4
Δ_F	0.0	-0.3	-0.7	-1.3	-1.9
Δ_X	-0.5	-4.7	-4.7	-2.6	-1.0
Percentage of men in common support	99.9	97.6	93.6	75.9	57.9
Percentage of women in common support	100.0	98.7	96.3	74.5	61.6

Source: Based on data from 1994–2006 household surveys conducted by the Colombian National Statistical Agency.

Note: Δ_M (Δ_F) is the part of the earnings gap attributed to the existence of men (women) with combinations of characteristics that are not met by any women (men). Δ_X is the part of the earnings gap attributed to differences in the observable characteristics of men and women over the "common support." Δ_0 is the part of the earnings gap that cannot be attributed to differences in characteristics of the individuals. It is typically attributed to a combination of both unobservable characteristics and discrimination. The sum of these components equals the total earnings gap ($\Delta_M + \Delta_F + \Delta_X + \Delta_0 = \Delta$).

The overall gender earnings gap is larger during the first period than in the other two. The pattern remains after controlling for observable individual demographic characteristics. In fact, most of the gap remains unexplained after matching by the whole set of demographics. The second most important element, but an order of magnitude smaller, is the one that exists because women fail to achieve certain combinations of characteristics that men do. These characteristics—that men have, but women do not—are in well-paid segments of the labor market.

Investigating the effect of job–related individual characteristics on top of the demographics reported in table 8.3 is not a simple task because of the "curse of dimensionality."[3] In order to leave space for the inclusion of job-related characteristics, the analysis ignores some demographic characteristics.

Table 8.4 uses the set of demographic matching variables that includes year, city, age, and education and adds the job–related characteristics one by one (as opposed to cumulatively, as done in table 8.3). The new variables considered are small firm (dummy equal to 1 if firm has no more than five workers); economic sector (primary, secondary, or tertiary); occupation category; type of employment (self-employed, employer, or employee); formality status (a dummy variable taking the value 1 for people covered by social security obtained from their labor relationship and 0 otherwise); and time commitment (part, full, or overtime). The last column includes all six job-related characteristics on top of the basic set of demographics.

The patterns are similar to the patterns shown in table 8.3. Most of the gender earnings gap is left unexplained by these observable characteristics. Furthermore, the unexplained gender gap after controlling for observable characteristics is frequently larger than the observed one. The one-by-one inclusion of job-related characteristics increases the magnitude of the component of the earnings gap attributable to the existence of men with characteristics that are not achieved by women (Δ_M). In the most dramatic case (the one obtained after adding type of employment to the demographic characteristics), this lack of "common support" in favor of men explains more than a third of the earnings gap in all three subperiods. For the two later periods, the role of type of employment accounts for about half of the observed gender earnings gap, partly because of the overrepresentation of women as domestic servants.

The component attributable to the existence of men with characteristics that are not achieved by women (Δ_M) plays a prominent role in explaining the gender gap when controlling for demographic characteristics alone. The component that reflects the existence of women with characteristics that are not achieved by men (Δ_F) is just as important when also controlling for job-related characteristics. This finding implies greater gender segmentation in job-related characteristics, particularly regarding job type and hours worked.

Table 8.4 Decomposition of Gender Earnings Gap in Colombia after Controlling for Demographic and Job Characteristics, 1994–2006
(percent)

	Demographic set	& Small firm	& Sector	& Occupation	& Type of employment	& Formality	& Time worked	Full set
1994–98								
Δ	18.3	18.3	18.3	18.3	18.3	18.3	18.3	18.3
Δ_0	19.9	20.3	19.3	23.4	16.0	20.3	24.0	19.9
Δ_M	1.8	3.0	2.9	1.8	7.4	3.1	4.0	1.0
Δ_F	-0.1	-0.7	-0.3	-0.1	2.3	-0.5	-2.6	2.3
Δ_X	-3.3	-4.3	-3.6	-6.9	-7.4	-4.6	-7.1	-4.9
Percentage of men in common support	97.4	92.4	90.3	93.2	83.7	93.0	88.9	29.6
Percentage of women in common support	99.3	97.3	96.9	97.3	84.6	97.1	91.1	38.6

(continued next page)

Table 8.4 (continued)

	Demographic set	& Small firm	& Sector	& Occupation	& Type of employment	& Formality	& Time worked	Full set
2000–01								
Δ	13.8	13.8	13.8	13.8	13.8	13.8	13.8	13.8
Δ_0	15.4	15.4	14.6	17.7	12.7	16.6	20.4	20.1
Δ_M	2.4	4.1	3.5	2.8	8.8	3.7	5.8	-5.9
Δ_F	-0.7	-1.9	-1.5	-0.7	0.2	-1.4	-3.5	5.3
Δ_X	-3.4	-3.8	-2.8	-6.0	-8.0	-5.1	-8.9	-5.7
Percentage of men in common support	96.9	91.8	88.9	91.9	83.0	92.1	86.8	23.9
Percentage of women in common support	98.7	96.1	95.1	95.8	80.0	96.0	88.1	28.7

(continued next page)

Table 8.4 (continued)

	Demographic set	& Small firm	& Sector	& Occupation	& Type of employment	& Formality	& Time worked	Full set
2002–06								
Δ	13.5	13.5	13.5	13.5	13.5	13.5	13.5	13.5
Δ_0	17.5	18.0	16.7	19.9	14.5	17.3	21.2	17.9
Δ_M	1.1	1.6	1.6	0.6	6.8	1.3	2.8	-7.2
Δ_F	-0.3	-1.2	-0.7	-0.4	1.8	-0.5	-1.9	10.5
Δ_X	-4.7	-4.8	-4.0	-6.6	-9.6	-4.5	-8.5	-7.7
Percentage of men in common support	97.6	92.5	89.4	92.6	83.6	93.3	88.5	25.8
Percentage of women in common support	98.7	95.8	95.0	95.8	78.9	95.2	86.4	28.7

Source: Based on data from 1994–2006 household surveys conducted by the Colombian National Statistical Agency.

Note: Δ_M (Δ_F) is the part of the earnings gap attributed to the existence of men (women) with combinations of characteristics that are not met by any women (men). Δ_X is the part of the earnings gap attributed to differences in the observable characteristics of men and women over the "common support." Δ_0 is the part of the earnings gap that cannot be attributed to differences in characteristics of the individuals. It is typically attributed to a combination of both unobservable characteristics and discrimination. The sum of these components equals the total earnings gap ($\Delta_M + \Delta_F + \Delta_X + \Delta_0 = \Delta$).

The addition of all job-related characteristics to the basic set of demo-graphics yields a negative Δ_M component and a positive Δ_F, implying that the presence of barriers to women's access to certain job profiles works in opposite directions at both extremes of the earnings distribution. The combinations of human capital characteristics that women fail to achieve (that is, the characteristics of the men that are not part of the common support) are not linked to higher earnings than those of matched men. Women who combine human capital characteristics for which there are no comparable men earn less than women without such combinations of characteristics.

Who are the women and men in and out of the common support of observable characteristics? The results in table 8.5 indicate that men out of the common support are married, older, and less educated than other men; are self-employed or employers in the secondary sector or blue-collar workers in small and less formal firms; and work more overtime than other men. There is no clear pattern indicating that out-of-support men share human capital characteristics that are better rewarded than those of other men.

Women out of the common support are older, less educated, more likely to be separated, and more likely to be domestic servants or self-employed than women in the common support. They tend to work at both extremes (part time and overtime), in smaller firms with less formality, as blue-collar workers in the tertiary sector. Unmatched women thus seem to have combinations of human capital characteristics that are less rewarded than those of women in the common support.

Exploring the Unexplained Component of the Gender Earnings Gap

Figure 8.1 shows the decomposition of the gender earnings gap after matching on the set of demographic variables, year by year. It illustrates the narrowing of the unexplained gender earnings gap during the period of analysis. However, the reduction is not statistically significant (Hoyos, Ñopo, and Peña 2010).

The unexplained gap can be analyzed along different segments of the labor market. Most cities show similar unexplained gender earnings gaps. The only statistically significant differences in unexplained gaps are between Medellín on the one hand and Bucaramanga and Pereira on the other (the gap is smaller in Medellín).

Younger people show smaller earnings gaps than people in middle age. The unexplained gaps are highly dispersed among people 55–65 years old. The unexplained gap along education categories is very similar to that of the whole distribution: it is larger among people in the low (incomplete

Table 8.5 Demographic and Job Characteristics of Matched and Unmatched Samples of Men and Women in Colombia's Labor Force, 2002–06
(*percent*)

	Matched women and men	Unmatched women	Unmatched men
Real hourly earnings (1998 Colombian pesos)		1,979	2,337
Personal characteristics			
Age			
18 to 24	20.6	17.0	16.3
25 to 34	39.1	29.2	29.2
35 to 44	27.8	29.0	26.1
45 to 54	10.8	18.0	18.4
55 to 65	1.7	6.9	10.0
Education			
None or primary incomplete	3.1	13.0	13.4
Primary complete or secondary incomplete	31.3	37.0	41.0
Secondary complete or tertiary incomplete	50.1	35.8	33.3
Tertiary complete	15.5	14.3	12.4
Presence of children in the household	20.9	20.3	25.5
Marital status			
Cohabiting	18.0	18.6	29.0
Married	26.6	25.6	38.3
Widowed, divorced, or separated	18.5	23.7	6.6
Single (never married)	37.0	32.1	26.2
Presence of other household member with labor income	76.2	74.5	63.2
Job characteristics			
Type of employment			
Employer	0.5	4.0	8.3
Self-employed	19.1	28.7	32.9

(continued next page)

Table 8.5 (continued)

	Matched women and men	Unmatched women	Unmatched men
Private employee	72.5	42.1	51.9
Public employee	7.3	7.8	6.6
Domestic servants	0.6	17.4	0.4
Time worked			
Part time	6.6	25.6	9.5
Full time	71.3	43.8	42.2
Overtime	22.1	30.6	48.3
Small firm	26.3	61.8	55.6
Formality	73.3	47.2	48.0
Economic sector			
Primary	0.1	1.1	2.6
Secondary	26.0	19.2	33.6
Tertiary	73.9	79.7	63.8
Occupation			
White collar	60.6	46.7	37.1
Blue collar	39.4	53.3	62.9

Source: Based on data from 2002–06 household surveys conducted by the Colombian National Statistical Agency.

secondary) and high (complete tertiary) education groups and smaller for people with intermediate education (complete secondary or incomplete tertiary). The unexplained gaps are also smaller among widows, public employees, full-time workers, workers in construction and transportation, white-collar workers, workers at larger firms, and formal sector workers.

The unexplained gender earnings gaps are smaller than average for middle-income earners, larger than average at both extremes of the earnings distribution, and slightly larger than average at the bottom of the earnings distribution (figure 8.2). What generates the observed U–shape in both the observed and unexplained gender earnings gaps? The minimum earnings may be behind the lower levels of the unexplained gender earnings gap in the middle of the distribution. Because people at the middle of the distribution are close to the minimum earnings (in the sample, 52 percent of men and 58 percent of women earn earnings less than or equal to the minimum wage), the minimum earnings may exert a gender–equalizing effect on intermediate–paying jobs. The "bite" of the

Figure 8.1 Decomposition of Gender Earnings Gap in Colombia after Controlling for Demographic and Job Characteristics, 1994–2006

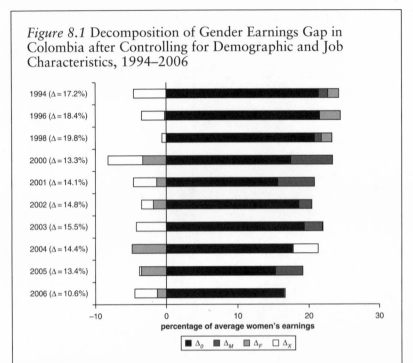

Source: Based on data from 1994–2006 household surveys conducted by the Colombian National Statistical Agency.

Note: Δ_M (Δ_F) is the part of the earnings gap attributed to the existence of men (women) with combinations of characteristics that are not met by any women (men). Δ_X is the part of the earnings gap attributed to differences in the observable characteristics of men and women over the "common support." Δ_0 is the part of the earnings gap that cannot be attributed to differences in characteristics of the individuals. It is typically attributed to a combination of both unobservable characteristics and discrimination. The sum of these factors equals the total earnings gap ($\Delta_M + \Delta_F + \Delta_X + \Delta_0 = \Delta$).

minimum earnings varies along the income distribution. It barely affects the earnings of people earning less than the minimum, usually informal workers; is very binding at and around the level of the minimum wage; and loses importance as one moves up the income distribution curve toward high earners (Cunningham 2007).

After controlling for the demographic set of observable characteristics, the unexplained gap is slightly larger than when matching on a smaller set of characteristics, especially at the upper end of the earnings distribution. After controlling for the full set of demographic and job characteristics, the situation is similar: the unexplained gaps above the median of the

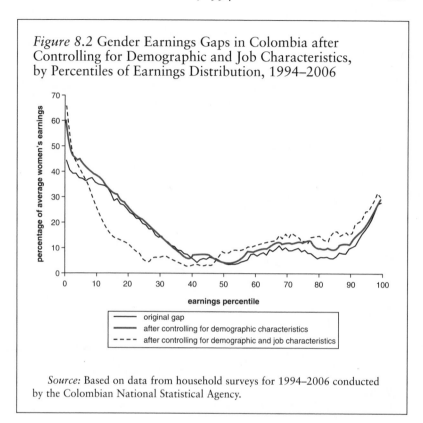

Figure 8.2 Gender Earnings Gaps in Colombia after Controlling for Demographic and Job Characteristics, by Percentiles of Earnings Distribution, 1994–2006

Source: Based on data from household surveys for 1994–2006 conducted by the Colombian National Statistical Agency.

earnings distributions are larger than they are for the smaller set of characteristics. The novelty arises below the median of the earnings distributions. There, the unexplained gaps are substantially smaller than the gaps observed with the other sets of matching characteristics. Thus, observable characteristics do a better job of explaining gender earnings differentials at the lower end of the earnings distribution.

The results presented in this chapter suggest that the gender earnings gap in Colombia is unexplained largely by differences in observable characteristics, both demographic and job related. The gap that remains unexplained after accounting for these differences displays a *U*-shape with respect to earnings: it is smaller for middle-income individuals and larger at both extremes of the earnings distribution. This shape may reflect the gender-equalizing effect of the minimum wage.

The largest unexplained earnings gaps are found among less educated people and people who work part time, in the primary sector and entertainment or household services, at small firms or in the informal sector, and as domestic or blue-collar workers. Among people with these characteristics, two distinct profiles are evident. One consists of low-productivity individuals, the other comprises women who, in need of flexibility to participate in the labor market, have to work under arrangements of precarious attachment to the market. Some women seem to be confined to combinations of human capital characteristics that are less well rewarded than those of the rest of the labor force.

Policy implications regarding the potential effectiveness—or ineffectiveness—of different measures to narrow the gender earnings gaps can be derived from these results. First, the gender earnings gap may reflect discrimination. Some observers argue that discrimination will decrease over time on its own, as society becomes accustomed to women in the working force. The high participation rates of women in Colombia and the fact that the gender earnings gap has changed little in the last decade suggest that this channel may not be effective.

Like Colombia, Brazil has implemented policies to reduce inequalities. It has addressed both gender inequality and inequalities faced by its large Afro–descendant population. Chapter 9 examines the evolution of the gender earnings gaps in Brazil.

Notes

1. Statistical discrimination is a theory of why women or minorities are paid lower earnings. It occurs when rational agents use aggregate group characteristics to evaluate individual characteristics, which leads agents belonging to different groups to be treated differently. If, for example, firms believe that women of child-bearing age are more likely to have babies, and therefore have breaks during their careers, than older women, they would pay such women less, to account for the higher probability of losing them.

2. For a description of the methodology used in this chapter, see chapter 2.

3. The curse of dimensionality refers to the fact that the likelihood of finding female–male matches decreases as the number of control variables (the "dimension") increases. This is a problem because researchers would like to use the maximum number of observable characteristics in order to control the scope of the role of unobservable factors in explaining the earnings gap.

References

Abadía, L. K. 2005. "Discriminación salarial por sexo en Colombia: un análisis desde la discriminación estadística." Documentos de Economía 17, Pontificia Universidad Javeriana, Bogotá.

Amador, D., and R. Bernal. 2009. "Marriage vs. Cohabitation: The Effects on Children's Well–Being." Universidad de los Andes, Bogotá.

Angel–Urdinola, D., and Q. Wodon. 2006. "The Gender Wage Gap and Poverty in Colombia." *Labour* 20 (4): 721–39.

Badel, A., and X. Peña. 2009 "Decomposing the Gender Gap with Sample Selection Adjustment: Evidence from Colombia." Universidad de Los Andes, Bogotá. http://ximena.pena.googlepages.com/gender.pdf.

Bernat, L. F. 2007. "¿Quiénes son las mujeres discriminadas? enfoque distributivo de las diferencias salariales por género" *Borradores de Economía y Finanzas* 13, Universidad Icesi, Cali, Colombia.

Cunningham, W. 2007. *Minimum Wages and Social Policy: Lessons from Developing Countries*. Washington, DC: World Bank.

Fernández, P. 2006. "Determinantes del diferencial salarial por género en Colombia, 1997–2003." *Desarrollo y Sociedad* 58 (2): 165–208.

Hoyos, A., H. Ñopo, and Ximena Peña. 2010. "The Persistent Gender Earnings Gap in Colombia, 1994–2006." IZA Discussion Paper 5073, Institute for the Study of Labor, Bonn, Germany.

Sabogal, A. 2009. "Brecha salarial por género y ciclo económico en Colombia." Universidad de los Andes, Bogotá.

Tenjo, J. 1993. "1976–1989: cambios en los diferenciales salariales entre hombres y mujeres." *Planeación y Desarrollo* 24: 103–16.

Tenjo, J., R. Ribero, and L. Bernat. 2006. "Evolución de las diferencias salariales de género en seis países de América Latina." In *Mujeres y trabajo en América Latina*, ed. C. Piras, 149–98. Washington, DC: Inter–American Development Bank.

9

Promoting Equality in the Country with the Largest Earnings Gaps in the Region: Brazil 1996–2006

Promoting gender and racial equality has been one of Brazil's major challenges in recent years. Some observers believe that this challenge has begun to be met; others believe that the work of implementing effective policies has just started. Disentangling group inequalities in Brazil will help researchers inform public policies.

This chapter analyzes the composition and evolution of gender earnings differentials over a decade (1996–2006), using the National Household Sample Survey (PNAD) conducted by the Brazilian Institute of Geography and Statistics and the matching comparison methodology described in chapter 2. The analysis is restricted to workers 15–65 years recording nonzero earnings. The variable of analysis is hourly earnings at the primary occupation.

What Does the Literature Show?

Camargo and Serrano (1983) investigate gender pay differentials, specifying earnings equations using not only personal characteristics, such as level of

This chapter was adapted from "Gender and Racial Wage Gaps in Brazil 1996–2006: Evidence Using a Matching Comparisons Approach," Luana Marquez Garcia, Hugo Ñopo, and Paola Salardi, RES Working Paper 4626, Inter-American Development Bank, 2009.

Luana Marquez Garcia is a young professional at the Inter-American Development Bank. Paola Salardi is a research fellow in the Economics Group at the University of Sussex, in Brighton, United Kingdom.

education, but also aspects of sectoral features, such as concentration, capital intensity, and size. Their findings suggest that the structure of economic sectors plays a negligible role in the determination of women's earnings.

One of the first studies to explore gender pay gaps using the Blinder-Oaxaca decomposition is Birdsall and Fox (1985). Extracting a 1 percent sample from the 1970 Brazilian census focused on a specific occupational category (school teachers), they find that the explained component of the gap is greater than the unexplained component. As 74 percent of the earnings gap can be explained, the authors claim that job discrimination (a proxy measured by the unexplained component) does not represent the main source of gender earnings differentials for school teachers.

Stelcner et al. (1992) examine gender differentials in earnings using the 1980 census by correcting the earnings equation estimations for selection bias. They find that unexplained components are larger than the total earnings differential and that a negative explained component reflects women's better endowments (such as education).

Exploring differences in the formal and informal labor market, Tiefenthaler (1992) finds that gender earnings differentials tend to be larger in the formal sector. The unexplained component dominates in the formal sector, whereas the explained component dominates in the informal sector. This finding is supported by evidence that better educated women tend to work in formal occupations.[1]

Barros, Ramos, and Santos (1995) investigate the role played by education and occupational structure in the evolution of gender differentials. In addition to confirming previous results on the effect of education on gender pay gaps, they provide evidence for the "glass ceiling" phenomenon, which prevents women from reaching managerial positions.

Ometto, Hoffmann, and Alves (1999) use the Blinder-Oaxaca decomposition technique as revised by Brown, Moon, and Zoloth (1980), which isolates the extent of gender pay gaps caused by interoccupation and intraoccupation differentials. They find that gender earnings gaps in Pernambuco are mainly the result of intraoccupational differentials. In contrast, in wealthier São Paulo, both kinds of differentials play a role.

Leme and Wajnman (2000) confirm findings of previous studies that education cannot explain gender pay gaps in Brazil. Returns to education favor women; gender earnings gaps thus reflect the unexplained component, not endowment differences. They find that returns to education are more favorable to women born after the 1950s, a finding compatible with improvements in women's educational attainment over time.

Arabsheibani, Carneiro, and Henley (2003) show that gender differentials in earnings decreased markedly over time, mainly because of the decline in the explained component. Women's endowments, particularly educational achievement, have had an important effect.

Loureiro, Carneiro, and Sachshida (2004) find larger earnings gaps in urban areas than in rural areas. When the Blinder-Oaxaca decomposition is used, unexplained components generally dominate gender differentials. These findings do not hold, however, once the sample is restricted to a more homogenous occupational group, such as school teachers (Birdsall and Fox 1985). Although gender earnings gaps have shrunk over time, the unexplained component has tended to increase (Arabsheibani, Carneiro, and Henley 2003).

The Role of Individual Characteristics in Explaining the Earnings Gap

Table 9.1 presents the average characteristics of men and women who were either matched or not matched based on their individual characteristics.[2] The matching was done based on six combinations of human capital and labor market characteristics. The first set includes only the number of years of schooling. The second set adds age and education, the third adds region,[3] the fourth adds occupation, the fifth adds sector, and the sixth adds a variable that identifies whether the individual works in the formal sector. The sequence in which extra variables were added to the set of controlling characteristics was chosen so that it leaves to the last sets variables that may end up being endogenous in a model of earnings determination à la Mincer (a pricing equation or hedonic earnings function revealing how the labor market rewards productive attributes such as schooling and work experience).

There are significant differences in characteristics of men and women that are and are not matched. The age patterns are similar, although unmatched individuals are likely to be older. Unmatched women are on average better educated than unmatched men over time. In 1996, 9.2 percent of unmatched women completed more than 15 years of education, compared with 6.2 percent of unmatched men; in 2006 these percentages increased to 16.6 percent for unmatched women and 7.6 percent for unmatched men.

Unmatched men are more likely to be nonwhite and to live in rural areas. The regional distribution of matched and unmatched individuals does not differ, with the South-East and the North-East showing the highest densities.

Labor characteristics reveal interesting differences by gender: in 1996, 14.0 percent of unmatched women worked as professionals and 77.3 percent worked at the intermediate level. In contrast, only 5.2 percent of unmatched men were professionals, and 67.5 percent were blue-collar workers. Over time, the number of unmatched individuals working as professionals increased, to 22.7 percent for women and 17.5 percent for men. In addition, unmatched men were more likely to be employed in the informal sector and concentrated in economic activities such as agriculture

Table 9.1 Demographic and Job Characteristics of Matched and Unmatched Samples of Men and Women in Brazil's Labor Force, 1996 and 2006 (percent)

Characteristics	1996			2006		
	Unmatched women	Unmatched men	Matched women and men	Unmatched women	Matched men	Matched women and men
Personal characteristics						
Age						
15–24	28.2	26.6	27.2	19.7	22.4	25.9
25–34	27.5	27.3	31.0	26.8	26.7	29.2
35–44	24.9	23.4	24.9	26.4	24.9	24.8
45–54	13.6	15.0	12.5	19.1	17.7	14.7
55–65	5.8	7.8	4.4	8.0	8.3	5.3
Years of education						
Less than 4	28.4	33.7	27.9	19.5	25.7	19.4
4–10	59.2	58.9	59.8	58.6	64.8	60.4
11–15	3.3	1.3	1.2	5.4	1.9	2.5
More than 15	9.2	6.2	11.1	16.6	7.6	17.7
Ethnicity (white)	54.3	52.9	55.7	51.3	44.8	49.3
Urban	92.1	84.6	84.9	93.4	85.7	87.6

Table 9.1 (continued)

Characteristics	1996			2006		
	Unmatched women	Unmatched men	Matched women and men	Unmatched women	Matched men	Matched women and men
Regions						
North	10.9	9.0	4.1	14.9	15.3	10.3
North-East	22.4	23.0	32.1	21.3	25.2	31.5
South-East	29.9	33.7	40.1	25.9	28.2	33.9
South	21.4	19.7	16.8	21.5	16.5	15.4
Central-West	15.4	14.5	7.0	16.3	14.8	8.9
Job characteristics						
Formal job	45.3	44.9	50.9	42.6	43.9	52.7
Occupation						
Professional	14.1	5.2	14.4	22.7	17.5	23.7
Intermediate	77.3	27.3	49.6	69.2	19.0	51.5
Blue collar	8.6	67.5	36.0	8.1	63.6	25.0
Agriculture	0.7	15.6	13.0	1.0	13.7	10.2
Construction	0.6	19.8	0.3	1.2	21.8	0.2
Social services	71.0	20.2	46.5	55.4	13.0	45.4

Source: Based on data from 1996 and 2006 PNAD.

and construction. Among unmatched women, 71.0 percent were employed in social services.

Figure 9.1 reports the decomposition of gender earnings gaps using the full set of characteristics.[4] The total gap shrinks by 13 percent, from 52 percent in 1996 to 39 percent in 2006. The dominance of the unexplained component is striking: the main portion of the gender earnings gap (Δ) is unexplained even when the full set of characteristics is included as controls. In fact, the part of the gap that cannot be attributed to differences in characteristics of the individuals (Δ_0) is much higher than the total earnings gap. The explained component (Δ_X)—attributed to differences in observable characteristics—is always negative for gender earnings differentials. This negative sign is explained by women's better endowments, particularly in terms of educational achievement.

Although the total gender earnings gap decreased over time, the change resulted mainly from the decrease in explained differences rather than

Figure 9.1 Decomposition of Gender Earnings Gaps in Brazil after Controlling for Demographic and Job Characteristics, 1996–2006

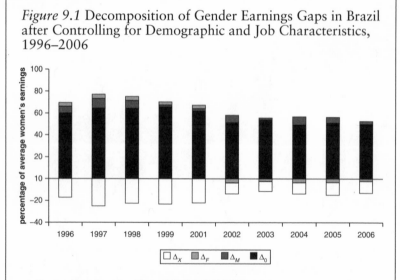

Source: Based on data from 1996–2006 PNAD.

Note: Δ_M (Δ_F) is the part of the earnings gap attributed to the existence of men (women) with combinations of characteristics that are not met by any women (men). Δ_X is the part of the earnings gap attributed to differences in the observable characteristics of men and women over the "common support." Δ_0 is the part of the earnings gap that cannot be attributed to differences in characteristics of the individuals. It is typically attributed to a combination of both unobservable characteristics and discrimination. The sum of these components equals the total earnings gap ($\Delta_M + \Delta_F + \Delta_X + \Delta_0 = \Delta$).

a drop in the unexplained component. The portion of the earnings gap attributable to unmatched individuals is negligible. In particular, the small size of Δ_M—the part of the earnings gap caused by the existence of men with combinations of characteristics that are not met by any woman— highlights the limited extent of men's advantage.

Exploring the Unexplained Component of the Gender Earnings Gap

Table 9.2 reports gender earnings gaps by characteristic, considering only the first year (1996) and last year (2006) of the period under study.[5] Earnings gaps increased with age, becoming larger at higher levels of education and for top job positions. The gap for the youngest cohort was much smaller than for other age cohorts. This finding may be explained by the fact that many young people are still in school. In the construction sector, women tend to earn higher earnings than men. The unexplained component is greater than the total earnings gap for most subgroups considered, as it is for the whole sample. For higher levels of education and job position, Δ_0 is smaller than the total differential. In these cases, the number of people out of support tends to be greater, and the earnings gap is explained largely by differences in characteristics in and out of support. Gender earnings gaps are larger among whites than nonwhites, and they are larger in urban regions than in national averages. Geographically, the gaps are higher in the South and South-East.

The analysis is enriched by considering unexplained earnings differentials in individual income. Earnings are rescaled such that average women's earnings are normalized to 100 in each year. This change neutralizes nominal changes in earnings, so that real changes in the gaps are evident. At each percentile of the earnings distribution, the earnings of the representative men and women in each distribution are compared and the earnings gap computed. Figure 9.2 reports the entire distribution for both total and unexplained gender earnings gaps, after controlling for the richer set of observable characteristics. The gender earnings gap, particularly the unexplained gap, displays a *U*-shape along the earnings distribution. The unexplained gap tends to be larger at the bottom of the distribution: low-earning women suffer larger differentials.

Observable individual characteristics cannot completely account for gender earnings gaps in Brazil. Unexplained gender earnings gaps increase with workers' age and education; they are larger among professionals and among people living in the South-East. The unexplained gender earnings gap is highest among the poor, lowest among middle-income earners, and higher among those with high income.

Table 9.2 Original and Unexplained Gender Earnings Gap in
Brazil, by Demographic and Job Characteristics,
1996 and 2006
(percent)

	1996		2006	
	Δ	Δ_0	Δ	Δ_0
Personal characteristics				
Age				
15–24	15.3	22.3	11.0	15.6
25–34	44.4	66.2	30.4	45.1
35–44	72.0	81.5	50.4	66.6
45–54	96.6	88.4	66.9	82.5
55–65	70.8	48.2	68.2	69.0
Years of education				
Less than 4	27.4	23.2	22.0	18.9
4–10	56.0	44.8	39.1	28.8
11–15	141.7	129.9	118.3	68.3
More than 15	277.0	149.4	207.9	140.3
White	71.2	72.4	57.6	63.5
Urban	63.0	63.5	47.3	52.4
Regions				
North	37.3	50.3	28.7	43.9
North-East	31.7	44.6	20.6	35.8
South	63.9	70.3	53.2	60.1
South-East	64.9	67.9	54.7	53.8
Central-West	49.0	64.2	41.7	69.3
Job characteristics				
Formal job	41.6	62.3	29.7	54.0
Type of occupation				
Professionals	202.8	97.6	120.0	109.5
Intermediate	133.3	55.9	32.4	27.7
Blue collar	40.1	43.6	31.6	33.6
Agriculture	24.5	18.3	24.0	21.4
Construction	–47.0	31.1	–113.0	–145.9

(continued next page)

Table 9.2 (continued)

	1996		2006	
	Δ	Δ₀	Δ	Δ₀
Social services	95.9	65.6	95.4	58.4
Total	**52.2**	**60.0**	**39.1**	**49.8**

Source: Based on data from 1996–2006 PNAD.

Note: Δ is the total earnings gap. Δ_0 is the part of the earnings gap that cannot be attributed to differences in characteristics of the individuals. It is typically attributed to a combination of both unobservable characteristics and discrimination.

Figure 9.2 Original and Unexplained Gender Earnings Gap in Brazil, by Percentiles of Earnings Distribution, 1996–2006

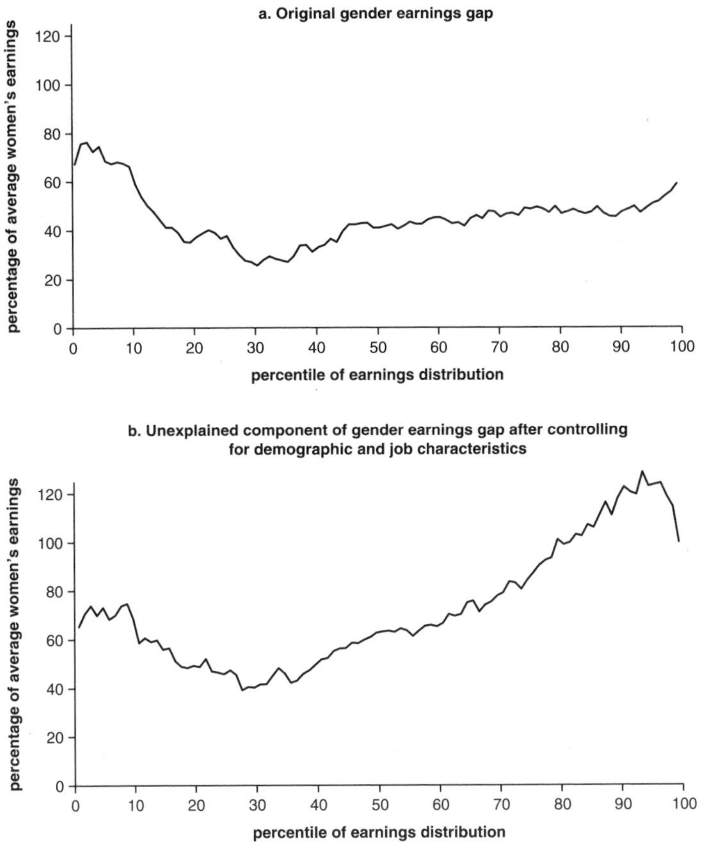

Source: Based on data from 1996–2006 PNAD.

Brazil has a large Afro-descendant population, which faces inequalities that may be comparable to the inequalities faced by women. This issue is addressed in chapter 14.

Notes

1. Kassouf (1997, 1998) and Silva and Kassouf (2000) correct the earnings equation estimation for participation in the formal and informal labor market sectors.
2. For a description of the methodology used in this chapter, see chapter 2.
3. The regions are North (Rondônia, Acre, Amazonas, Roraima, Parà, Amapà, Tocantins); North-East (Maranhão, Piauì, Cearà, Rio Grande do Norte, Paraiba, Pernambuco, Alagoas, Sergipe, Bahia); South-East (Minas Gerais, Espìrito Santo, Rio de Janeiro, São Paulo); South (Paraná, Santa Catarina, Rio Grande do Sul); and Central-West (Mato Grasso do Sul, Mato Grosso, Goiás, Distrito Federal).
4. For graphs reporting different sets of controls, see Garcia, Ñopo, and Salardi (2009). The results are qualitatively similar to those reported here.
5. Only results for the first and last year are reported, because the trend over the decade is fairly stable and smoothly decreasing. For all subsamples of population, both explained and unexplained earnings gaps decrease over time.

References

Arabsheibani, G. R., F. G. Carneiro, and A. Henley. 2003. "Gender Wage Differentials in Brazil: Trends over a Turbulent Era." Policy Research Working Paper 3148, World Bank, Washington, DC.

Barros, R., L. Ramos, and E. Santos. 1995. "Gender Differences in Brazilian Labor Markets." In *Investment in Women's Human Capital*, ed. T. P. Schultz, 345–79. Chicago: University of Chicago Press.

Birdsall, N., and M. L. Fox. 1985. "Why Males Earn More: Location and Training of Brazilian Schoolteachers." *Economic Development and Cultural Change* 33 (3): 533–56.

Brown, R. S., M. Moon, and B. S. Zoloth. 1980. "Incorporating Occupational Attainment in Studies of Male-Female Earnings Differentials." *Journal of Human Resources* 15 (1) 3–2.

Camargo, J. M., and F. Serrano. 1983. "Os dois mercados: homens e mulheres na indústria Brasileira." *Revista Brasileira de Economía* 34: 435–48.

García, L. M., H. Ñopo, and P. Salardi. 2009. "Gender and Racial Wage Gaps in Brazil 1996–2006: Evidence Using a Matching Comparisons Approach." RES Working Paper 4626, Inter-American Development Bank, Research Department, Washington, DC.

Kassouf, A. L. 1997. "Retornos à escolaridade e ao treinamento nos setores urbano e rural do Brasil." *Revista de Economia e Sociologia Rural* 35 (2): 59–76.

———. 1998. "Wage Gender Discrimination and Segmentation in the Brazilian Labour Market." *Brazilian Journal of Applied Economics* 2 (2): 243–69.

Leme, M. C., and S. Wajnman. 2000. "Tendencias de coorte nos diferenciais de rendimentospor sexo." In *Desigualdade e pobreza no Brasil*, org. R. Henriques, 251–70. Instituto de Pesquisa Econômica Aplicada, Rio de Janeiro.

Loureiro, P. R. A., F. G. Carneiro, and A. Sachsida. 2004. "Race and Gender Discrimination in the Labor Market: An Urban and Rural Sector Analysis for Brazil." *Journal of Economic Studies* 31 (2): 129–43.

Ometto, A. M. H., R. Hoffmann and M. C. Alves. 1999. "Participação da mulher no mercado de trabalho: discriminação em Pernambuco e São Paulo." *Revista Brasileira de Economia* 53 (3): 287–322.

Silva, N. D. V., and A. L. Kassouf. 2000. "Mercados de trabalho formal e informal: uma analise da discriminação e da segmentação." *Nova Economía* (1): 41–47.

Stelcner, M., J. B. Smith, J. A. Breslaw, and G. Monette. 1992. "Labor Force Behavior and Earnings of Brazilian Women and Men, 1980." *Case Studies of Women's Employment and Pay in Latin America*, Vol. 2 of ed. G. Psacharopoulos and T. Zatiris, 39–88. Washington, DC: World Bank.

Tiefenthaler, J. 1992. "Female Labor Force Participation and Wage Determination in Brazil 1989." *Case Studies of Women's Employment and Pay in Latin America*, Vol. 2 of ed. G. Psacharopoulos and T. Zatiris, 89–118. Washington, DC: World Bank.

10

Gender Earnings Gaps in a Country with a Large Indigenous Population: Ecuador 2003–07

Ecuador has made important advances in reducing gender disparities and addressing gender-related development issues. The country's gender disparities in education and labor force participation have continued to close. Women's labor force participation has steadily increased since the 1980s, and women have made significant advances in professional, managerial, and technical fields (Correia and Van Bronkhorst 2000.) In rural areas, women continue to play an important role in subsistence farming and commercial agriculture. However, gender disparities in educational and employment opportunities are still significant, particularly among indigenous people.

This chapter analyzes the gender earnings gap in Ecuador, using data from the Survey on Employment, Unemployment, and Underemployment (Encuesta de Empleo, Desempleo, y Subempleo [ENEMDU]), conducted annually by the Instituto Nacional de Estadísticas y Censos de Ecuador (National Institute of Statistics and Census of Ecuador, INEC). The sample studied includes 15 to 65-year-old employers, employees, and the self-employed reporting positive earnings (measured as hourly earnings) who lived in the coastal, highland, and Amazon regions of Ecuador. (Chapter 15 examines the indigenous earnings gap in Ecuador.)

This chapter was adapted from "Ethnic and Gender Wage Gaps in Ecuador," Lourdes Gallardo and Hugo Ñopo, RES Working Paper 4625, Inter-American Development Bank, 2009.

Lourdes Gallardo is an investment officer at the Inter-American Development Bank.

What Does the Literature Show?

Correia and Van Bronkhorst (2000) document that Ecuador's disparities in educational and labor force participation have continued to close.
García-Aracil and Winter (2006) document that endowments account for
slightly less than half of the total earnings differentials between men and
women in Ecuador. This means that more than half of the earnings dis-
parity is unexplained by observable human capital characteristics. García-
Aracil and Winter conclude that equalizing educational opportunities for
girls would only marginally reduce gender earnings differentials. However,
in the case of indigenous women, equalizing educational opportunities
would be important in reducing the earning differential with other groups
(other studies, focused on ethnic minorities, are addressed in chapter 15).

How Do Male and Female Workers Differ?

Table 10.1 reports educational completion rates for men and women. On
average, women's educational attainment slightly surpasses that of men.
In addition, larger percentages of women have both higher education and
no education. Gender differences did not change much during the period
of analysis.

Table 10.2 presents average hourly earnings for indigenous and nonindigenous men and women between 2003 and 2007. It shows that the
gender earnings gap for 2007 (7.4 percent) is much smaller than the indigenous earnings gap (44.9 percent).

Table 10.1 Educational Attainment by Men and Women in Ecuador's
Labor Force, 2003 and 2007
(percent)

Level of education	2003		2007	
	Men	*Women*	*Men*	*Women*
None	5.3	7.8	4.1	6.1
Pre-school	0.3	0.3	0.3	0.4
Basic	52.2	48.3	53.3	49.9
Bachillerato[a]	28.7	28.8	27.5	27.6
Tertiary	13.5	14.7	14.8	16.0
Total	**100**	**100**	**100**	**100**

Source: Based on data from 2003–07 ENEMDU.
a. Equivalent to last three years of high school.

Table 10.2 Average Hourly Earnings for Indigenous and Nonindigenous Men and Women in Ecuador, 2003–07 *(current U.S. dollars)*

Gender	2003	2004	2005	2006	2007
Women	1.0	1.1	1.1	1.3	1.4
Men	1.1	1.2	1.2	1.4	1.5
Gender earnings gap (percent)	7.1	11.2	7.8	9.2	7.4
Ethnicity	2003	2004	2005	2006	2007
Ethnic minorities	0.8	0.8	0.9	0.9	1.0
Nonminorities	1.1	1.2	1.3	1.4	1.5
Ethnic earnings gap (percent)	44.9	48.7	45.4	48.2	44.9

Source: Based on data from 2003–07 ENEMDU.

The Role of Individual Characteristics in Explaining the Gender Earnings Gap

Men and women in the sample were matched on four combinations of human capital characteristics.[1] The first combination includes area (rural or urban), education, ethnicity, and age. The second adds a dummy variable that identifies whether the respondent is the head of household. The third adds occupation (coded at the one-digit classification). The fourth adds a variable that reports whether the respondent's income is complemented by remittances from abroad.

Figure 10.1 presents the results of the decomposition. Gender earnings differentials range from 7.1 percent in 2003 to 11.2 percent in 2007. The contribution of the endowment of productive characteristics to the total earnings gap, Δ_X, is negative, indicating that despite having a better endowment of human capital characteristics, women earn less than men.

The component of the earnings gap attributed to the existence of men with observable characteristics that were not met by any woman (Δ_M) was small over the whole period but slightly higher in 2007 than in 2003. This result may suggest the existence of a glass ceiling effect, as there are men with combinations of observable characteristics for whom there are no comparable women and these men earn earnings that are, on average, higher than the earnings of the rest of the population.

Figure 10.1 Decomposition of Gender Earnings Gap in
Ecuador, 2003–07

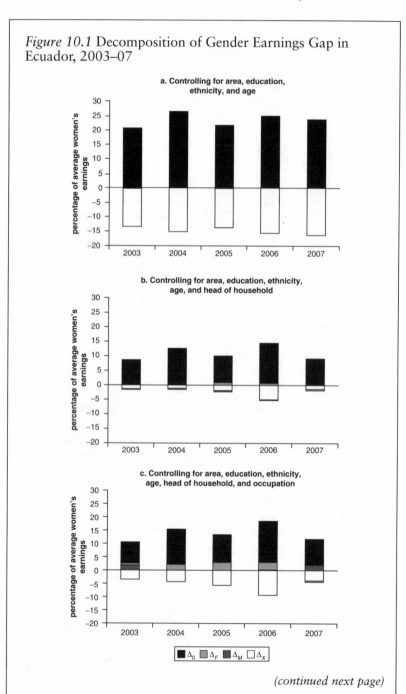

a. Controlling for area, education,
ethnicity, and age

b. Controlling for area, education, ethnicity,
age, and head of household

c. Controlling for area, education, ethnicity,
age, head of household, and occupation

Δ_0 Δ_F Δ_M Δ_X

(continued next page)

Figure 10.1 (continued)

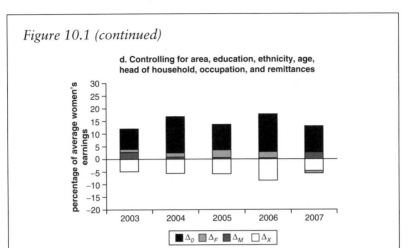

d. Controlling for area, education, ethnicity, age, head of household, occupation, and remittances

Source: Based on data from 2003–07 ENEMDU.

Note: Δ_M (Δ_F) is the part of the earnings gap attributed to the existence of men (women) with combinations of characteristics that are not met by any women (men). Δ_X is the part of the earnings gap attributed to differences in the observable characteristics of men and women over the "common support." Δ_0 is the part of the earnings gap that cannot be attributed to differences in characteristics of the individuals. It is typically attributed to a combination of both unobservable characteristics and discrimination. The sum of these components equals the total earnings gap ($\Delta_M + \Delta_F + \Delta_X + \Delta_0 = \Delta$).

In 2006, the component of the earnings gap attributed to the existence of women with observable characteristics that were not met by any men (Δ_F) accounted for a larger proportion of the earnings differential than Δ_M. This finding suggests the existence of a large "maid effect"—that is, the presence of many indigenous women in the segments of the labor markets that work as maids. This contrasts with the "chief executive officer (CEO) effect," which refers to the fact that men and not woman tend to be CEOs. A large maid effect indicates that on average, women's earnings are lower than the earnings of the rest of the population.

Exploring the Unexplained Component of the Gender Earnings Gap

All combinations of human capital characteristics used in the matching exercise show that the unexplained component of the gap accounts for most of the earning differential between men and women. Figure 10.2 shows the distribution of the unexplained component for different percentiles of the earnings distribution for women and men. The unexplained component is larger at the lower end of the income distribution. Introducing the head of household control into the matching reduces the unexplained component by more than half. This effect is particularly strong between the 80th and 90th percentile of the income distribution, where being the head of household somewhat eliminates the unexplained component. At the low end of the income distribution, the occupational variable has a significant effect on reducing the unexplained component. Occupational sorting thus plays an important role in determining gender earnings gaps among lower-income workers, whereas heading a household matters more for higher-income workers. Different policy approaches are needed to combat gender disparities in labor markets for different segments of the earnings distribution.

As in other countries, observable differences between men and women do not explain gender earnings gaps in Ecuador, suggesting that gender inequalities in labor markets there cannot be reduced through policies that improve human capital endowments for women. Instead, action must be oriented toward changing practices that may discriminate against women.

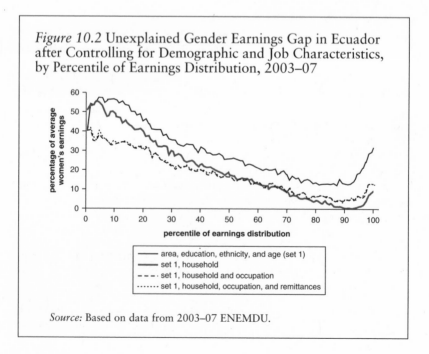

Figure 10.2 Unexplained Gender Earnings Gap in Ecuador after Controlling for Demographic and Job Characteristics, by Percentile of Earnings Distribution, 2003–07

Source: Based on data from 2003–07 ENEMDU.

Ecuador has a large indegenous population, which faces high inequalities in the labor markets. This issue is addressed in chapter 15.

Note

1. For a description of the methodology used in this chapter, see chapter 2.

References

Correia, M., and B. Van Bronkhorst. 2000. *Ecuador: Gender Review: Issues and Recommendations*. Washington, DC: World Bank.

Gallardo, L., and H. Ñopo. 2009. "Ethnic and Gender Wage Gaps in Ecuador." RES Working Paper 4625, Inter-American Development Bank, Research Department, Washington, DC.

García-Aracil, A., and C. Winter. 2006. "Gender and Ethnicity Differentials in School Attainment and Labor Market Earnings in Ecuador." *World Development* 34 (2): 289–307.

11

Gender Earnings Gaps in Central American Countries, 1997–2006

Central America has a relatively young labor force (29 percent under 25), in which women are underrepresented (38 percent of the labor force). The average unemployment rate in Central American countries was 4.3 percent in 2008, 4.8 percent for women and 4.1 percent for men. Almost two-fifths of the economically active labor force lives in rural areas, where the unemployment rate was 3.1 percent (the rate in urban areas was 5.1 percent). Educational achievement is low, with 39 percent of the labor force not having completed primary education and 58 percent having no more than a primary education.

This chapter presents a general picture of Central America, using a pooled database for four countries: Costa Rica, El Salvador, Honduras, and Nicaragua. The pooled dataset includes data for three points in time: the mid-1990s, the early 2000s, and the mid-2000s. The countries are then analyzed individually using the same surveys and years as in the pooled dataset (Enamorado,

This chapter was adapted from the following sources: "Gender Wage Gaps in Central American Countries: Evidence from a Non-Parametric Approach," Ted Enamorado, Ana Carolina Izaguirre, and Hugo Ñopo, RES Working Paper 4639, Inter-American Development Bank, 2009; "Gender and Ethnic Wage Gaps in Guatemala from a Matching Comparisons Perspective," Hugo Ñopo and Alberto Gonzales, RES Working Paper 4587, Inter-American Development Bank, 2008; and Hugo Ñopo and Alberto Gonzales, "Brechas salariales por género y etnicidad," in *Más crecimiento, más equidad*, ed. Ernesto Stein, Osmel Manzano, Hector Morena, and Fernando Straface, Banco Interamericano de Desarrollo, 265–98, 2009.

Ted Enamorado is a PhD student in the department of political science at Vanderbilt University, in Nashville, TN. Ana Carolina Izaguirre is a researcher at the Inter-American Development Bank. Alberto Gonzales is a PhD student in the department of economics at the University of Virginia in Charlottesville.

Izaguirre, and Ñopo 2009). An analysis for Guatemala is also included (see Ñopo and Gonzales 2008).[1] Earnings are measured as hourly earnings.

What Does the Literature Show?

Psacharopoulos and Tzannatos (1993) were among the first to address gender disparities in Central America. Using historical census data and household surveys in a set of Latin American countries including Costa Rica and Honduras, they find that gender differences in human capital characteristics cannot account for the observed earnings differentials between men and women. They also find that women in the public sector are paid more than their counterparts in the private sector and that pay is more unequal in the public sector than in the private sector. These differences reflect the fact that women in the public sector tend to be more educated than both women and men in the private sector.

Panizza and Qiang (2005) show similar results for Costa Rica and El Salvador, where they find a premium of more than 10 percent associated with working in the public sector. Although this premium is often larger for women than men, it still does not compensate for the wide overall gender earnings gap.

Dávila and Pagán (1999) analyze the sources of intercountry differences between Costa Rica and El Salvador in the gender earnings gap during the late 1980s from an occupational segregation approach. They report that women in both countries are underrepresented in occupational categories such as managerial, service, agricultural labor, and laborer occupational categories and overrepresented in professional, administrative support and clerical, and transportation jobs. They also find that differences in weekly hours worked and occupational attainment explain the differences in the gender earnings gap.

Using data for urban Costa Rica in 1989, 1993, and 1997, Deutsch et al. (2005) find that occupational segregation did not decrease during this period. Human capital endowments reduced the gender gap in earnings, but a larger problem involved returns to that human capital. Occupational segregation is much more severe among the less educated than the more educated. Furthermore, in all years studied, differences in earnings that cannot be explained by differences in human capital characteristics account for the largest portion of the earnings gap.

Corley, Perardel, and Popova (2005) show trends in low- and high-skilled occupational earnings across countries. They find that between 1990 and 2000, Nicaragua enjoyed particularly strong earnings growth in both high-skilled and low-skilled occupations. In El Salvador, the gender earnings gap in the manufacturing sector increased from 5 percent in 1996 to almost 16 percent in 2003. The opposite occurred in Costa Rica, where the gap narrowed from 28 percent in 1996 to 18 percent in 2006.

Pisani and Pagán (2004) conduct a similar exercise, focusing on high and low educational attainment groups. They find that workers in Nicaragua with higher levels of education were most likely to be employed in the much higher-paying formal sector; people with little education were most likely to be found in the low-paying informal sector. They also find that women earn less than men in both educational groups.

How Do Male and Female Workers Differ?

Table 11.1 presents statistics for each period in the pooled database for Costa Rica, El Salvador, Honduras, and Nicaragua. It shows relative hourly earnings by various sets of observable individual characteristics, normalizing them by the average women's earnings. Table 11.2 presents descriptive statistics of the distribution of these characteristics in the samples.

In circa 1997, men earn 8.9 percent more than women. This relation is reversed in circa 2001 and 2006: men earn 1.3 percent less than women in circa 2001 and 2.6 percent less in circa 2006. In circa 1997, men earn more than women at every age interval. In circa 2001 and 2006, for the population 15–34, women earn slightly more than men. In circa 1997, men earn more than women at every level of education. However, in circa 2001 and 2006, women at the bottom of the education distribution (no education or incomplete primary) earn more than men with the same educational level.

The original gender earnings gap differs by economic sector, type of employment, firm size, and other characteristics. However, these differences are just simple mean comparisons; they do not take into account gender differences in observable characteristics, which matter in the determination of earnings.

Women in the labor force are more educated than men. The proportion of women with tertiary education increased by 3.3 percentage points between circa 1997 and 2006, whereas the proportion for men increased by just 1.1 percentage points. The prevalence of self-employed people is greater for women in all three years. Women are more likely than men to work part time. There are also significant differences in economic sector by gender: women are concentrated in wholesale and retail trade and the hotel and restaurants sectors, whereas men are concentrated in agriculture, hunting, forestry, and fishing.

Women represent just 30–40 percent of the paid work force in Costa Rica, El Salvador, Honduras, and Nicaragua (for tables on each country, see Enamorado, Izaguirre, and Ñopo 2009). However, participation by women increased over the period examined, especially in Costa Rica and Honduras.

The countries in the pooled sample show patterns of gender schooling gaps similar to the patterns in the rest of the region, with a marked reversal in recent decades (see chapter 3). On average, women have about one more

Table 11.1 Relative Hourly Earnings of Men and Women in Central American Countries, by Demographic and Job Characteristics, Circa 1997–2006

	Circa 1997		Circa 2001		Circa 2006	
	Base: average women's earnings in each year and country = 100		Base: average women's earnings in each year and country = 100		Base: average women's earnings in each year and country = 100	
	Women	Men	Women	Men	Women	Men
All	100	108.9	100.0	98.7	100.0	97.4
Personal characteristics						
Age						
15–24	71.4	75.0	71.3	68.6	72.7	67.8
25–34	104.6	111.6	102.2	98.8	102.5	99.3
35–44	117.5	132.2	113.5	115.1	108.4	113.0
45–54	108.9	128.8	113.4	122.4	114.8	115.0
55–64	86.7	112.0	94.0	100.4	93.8	103.2
Education						
None	52.5	59.4	59.9	53.2	59.6	51.8
Primary incomplete	65.6	79.1	68.5	69.4	73.4	71.0
Primary complete	75.9	96.4	73.4	85.1	70.7	81.7
Secondary incomplete	85.0	105.3	79.7	91.7	76.4	86.9
Secondary complete	117.2	145.1	117.2	126.8	104.7	117.9

Table 11.1 (continued)

	Circa 1997		Circa 2001		Circa 2006	
	Base: average women's earnings in each year and country = 100		Base: average women's earnings in each year and country = 100		Base: average women's earnings in each year and country = 100	
	Women	Men	Women	Men	Women	Men
Tertiary incomplete	197.7	207.9	167.4	186.6	152.8	170.9
Tertiary complete	247.7	280.7	232.5	274.4	215.5	244.1
Presence of children (12 years or younger) in the household						
No	111.0	117.6	107.6	107.1	106.5	103.3
Yes	88.4	100.6	90.4	89.3	90.3	89.4
Presence of other household member with labor income						
No	97.5	111.2	98.6	98.5	104.3	98.4
Yes	100.9	107.3	100.5	98.9	98.4	96.8
Dependency						
More independents than dependents in the household	105.9	111.5	104.0	102.8	103.2	99.9

(continued next page)

Table 11.1 (continued)

	Circa 1997		Circa 2001		Circa 2006	
	Base: average women's earnings in each year and country = 100		Base: average women's earnings in each year and country = 100		Base: average women's earnings in each year and country = 100	
	Women	Men	Women	Men	Women	Men
Same independents as dependents in the household	100.2	116.2	101.5	100.0	101.1	100.8
More dependents than independents in the household	84.7	95.0	84.9	82.6	85.1	81.2
Urban						
No	82.0	86.6	84.8	74.2	82.6	74.6
Yes	108.0	125.9	105.8	116.1	106.7	112.6
Labor characteristics						
Type of employment						
Employer	143.0	161.0	172.8	144.8	138.2	152.4
Self-employed	80.1	99.7	81.6	83.0	82.4	84.6
Employee	107.5	106.4	106.3	99.0	106.8	96.8

Table 11.1 (continued)

	Circa 1997 Base: average women's earnings in each year and country = 100		Circa 2001 Base: average women's earnings in each year and country = 100		Circa 2006 Base: average women's earnings in each year and country = 100	
	Women	Men	Women	Men	Women	Men
Time worked						
Part time	120.5	136.0	115.1	121.1	114.5	113.3
Full time	115.6	114.2	109.9	100.7	107.3	100.9
Overtime	65.0	93.6	72.6	87.8	72.6	85.7
One job						
No	112.5	123.6	116.1	104.6	110.4	96.8
Yes	99.3	107.6	98.9	98.1	99.2	97.5
Small firm (five workers or less)						
No	132.4	125.1	130.6	119.0	129.8	114.8
Yes	73.7	92.3	77.0	80.4	74.2	75.4
Economic sector						
Agriculture, hunting, forestry, and fishing	54.9	67.2	60.1	55.0	58.1	52.9

(continued next page)

Table 11.1 (continued)

| | Circa 1997 | | Circa 2001 | | Circa 2006 | |
	Base: average women's earnings in each year and country = 100		Base: average women's earnings in each year and country = 100		Base: average women's earnings in each year and country = 100	
	Women	Men	Women	Men	Women	Men
Elementary manufacturing	77.2	100.0	74.0	92.5	74.0	94.4
Other manufacturing	116.3	120.2	96.8	102.7	105.3	102.0
Construction	132.0	102.4	134.0	93.8	114.0	89.6
Wholesale and retail trade and hotels and restaurants	87.0	119.3	91.5	105.3	89.6	103.3
Electricity, gas, water supply, transport, and communications	182.3	137.2	152.2	131.3	153.8	121.3
Financing, insurance, real estate, and business services	185.9	168.1	154.7	148.4	150.5	136.4
Public administration and defense	170.3	156.4	176.5	153.1	165.0	152.2
Education, health, and personal services	151.0	151.3	136.8	150.3	142.7	150.3

Source: Based on 1995–2007 national household surveys of Costa Rica, El Salvador, Honduras, and Nicaragua.

Table 11.2 Demographic and Job Characteristics of Central American Countries, 1997, 2001, and 2006
(percent)

	Circa 1997		*Circa 2001*		*Circa 2006*	
	Women	*Men*	*Women*	*Men*	*Women*	*Men*
Real Earnings						
Personal characteristics						
Age						
15–24	22.7	26.9	21.0	25.5	19.0	24.9
25–34	30.7	28.8	29.2	27.4	28.6	27.5
35–44	26.5	22.4	26.6	23.2	27.0	22.4
45–54	14.0	14.5	16.4	15.7	18.0	16.3
55–64	6.0	7.5	6.9	8.3	7.4	9.0
Education						
None	10.4	11.9	9.3	11.2	7.4	8.8
Primary incomplete	26.3	29.4	24.8	28.0	21.5	24.2
Primary complete	18.6	21.7	18.4	22.8	18.0	23.4
Secondary incomplete	12.6	14.2	13.0	14.0	15.5	17.4
Secondary complete	17.7	12.7	17.6	13.0	17.5	13.8
Tertiary incomplete	8.0	5.7	9.6	6.4	10.5	6.8
Tertiary complete	6.5	4.4	7.2	4.7	9.7	5.5

(continued next page)

Table 11.2 *(continued)*

	Circa 1997		Circa 2001		Circa 2006	
	Women	*Men*	*Women*	*Men*	*Women*	*Men*
Presence of children (12 years or younger) in the household						
No	51.3	48.5	59.8	52.9	59.8	57.6
Yes	48.8	51.5	44.1	47.2	40.2	42.4
Presence of other household member with labor income						
No	26.2	39.7	25.3	38.2	27.1	38.5
Yes	73.8	60.3	74.8	61.8	72.9	61.5
Dependency						
More independents than dependents in the household	59.9	62.6	64.7	65.5	68.4	70.0
Same independents as dependents in the household	16.7	16.6	16.6	16.6	15.7	15.9
More dependents than independents in the household	23.3	20.8	18.7	17.9	15.9	14.0

Table 11.2 (continued)

	Circa 1997		Circa 2001		Circa 2006	
	Women	*Men*	*Women*	*Men*	*Women*	*Men*
Urban						
No	30.7	43.3	27.6	41.4	27.7	40.0
Yes	69.3	56.7	72.4	58.6	72.3	60.0
Job characteristics						
Type of employment						
Employer	2.5	7.3	3.0	8.0	3.0	6.0
Employee	67.0	70.7	63.5	67.5	65.3	72.0
Self-employed	30.5	22.0	33.5	24.5	31.7	22.0
Time worked						
Part time	23.7	11.7	25.0	12.7	26.1	13.2
Full time	43.2	50.0	44.5	51.6	47.4	53.2
Overtime	33.0	38.3	30.2	35.6	26.5	33.7
One job						
No	5.6	8.0	6.3	9.6	6.8	8.5
Yes	94.4	92.0	93.7	90.3	93.2	91.5

(continued next page)

Table 11.2 (continued)

	Circa 1997		Circa 2001		Circa 2006	
	Women	*Men*	*Women*	*Men*	*Women*	*Men*
Small firm (five workers or less)						
No	44.9	50.5	43.0	47.4	44.4	50.3
Yes	55.2	49.5	57.0	52.6	46.2	44.4
Not reported	–	–	–	–	9.5	5.3
Economic sector						
Agriculture, hunting, forestry, and fishing	4.6	28.2	2.8	27.8	3.3	24.6
Elementary manufacturing	17.3	8.3	16.5	7.5	15.6	7.7
Other manufacturing	2.7	7.3	2.6	7.4	2.5	7.2
Construction	0.3	10.2	0.5	10.5	0.4	11.7
Wholesale and retail trade and hotels and restaurants	31.2	19.4	31.7	19.4	32.7	20.4

Table 11.2 (continued)

	Circa 1997		Circa 2001		Circa 2006	
	Women	*Men*	*Women*	*Men*	*Women*	*Men*
Electricity, gas, water supply, transport, and communications	1.45	8.37	1.76	8.85	1.98	9.26
Financing, insurance, real estate, and business services	3.13	3.52	4.79	4.85	4.99	5.89
Public administration and defense	4.95	5.82	4.67	5.00	4.59	5.05
Education, health, and personal services	19.13	8.10	20.91	7.74	19.95	6.85
Domestic servants	15.33	0.82	13.74	0.98	13.99	1.17

Source: Based on 1995–2007 national household surveys of Costa Rica, El Salvador, Honduras, and Nicaragua.

year of schooling than their male counterparts. In Costa Rica, about half of workers report being a head of household. This percentage is slightly smaller in El Salvador, Honduras, and Nicaragua. Marital arrangements are similar across countries and stable over time. Except in El Salvador in 1995, about 1 in 4 workers is single and about 5–6 in 10 workers are in a (formal or informal) marital union.[2] Age groups display similar patterns across countries, with almost 40 percent of the sample in each country between the ages of 25 and 40.

Descriptive statistics for Guatemala for 2000, 2004, and 2006 show that the gender composition of the labor market was stable over the period of analysis (see Ñopo and Gonzales 2008).[3] About 70 percent of workers in Guatemala are men, and this share did not change significantly during the period of analysis. Participation by gender is more balanced in urban (60 percent men) than in rural (80 percent men) areas. Real monthly earnings (expressed in 2006 quetzals) declined slightly for men and remained constant for women during 2000–06. As a result, the gender earnings gap narrowed, from 28 percent to 18 percent, during this period. Average urban earnings are almost twice average earnings in rural areas, but the decline in men's average earnings was more pronounced in urban areas. There are no significant differences in gender gaps between urban and rural areas, except in 2000.

Monthly earnings differ widely by educational attainment. The ratio between average earnings of people with university degrees and people with less than secondary education is five to one, although this gap has been closing since 2000. Income disparities between the least educated and most educated are in line with the findings of Auguste, Artana, and Cuevas (2007), who find that the returns to education in Guatemala are among the highest in Latin America.

Among employed people in Guatemala, women have about one year more education than men. This result is in apparent contradiction with the findings reported in chapter 3, which indicate that Guatemalan men from recent cohorts are more educated than women. The results presented in this chapter refer only to the working population. The difference between the two results may reflect the nonrandom selection of men and women into the labor market. Given their more limited opportunities to participate in labor markets, women may be acquiring more education to compete with men for jobs.

The Role of Individual Characteristics in Explaining the Earnings Gap

Figure 11.1 shows the evolution of the original gender earnings gap by country. Except for Costa Rica, the earnings gap decreased between circa

Figure 11.1 Gender Earnings Gap in Central American
Countries, Circa 1997–2006

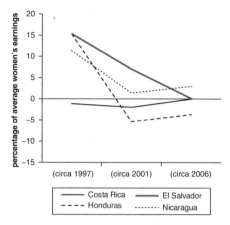

Source: Based on 1995–2007 national household surveys of Costa Rica, El
Salvador, Honduras, and Nicaragua.

1997 and circa 2006. The widest gaps appear in circa 1997 in El Salvador
and Honduras, circa 2001 in Guatemala, and circa 2006 in Nicaragua. In
circa 2006, the original gender earnings gap is not statistically different
from zero in Costa Rica and El Salvador.

Table 11.3 decomposes the gender earnings gap using the matching
methodology described in chapter 2. Six observable demographic characteristics are considered as controls.

In circa 1997, men earn 8.9 percent more than women. After controlling for age, most of the gender earnings gap remains unexplained. Adding
education to the controls, the unexplained earnings gap (Δ_0)—the part of
the earnings gap that cannot be attributed to differences in characteristics
of individuals—is considerably larger than the total earnings gap (Δ). The
component that captures differences in observable characteristics (Δ_x) is
negative, reflecting the fact that women have more education than men.
After adding new characteristics to the set of controls, the unexplained
component of the earnings gap remains constant.

Matching by demographic characteristics, the unexplained earnings gap
is 18.3 percent (that is, if men and women had the same distribution of
observable demographic characteristics, men would earn 18.3 percent more
than women). The total earnings gap is smaller than the unexplained earnings gap because women have characteristics that are better remunerated

Table 11.3 Decomposition of Gender Earnings Gap in Central America after Controlling for Demographic Characteristics, Circa 1997
(percent)

	Circa 1997—Guatemala not included					
	Age	*+ Education*	*+ Presence of children in the household*	*+ Presence of other household member with labor income*	*+ Dependency*	*+ Urban*
Δ	8.9	8.9	8.9	8.9	8.9	8.9
Δ_0	11.7	18.9	18.2	16.8	16.6	18.3
Δ_M	0.0	0.9	1.1	1.7	1.7	-1.7
Δ_F	0.0	-0.3	-0.5	-1.5	-2.5	-1.9
Δ_X	-2.8	-10.7	-9.9	-8.1	-6.9	-5.9
Percentage of men in the common support	100.0	98.5	96.0	89.2	72.9	59.5
Percentage of women in the common support	100.0	99.5	98.7	95.8	83.6	74.0

Source: Based on circa 1997 national household surveys of Costa Rica, El Salvador, Honduras, and Nicaragua.

Note: Δ_M (Δ_F) is the part of the earnings gap attributed to the existence of men (women) with combinations of characteristics that are not met by any women (men). Δ_X is the part of the earnings gap attributed to differences in the observable characteristics of men and women over the "common support." Δ_0 is the part of the earnings gap that cannot be attributed to differences in characteristics of the individuals. It is typically attributed to a combination of both unobservable characteristics and discrimination. The sum of these components equals the total earnings gap ($\Delta_M + \Delta_F + \Delta_X + \Delta_0 = \Delta$).

in the labor market (Δ_X = –5.9 percent) and because of differences in the "common support" of characteristics. Unmatched men earn lower earnings than matched men (Δ_M = –1.6 percent), and unmatched women earn higher earnings than matched women (Δ_F = –1.9 percent). This pattern is the same in all periods, except for the reversal of the gap in favor of women reported earlier.

Table 11.4 compares results for each country after matching on two sets of individual characteristics. The first set considers only area and education; the second adds age, head of household, marital status, and occupation. Costa Rica stands out as a country with a negative gender earnings gap, although the gap is relatively small (and likely not statistically different from zero). Nicaragua has a small positive gender earnings gap. Honduras shows a slightly larger gender earnings gap, and El Salvador is the country in the sample with the largest gap. The set of countries can thus be grouped into countries with small gender earnings gaps (Costa Rica and Nicaragua) and countries with larger gender earnings gaps (El Salvador and Honduras).

In all four countries, the unexplained component of the gap exceeds the original measure of the gender earnings gap. This result is a consequence of the fact that women have more years of education than men. The extent to which Δ_0 exceeds Δ varies across countries and time. For the two countries with large earnings gaps (El Salvador and Honduras), the portion of the gap that cannot be explained by gender differences in observed characteristics tends to be closer to the total earnings gap in the mid-1990s than in later years, especially when controlling for the broader set of individual characteristics. For countries with smaller gaps (Costa Rica and Nicaragua), the unexplained components are larger than the original earnings gaps. Regarding the out-of-common-support components, in most cases Δ_M is positive and Δ_F is negative. In the two countries with larger earnings gaps, Δ_M dominates Δ_F; in the two countries with small earnings gaps, the opposite is true.

The rural earnings gap has a larger unexplained component than the national gap in three of the four countries (the exception being El Salvador) (for tables reporting these results, see Enamorado, Izaguirre, and Ñopo 2009). The national findings on out-of-common-support components prevail in rural areas, in both the high and low earnings gap countries. For the urban earnings gap decomposition, the situation changes slightly. In Costa Rica and Nicaragua (countries with low earnings gaps), the unexplained component of the gap is larger than the original gap. In Honduras and El Salvador (countries with high earnings gaps), the situation resembles a traditional gender earnings gap decomposition: the unexplained component is no longer larger than the original gap.

Regarding the out-of-common-support components for the low earnings gap countries, in Nicaragua, the pattern observed at the national and rural

Table 11.4 Decomposition of Gender Earnings Gaps in Central American Countries after Controlling for Demographic Characteristics, Various Years
(percent)

Period	Costa Rica		El Salvador		Honduras		Nicaragua	
	Area and education	Urban, education, age, head of household, marital status, and occupation	Area and education	Urban, education, age, head of household, marital status, and occupation	Area and education	Urban, education, age, head of household, marital status, and occupation	Area and education	Urban, education, age, head of household, marital status, and occupation
Circa 1997								
Δ	−1.9	−1.9	24.7	24.7	11.4	11.4	5.1	5.1
Δ_0	14.6	11.8	30.1	22.9	26.0	10.1	22.3	30.1
Δ_M	0.0	22.9	0.0	21.4	0.1	10.7	0.0	15.0
Δ_F	0.0	−28.7	−0.1	−12.1	0.0	−4.9	0.0	−24.6
Δ_X	−16.5	−7.8	−5.3	−7.5	−14.8	−4.5	−17.2	−15.4
Circa 2001								
Δ	−3.5	−3.5	12.9	12.9	0.0	0.0	−4.6	−4.6
Δ_0	15.7	7.8	16.7	11.0	16.4	8.9	12.9	18.6
Δ_M	0.0	15.2	0.1	15.9	0.0	8.3	0.0	9.9
Δ_F	0.0	−19.2	−0.1	−3.9	0.0	−8.2	−0.1	−17.5
Δ_X	−19.2	−7.3	−3.9	−10.0	−16.5	−9.0	−17.4	−15.5

Table 11.4 *(continued)*

Period	Costa Rica		El Salvador		Honduras		Nicaragua	
	Area and education	*Urban, education, age, head of household, marital status, and occupation*	*Area and education*	*Urban, education, age, head of household, marital status, and occupation*	*Area and education*	*Urban, education, age, head of household, marital status, and occupation*	*Area and education*	*Urban, education, age, head of household, marital status, and occupation*
Circa 2006								
Δ	-2.9	-2.9	14.3	14.3	2.6	2.6	2.6	2.6
Δ_0	17.2	12.2	20.6	20.5	14.2	12.3	20.3	16.4
Δ_M	0.0	7.8	0.1	-9.3	0.1	7.5	0.1	11.6
Δ_F	0.0	-7.2	-0.2	4.8	0.0	-7.3	0.0	-14.8
Δ_X	-20.2	-15.7	-6.1	-1.6	-11.6	-9.9	-17.8	-10.5

Source: Based on 1995–2007 national household surveys of Costa Rica, El Salvador, Honduras, and Nicaragua.

Note: Δ_M (Δ_F) is the part of the earnings gap attributed to the existence of men (women) with combinations of characteristics that are not met by any women (men). Δ_X is the part of the earnings gap attributed to differences in the observable characteristics of men and women over the "common support." Δ_0 is the part of the earnings gap that cannot be attributed to differences in characteristics of the individuals. It is typically attributed to a combination of both unobservable characteristics and discrimination. The sum of these components equals the total earnings gap ($\Delta_M + \Delta_F + \Delta_X + \Delta_0 = \Delta$).

levels remains when controls are added for the urban sample. In contrast, in Costa Rica, the relationship between Δ_F and Δ_M changes, with Δ_M now dominating Δ_F. In El Salvador and Honduras, the results for the national and rural samples (that is, Δ_M dominating Δ_F) reverses in the mid-2000s.

The earnings gaps in Guatemala were decomposed for the entire working population and for urban and rural working populations. Only the decompositions for the entire population that control for age, marital status, and education are shown, because they are closer to the controls used in the other countries (figure 11.2).[4] About half of the earnings gaps are explained by differences in the distribution of characteristics, both where these distributions are comparable for men and women (Δ_X) and where they are not (Δ_F and Δ_M).

The components that control for the lack of common support between men and women are very small and not statistically significant in most combinations. Only in the last set of controls do Δ_M and Δ_F play important roles. This result is very similar to the results for Chile (chapter 7) and Peru (chapter 5). Age, marital status, and education provide enough

Figure 11.2 Decomposition of Gender Earnings Gap in Guatemala after Controlling for Age, Marital Status, and Education, 2000–06

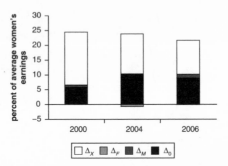

Source: Based on data from the 2000 and 2006 ENCOVI and 2004 ENEI.
Note: Δ_M (Δ_F) is the part of the earnings gap attributed to the existence of men (women) with combinations of characteristics that are not met by any women (men). Δ_X is the part of the earnings gap attributed to differences in the observable characteristics of men and women over the "common support." Δ_0 is the part of the earnings gap that cannot be attributed to differences in characteristics of the individuals. It is typically attributed to a combination of both unobservable characteristics and discrimination. The sum of these components equals the total earnings gap ($\Delta_M + \Delta_F + \Delta_X + \Delta_0 = \Delta$).

information to assess the unexplained gender earnings gap. Of these three variables, it is education that drives gender earnings gaps.

The decomposition of the national earnings gap is largely similar to the decomposition in urban areas. In contrast, in rural areas, the decomposition is slightly different. The unexplained component accounts for about 80 percent of the earnings gap and the component attributable to unpaired women is negative. Apparently, segmentation (or segregation) operates negatively on women's earnings in urban areas and positively in rural areas.

Exploring the Unexplained Component of the Gender Earnings Gap

The decompositions described in table 11.3 and figure 11.2 describe the mean gaps, without reference to either their distribution or variability.

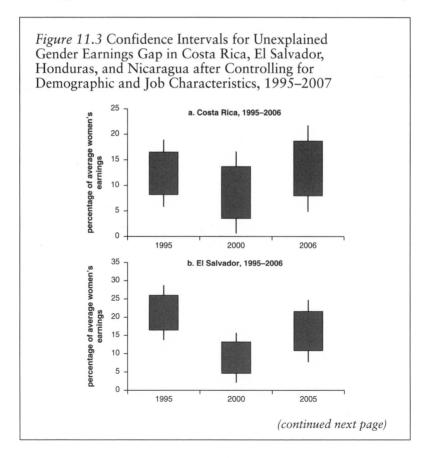

Figure 11.3 Confidence Intervals for Unexplained Gender Earnings Gap in Costa Rica, El Salvador, Honduras, and Nicaragua after Controlling for Demographic and Job Characteristics, 1995–2007

(continued next page)

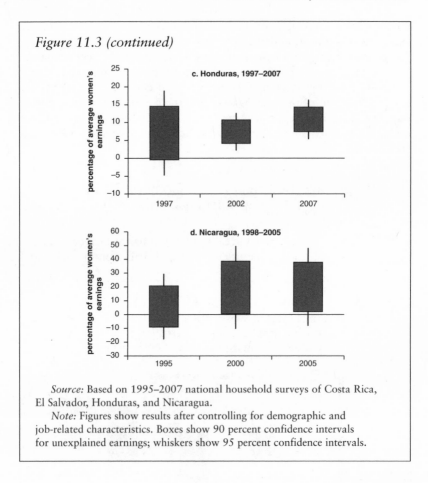

Figure 11.3 (continued)

Source: Based on 1995–2007 national household surveys of Costa Rica, El Salvador, Honduras, and Nicaragua.
Note: Figures show results after controlling for demographic and job-related characteristics. Boxes show 90 percent confidence intervals for unexplained earnings; whiskers show 95 percent confidence intervals.

Figure 11.3 presents confidence intervals for the unexplained component of the gender earnings gap that remains after controlling for the full set of individual characteristics (area, education, age, household head, marital status, and occupation) for Costa Rica, El Salvador, Honduras, and Nicaragua. The extremes of the boxes represent 90 percent confidence intervals for the mean unexplained gender earnings gaps; the whiskers represent 95 percent confidence intervals (for figures at the urban and rural levels, see Enamorado, Izaguirre, and Ñopo 2009). Although the hypothesis that the gender earnings gaps remained constant over time cannot be statistically ruled out, the figures show a narrowing in the gaps between the mid-1990s and 2000, after which the gaps widen.

The following subsections present the results for the empirical distributions of the unexplained earnings gap for each country, using the latest survey data available and three different sets of individual characteristics: first, area; second, area, education, and age; and third, area, education, age, household head, marital status, and occupation.

Costa Rica

The unexplained part of the gender earnings gap in Costa Rica is larger at the lowest percentiles; gaps are close to zero after the 57th percentile (figure 11.4). After controlling by more characteristics, the gaps remain about 20 percent. At the upper extreme of the earnings distribution, after controlling by the full set of characteristics, the earnings gaps narrow, approaching zero.

El Salvador

Much of the unexplained gaps in El Salvador appears at the bottom of the earnings distribution (figure 11.5). Qualitatively, the plots for the

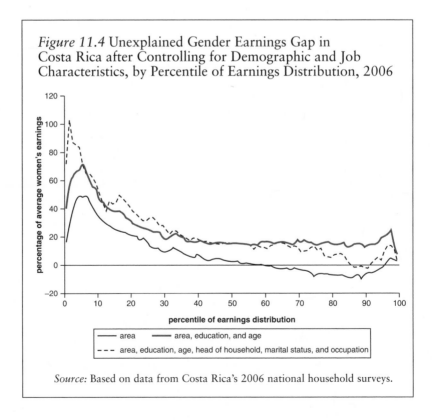

Figure 11.4 Unexplained Gender Earnings Gap in Costa Rica after Controlling for Demographic and Job Characteristics, by Percentile of Earnings Distribution, 2006

Source: Based on data from Costa Rica's 2006 national household surveys.

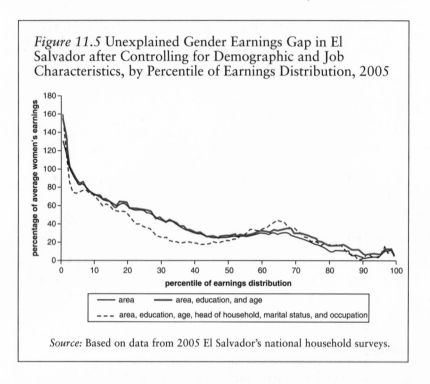

Figure 11.5 Unexplained Gender Earnings Gap in El Salvador after Controlling for Demographic and Job Characteristics, by Percentile of Earnings Distribution, 2005

Source: Based on data from 2005 El Salvador's national household surveys.

three sets of controls are similar. Between the 1st and 10th percentiles, the gaps are large but decrease rapidly, moving from 160 percent to 80 percent in these first 10 percentiles. Between the 11th and 55th percentiles, there is still a decrease of the gender gap along the percentiles, but the rate of decrease is slower, falling from 80 percent to 30 percent. In this interval, the use of extra controls (head of household, marital status, and occupation) reduces unexplained gap. Around the 65th percentile, there is a peak in unexplained earnings differences. Thereafter the gap declines, ending up with values close to zero at the top of the earnings distribution.

Guatemala

The unexplained component of the earnings gap is larger among low-income workers than among high-income workers in Guatemala (figure 11.6). The gap decreases rapidly, becoming negative after the 70th percentile of the earnings distribution, a sign of significant inequality

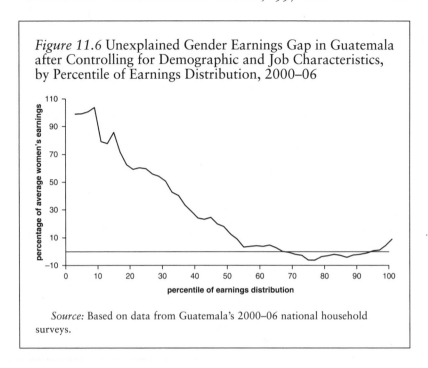

Figure 11.6 Unexplained Gender Earnings Gap in Guatemala after Controlling for Demographic and Job Characteristics, by Percentile of Earnings Distribution, 2000–06

Source: Based on data from Guatemala's 2000–06 national household surveys.

within social classes. This distribution is similar to that found in the other Central American countries.

Honduras

As in El Salvador, larger unexplained differences in earnings are found at the lower percentiles of the earnings distribution in Honduras (figure 11.7). At the lowest percentile of the earnings distribution the unexplained gender earnings gap is 60–100 percent, declining to 20–30 percent around the 40th percentile. For higher percentiles of the earnings distribution, the unexplained gender gap also decreases but at a slower rate. As in El Salvador, at the upper part of the earnings distributions (85th percentile and above), the unexplained gender earnings gap is almost zero for all three sets of controlling characteristics.

Nicaragua

The unexplained gender gaps in Nicaragua behave slightly differently from the other countries (figure 11.8). At the lowest percentiles of the earnings distributions, the gap is negative when the smaller sets of controls

Figure 11.7 Unexplained Gender Earnings Gap in Honduras after Controlling for Demographic and Job Characteristics, by Percentile of Earnings Distribution, 2007

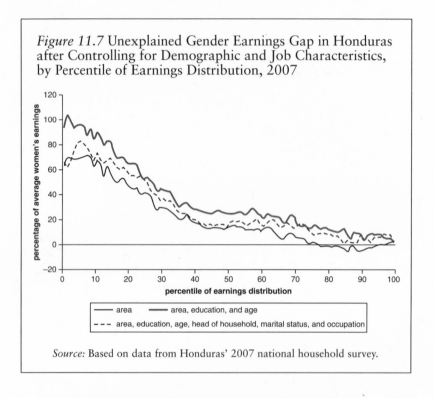

Source: Based on data from Honduras' 2007 national household survey.

are used; it is positive only for the set that controls for area, education, age, head of household, marital status, and occupation. The unexplained gap increases with earnings up to the 15th percentile. After that point, the gap decreases but at a slower rate than in Honduras and Guatemala, so that in statistical terms the unexplained gap can be assumed to be constant between the 30th and 95th percentiles.

Figures 11.4–11.8 show more similarities than differences in the distribution of unexplained gender differences in pay in the five countries. All five countries show larger gaps at the bottom of the earnings distribution and almost zero gaps at the top.

For this reason, in the remainder of the analysis, only results for the pooled database are shown. The pool selected corresponds to data for Costa Rica, El Salvador, Honduras, and Nicaragua in the latest time period for which data were available (circa 2006).

To what extent do unexplained gender earnings gaps (after controlling for the fullest set of observable characteristics) differ across different segments of labor markets? Figure 11.9 shows confidence intervals for the unexplained component of the gender earnings gap by area, age, years of

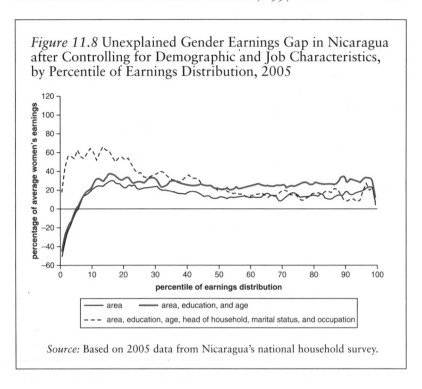

Figure 11.8 Unexplained Gender Earnings Gap in Nicaragua after Controlling for Demographic and Job Characteristics, by Percentile of Earnings Distribution, 2005

Source: Based on 2005 data from Nicaragua's national household survey.

education, marital status, head of household, and occupation. As before, the extremes of the boxes represent 90 percent confidence intervals for the mean unexplained gender earnings gaps, and the whiskers represent a 95 percent confidence interval.

The results illustrate that gender earnings gaps do not statistically differ in rural and urban areas (panel a). They decrease with age, becoming statistically indistinguishable from zero among the oldest cohort (people passed the traditional retirement age) (panel b). In contrast with other countries in Latin America, the unexplained gender earnings gap seems to be larger among people with 6–11 years of completed schooling (panel c). The unexplained gaps are smaller among widowed people, among whom the gap is negative at the 95 percent confidence level (panel d). Although the average unexplained gaps do not statistically differ between people who are heads of household and people who are not, the dispersion is greater among household heads (panel e). Unexplained gender earnings differences are large and dispersed among agricultural workers and negative among professionals (panel f). A similar analysis for Guatemala shows that the unexplained gender earnings gaps are larger among young people, people with higher education, people who

Figure 11.9 Confidence Intervals for Unexplained Earnings
Gaps in Central America after Controlling for Demographic
Characteristics, Circa 2006

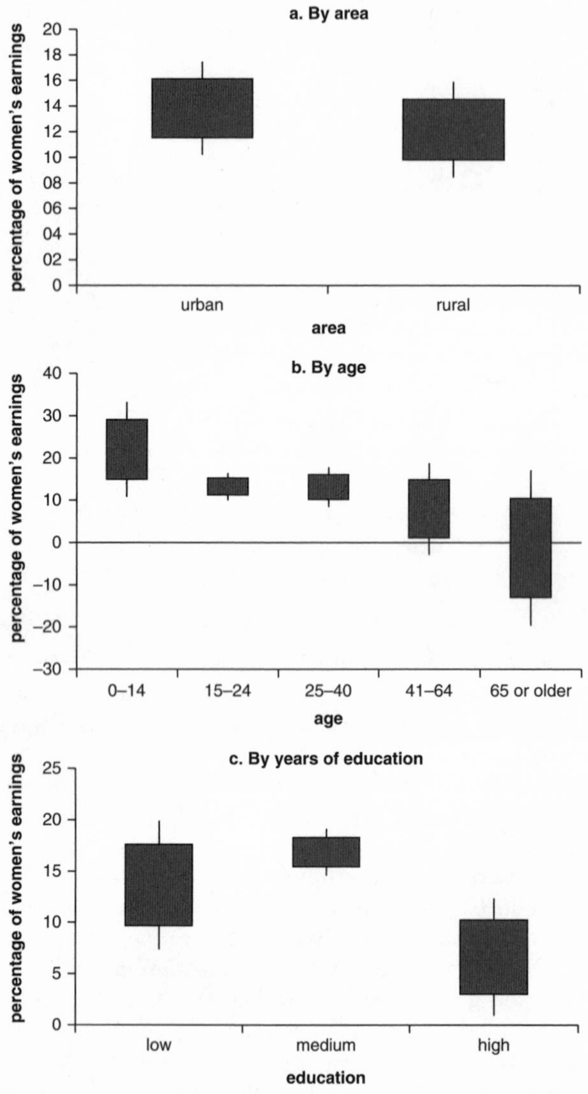

a. By area

b. By age

c. By years of education

(continued next page)

Figure 11.9 (continued)

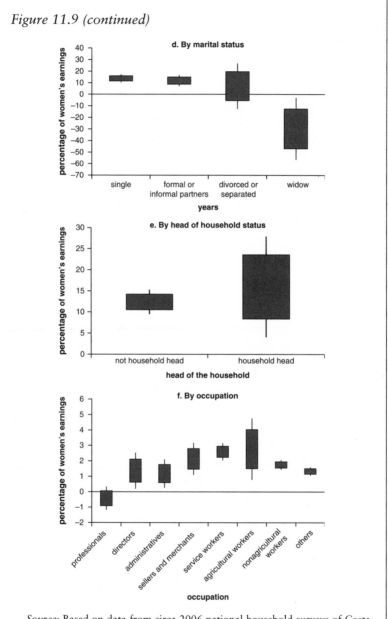

Source: Based on data from circa 2006 national household surveys of Costa Rica, El Salvador, Honduras, and Nicaragua.

Note: Figures show results after controlling for demographic and job-related characteristics. Boxes show 90 percent confidence intervals for unexplained earnings; whiskers show 99 percent confidence intervals.

are separated, migrants, and people living in the capital (Ñopo and Gonzales 2008).

This chapter portrays the evolution of gender earnings gaps in Central American countries during the past decade. Some trends suggest improvements in gender equity in labor markets: participation by women increased (particularly in Costa Rica and Honduras), and women acquired more years of schooling than men during the period under study. However, substantial gender earnings gaps persist. The results show a pattern in which the unexplained part of the gender earnings gaps is larger among poorer people than it is at the top of the income distribution. This pattern can be very harmful in countries with high incidences of poverty.

Notes

1. The population examined is working people between the ages of 15 and 65, except in Guatemala, where the working population is age 18–65.
2. The category of "informal union" was not included in the Salvadoran survey until 2000.
3. Data for 2000 and 2006 come from the National Survey of Living Conditions (Encuesta Nacional de Condiciones de Vida [ENCOVI]); data for 2004 come from the National Survey of Employment and Income (Encuesta Nacional de Empleo e Ingresos [ENEI]).
4. For urban and rural decompositions and for results using the other sets of controls refer to Ñopo and Gonzales (2008).

References

Auguste, S., D. Artana, and M. Cuevas. 2007. "Tearing Down the Walls: Growth and Inclusion in Guatemala." Inter-American Development Bank, Country Department Central America, Mexico, Panama, and Dominican Republic (CID), Washington, DC.

Corley, M., Y. Perardel, and K. Popova. 2005. *Wage Inequality by Gender and Occupation: A Cross-Country Analysis.* Geneva: International Labour Organization.

Dávila, A., and J. Pagán. 1999. "Gender Pay and Occupational-Attainment Gaps in Costa Rica and El Salvador: A Relative Comparison of the Late 1980s." *Review of Development Economics* 3 (2): 215–30.

Deutsch, R., A. Morrison, C. Piras, and H. Ñopo. 2005. "Working within Confines: Occupational Segregation by Sex for Three Latin American Countries." *Icfai University Journal of Applied Economics* 4 (3): 50–59.

Enamorado, T. A., C. Izaguirre, and H. Ñopo. 2009. "Gender Wage Gaps in Central American Countries: Evidence from a Non-Parametric Approach." RES Working Paper 4639, Inter-American Development Bank, Research Department, Washington, DC.

Ñopo, H., and A. Gonzales. 2008. "Gender and Ethnic Wage Gaps in Guatemala from a Matching Comparisons Perspectives." RES Working Paper 4588, Inter-American Development Bank, Research Department, Washington, DC.

———. 2009. "Brechas salariales por género y etnicidad." In *Más crecimiento, más equidad*, ed. Ernesto Stein, Osmel Manzano, Hector Morena, and Fernando Straface, 265–98. Banco Interamericano de Desarrollo.

Panizza, U., and C. Z.-W. Qiang. 2005. "Public-Private Wage Differential and Gender Gap in Latin America: Spoiled Bureaucrats and Exploited Women?" *Journal of Socioeconomics* 34 (6): 810–83.

Pisani, M. J., and J. A. Pagán. 2004. "Sectoral Selection and Informality: A Nicaraguan Case Study." *Review of Development Economics* 8 (4): 541–56.

Psacharopoulos, G., and Z. Tzannatos. 1993. "Economic and Demographic Effects on Working Women in Latin America." *Journal of Population Economics* 6 (4): 293–315.

12

The Understudied Caribbean: Barbados (2004) and Jamaica (2003)

The Caribbean is an understudied region in economic terms. On labor markets issues, the body of empirical research is small. This chapter attempts to fill this void by examining gender earnings gaps in Barbados and Jamaica, two large economies by Caribbean standards, with diverse labor market, social, and economic issues. The chapter focuses on these two countries for a number of reasons. First, both countries have reliable data for representative samples of workers at the national level. Second, the countries have many similarities and differences in terms of social, economic, and labor market issues. Examining gender earnings gaps for the two countries will illuminate peculiarities within the national labor markets, facilitating conjectures on whether the presence of gender earnings gaps is an endemic feature of Caribbean labor markets, as in the rest of Latin America and the world.

What Does the Literature Show?

Only a small number of studies examine gender gaps in the Caribbean.[1] A few studies investigate gender issues in labor markets in Barbados, Jamaica, and Trinidad and Tobago.

This chapter was adapted from "Gender Earnings Gaps in the Caribbean: Evidence from Barbados and Jamaica," Alejandro Hoyos, Annelle Bellony, and Hugo Ñopo, IDB Working Paper IDB-WP-210, Inter-American Development Bank, 2010.

Alejandro Hoyos is a consultant at the Poverty Reduction and Economic Management Network (PREM) at the World Bank. Annelle Bellony is a senior associate in the Education Division at the Inter-American Development Bank.

The evidence from the literature on the gender earnings gap generally indicates that women in Caribbean countries earn less on average than men. Scott (1992) finds that women in Jamaica earn on average 58 percent of men's earnings. Hotchkiss and Moore (1996) report that average earnings for women in Jamaica are 80 percent of men's earnings. The two studies are based on different data sources for the same period (the late 1980s), revealing the heterogeneity of results of studies of this kind. Whereas Scott uses labor force survey data, Hotchkiss and Moore use a special dataset compiled for a one-time tax project. Notwithstanding the discrepancy in the magnitude of the gender earnings gap, both studies find that the bulk of the gender earnings differential is unexplained by differences in individual characteristics.

Using the 1994 Continuous Household Sample Survey (CHSS) for Barbados, Coppin (1996) finds a women's/men's earnings ratio of 0.87.[2] Olsen and Coppin (2001) use the 1993 Continuous Sample Survey of the Population (CSSP) to estimate the gender earnings gap for Trinidad and Tobago. Their findings suggest that differences in human capital and other measured factors valued by the labor market do not do a good job of explaining earnings differentials. Terrell (1992) cites an unpublished study by Brendan (1991) that estimates the women's and men's earnings ratio for Haiti, derived from a 1987 survey of large-scale enterprises in Port-au-Prince, at 0.87. Furthermore, Sookram and Watson (2008) find evidence that workers in the informal sector suffer an earnings penalty, particularly women.

History and Development of Barbados and Jamaica

British colonization, from 1625–1966, dominates the history of Barbados, in the eastern part of the Caribbean archipelago. An estimated 90 percent of its 270,000 people are of African descent.

Like many other Eastern Caribbean countries, Barbados has a history of dependence on one crop as the main export commodity, in its case, sugarcane. The economy has evolved over time to focus primarily on services, particularly tourism and finance.

Jamaica, located in the western Caribbean, gained independence from the United Kingdom in 1962. It was a Spanish colony until 1655, when the British took control. Once the British settled in Jamaica, sugar production became the mainstay of the economy. First, African slaves and, later, Chinese and Indian indentured servants worked the land. Their descendants remain on the island, contributing to the ethnic diversity of the Jamaican people. The population of Jamaica is slightly less than 3 million. Tourism forms the mainstay of the economy, followed by bauxite and manufacturing.

The confluence of diverse ethnic groups resulted in the creation of the Jamaican Creole language, which is widely spoken. Use of Creole has contributed to low educational outcomes, especially among men (Ministry of Education, Youth, and Culture 2001).

In many respects, the historical and economic pasts of Barbados and Jamaica have followed the same trajectory. However, in terms of progress on social indicators, the two countries display some noteworthy differences.

Barbados has consistently ranked in the top 40 countries on the United Nations Human Development Index. In contrast, Jamaica ranked 100th on this index in 2007 (UNDP 2009). Both countries are home to two of the three campuses of the University of the West Indies (UWI), but the effect of the campuses is markedly different. Barbados has capitalized on the presence of the university: the government provides free tuition to qualified candidates as an investment in the future economic and social development of the country. Exposure to tertiary education, although low by international standards, is high for the Caribbean. In Jamaica, tertiary educational outcomes are much weaker, especially among men. The incidence of poverty is also much higher than in Barbados.

Barbados: Men in the Middle, Women at Both Ends

The data used in the analysis for Barbados are derived from the Continuous Labor Force Sample Survey (CLFSS) for 2004. The Barbados Statistical Service conducts the CLFSS quarterly. The data were purged to include only people between the ages of 15 and 64.

Data on labor earnings are coded in intervals. Coding the data in intervals imposes some challenges on the computation of gender earnings gaps, as the computation of average earnings requires assuming particular values for earnings within the given intervals. For simplicity, the lowest extreme of each earnings interval is assumed to be the representative value.

Figure 12.1 shows the distribution of men and women along the earnings intervals. The distribution for women is skewed to the left of the distribution for men. However, at the high end of the earnings distributions, there are almost no gender differences.

Women's labor force participation also varies with earnings. At the lower-middle portion of the earnings distribution, women make up less than 40 percent of the labor force. In contrast, at the two lowest extreme income brackets and the upper-middle part of the distribution, women account for more than 60 percent of the labor force (figure 12.2).

An additional challenge that the dataset imposes is that not only earnings but also hours worked per week are coded in intervals. Fortunately, almost three out of four male workers and four out of five female workers in Barbados work 40–44 hours a week.

There are some gender differences in the percentages of overtime workers: 20 percent of men and 10 percent of women fall within this

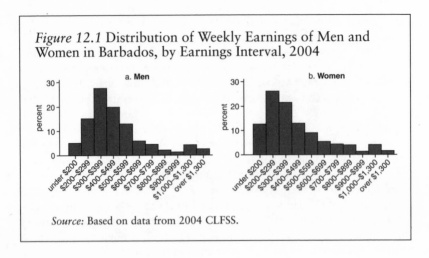

Figure 12.1 Distribution of Weekly Earnings of Men and
Women in Barbados, by Earnings Interval, 2004

Source: Based on data from 2004 CLFSS.

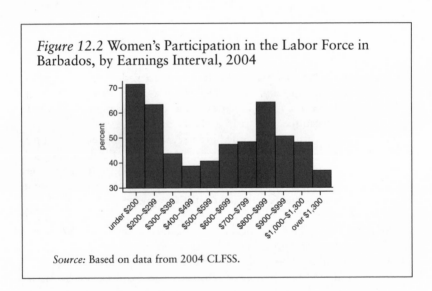

Figure 12.2 Women's Participation in the Labor Force in
Barbados, by Earnings Interval, 2004

Source: Based on data from 2004 CLFSS.

category. This difference complicates the calculation of hourly earnings.
The approach adopted here is to adjust the distributions so that weekly
hours worked are the same for men and women.

Table 12.1 provides the descriptive statistics used in the analysis. It shows
that the average gender earnings gap in Barbados reaches 18.9 percent of
average women's earnings.

Regarding age, the data indicate a slight predominance of men at both
extremes of the age distribution, with a predominance of women among

Table 12.1 Demographic and Job Characteristics and Relative
Earnings of Men and Women in Labor Force in Barbados, 2004

| | Composition (%) | | Earnings index (Base: average women's earnings = 100) | |
	Men	Women	Men	Women
All	100	100	118.9	100.0
Personal characteristics				
Age				
15–24	13.9	10.8	75.4	66.7
25–34	23.7	24.8	107.2	98.0
35–44	27.7	31.0	127.5	107.4
45–54	23.6	24.0	134.9	108.1
55–64	11.1	9.3	142.0	99.4
Education				
None	1.3	0.9	97.6	80.0
Primary	16.1	12.4	89.0	57.7
Secondary	60.0	58.9	107.3	79.0
Tertiary	22.6	27.8	171.2	165.7
Presence of children (12 years or younger) in household				
No	75.5	70.0	115.2	98.4
Yes	24.5	30.0	130.6	103.9
Presence of other household member with labor income				
No	28.7	23.0	118.3	107.7
Yes	71.3	77.0	119.2	97.5
Stratum (based on socioeconomic development)				
1 (urban)	32.8	32.4	111.9	93.5
2 (mixed)	28.3	29.5	124.8	101.2
3 (mixed)	22.2	23.7	125.5	111.3
4 (rural)	16.7	14.5	113.9	93.6
Job characteristics				
Type of employment				
Employer	1.0	0.4	151.9	117.8
Self-employed	17.1	7.9	135.5	104.9

(continued next page)

Table 12.1 (continued)

	Composition (%)		Earnings index (Base: average women's earnings = 100)	
	Men	Women	Men	Women
Public employee	21.9	25.6	138.5	134.4
Private employee	60.0	66.1	107.7	85.9
Occupation				
Legislators and senior officials	6.5	6.8	189.7	169.9
Professionals	8.2	14.3	203.6	185.2
Technicians and associate professionals	10.1	6.4	157.7	122.7
Clerks	4.9	19.8	121.0	111.6
Service, shop, and market sales workers	12.2	26.8	103.0	66.0
Skilled agricultural and fishery workers	4.4	1.0	83.5	52.8
Craft and related trades workers	23.8	3.0	108.2	67.1
Plant and machine operators and assemblers	8.9	2.8	103.2	58.6
Elementary occupations	21.0	19.1	77.1	52.5
Economic sector				
Agriculture and mining	4.9	3.5	98.7	61.2
Manufacturing	6.2	6.4	105.7	69.1
Electricity, gas, and water	2.1	1.9	127.1	88.5
Construction	17.6	1.0	104.3	110.9
Wholesale and retail trade and hotels and restaurants	12.1	17.8	107.1	73.1
Transport, storage, and communication	14.2	14.8	116.3	91.2
Finance, insurance, real estate, and business services	22.8	30.2	126.1	101.4

(continued next page)

Table 12.1 (continued)

	Composition (%)		Earnings index (Base: average women's earnings = 100)	
	Men	Women	Men	Women
Community, social, and personal services	20.0	24.5	139.8	135.4
Experience				
Less than 1 year	8.6	11.1	87.2	69.6
1–5 years	33.7	38.6	104.0	91.8
6–10 years	20.1	20.6	114.8	98.6
11–15 years	11.7	9.8	128.6	106.5
16–20 years	7.8	5.9	132.7	117.2
20 or more years	18.1	14.0	154.8	139.3

Source: Based on data from 2004 CLFSS.

middle-age (25–54) workers. The data also show that earnings evolve with age in a monotonic way for men whereas women's earnings increase monotonically up to age 54, after which they decline slightly.

Women's educational achievement surpasses that of men: 27.8 percent of women and 22.6 percent of men completed university. However, at every level of education, men earn more than women. Average earnings for women with no, primary, or secondary education are statistically similar; earnings for women increase markedly only for women with university education.

The incidence of children and other labor income earners in the household is higher among women than among men. The earnings premium linked to children living in the household is larger for men than for women, however. The earnings premium linked to the presence of other labor income earners at home is nonexistent for men and negative for women—that is, women who are the sole income earners in their households tend to have higher earnings than women who live with another earner.

In the sample design, the 11 parishes in Barbados were grouped into four strata based on socioeconomic development and geographical proximity.[3] For this chapter, the four strata were reclassified as urban, mixed, and rural. Stratum 1 contains the capital city (Bridgetown), which is classified as urban. Strata 2 and 3 contain parishes that are both suburban and rural (defined as areas with low population density); they are classified as mixed. Stratum 4, which includes the parishes farthest from Bridgetown, is classified as rural. Earnings are higher in the two mixed strata than in the other two strata for both men and women. This finding reflects the socioeconomic make-up of these regions.

The majority of workers in Barbados (82 percent of men and 92 percent of women) are employees. As in most labor markets, most employers are men. Self-employment is also a category dominated by men in Barbados, in sharp contrast with the rest of the developing world, where it is dominated by women. The highest-earning men are employers; the highest-earning women work in the public sector.

The highest-paid occupational group consists of professionals (8 percent of men and 14 percent of women). The sectors of finance, insurance, real estate, and business services and community, social, and personal services have large shares of women workers (55 percent), with large gender gaps in the business sectors and almost no gaps among social workers.

The Role of Individual Characteristics in Explaining the Gender Earnings Gap

To what extent do the observed differences in earnings correspond to differences in observable characteristics that labor markets reward? What would the distribution of men's earnings look like if their distribution of observable characteristics were exactly the same as the distribution for women? What would the gender earnings gap be in this case?

Counterfactual situations are created using the matching technique described in chapter 2. Table 12.2 decomposes the earnings gap for various combinations of observable demographic characteristics. The combinations of characteristics are constructed so that each combination builds on the previous one by adding one characteristic.

The comparison of the decomposition exercises is analyzed next. First, the Barbados labor market tends to have a larger proportion of prime-age women than men. In a hypothetical world in which men and women have the same age distribution, the gender earnings gap would reach 20.4 percent of average women's earnings (up from the 18.9 percent observed).

A more pronounced result in the same direction is found when considering education as a second matching characteristic. The counterfactual gender earnings gap that would be observed in a world in which men and women have the same distribution of age and education in the labor market exceeds that observed in the real world by almost 7 percentage points, reaching 25.7 percent of average women's earnings.

Inclusion of the presence of children and other labor income earners in the household does not change the measure of unexplained gender differences in earnings much, but the components attributable to the existence of uncommon supports become pronounced, reaching about

Table 12.2 Decomposition of Earnings Gap in Barbados after Controlling for Demographic Characteristics, 2004
(percent)

	Age	+ Education	+ Presence of children in the household	+ Presence of other household member with labor income	+ Stratum
Δ	18.9	18.9	18.9	18.9	18.9
Δ_0	20.4	25.7	25.9	25.0	20.4
Δ_M	-2.6	-3.6	-10.8	-11.4	-10.4
Δ_F	2.7	2.2	9.8	10.8	11.0
Δ_X	-1.7	-5.4	-5.9	-5.5	-2.1
Percentage of women in common support	96.3	92.6	90.4	86.9	73.7
Percentage of men in common support	97.6	93.0	88.8	83.5	67.7

Source: Based on data from 2004 CLFSS.

Note: Δ_M (Δ_F) is the part of the earnings gap attributed to the existence of men (women) with combinations of characteristics that are not met by any women (men). Δ_X is the part of the earnings gap attributed to differences in the observable characteristics of men and women over the "common support." Δ_0 is the part of the earnings gap that cannot be attributed to differences in characteristics of the individuals. It is typically attributed to a combination of both unobservable characteristics and discrimination. The sum of these components equals the total earnings gap ($\Delta_M + \Delta_F + \Delta_X + \Delta_0 = \Delta$).

10 percent (positive for women and negative for men). Socioeconomic stratum reduces the measure of unexplained earnings gap, maintaining at the same 10 percent level the components attributed to the existence of uncommon supports.

The likelihood of finding matches falls as the number of matching characteristics increases (as shown in the last two rows of table 12.2). Linked to this result is the fact that the measures of the gender earnings gap can be attributed to the existence of men and women with unmatchable characteristics, whose number grows as the number of matching characteristics increases.

In contrast to what is typically observed in this decomposition in other countries in Latin American and the Caribbean, the Δ_M component (the part of the earnings gap attributed to the existence of men with combinations of characteristics that are not found in any women) is negative and the Δ_F component (the part of the earnings gap attributed to the existence of women with combinations of characteristics that are not met by any men) is positive. Men whose characteristics cannot be compared with those of women in the labor market tend to have lower earnings than men whose characteristics are matchable.

This pattern is shown in figure 12.3, which reports the percentages of unmatched women in each earnings bracket. The two extremes of the earnings distribution have the largest percentages of unmatched women. This result may suggest some segmentation in the labor market, in which there are low-earning men at the bottom extreme of the earnings distribution and high-earning women at the other extreme.

Table 12.3 adds job characteristics to the demographic characteristics used in table 12.2. The variables are added separately, in order to facilitate exploration of the effects of each variable and avoid the "curse of dimensionality."[4]

The results show that sector is the job characteristic that best explains the gender earnings gap. Inclusion of this variable as a matching characteristic reduces the unexplained component of the gap from 20.4 percent to 14.1 percent of average women's earnings. Thus, elimination of gender segregation by sector would reduce more than 6 percentage points of the gender earnings gap.

Another variable that helps explain gender earnings gaps in Barbados is experience. Elimination of gender differences in experience would reduce the gender earnings gap by about 2.5 percentage points.

Reduction of occupational segregation by gender would not reduce the gender earnings gap. On the contrary, elimination of gender occupational segregation is linked to an increase of more than 6 percentage points in the gender earnings gap.

Type of employment does not change the decomposition of the earnings gap. However, there are differences in unexplained earnings gaps across types of employment (as shown in the next section).

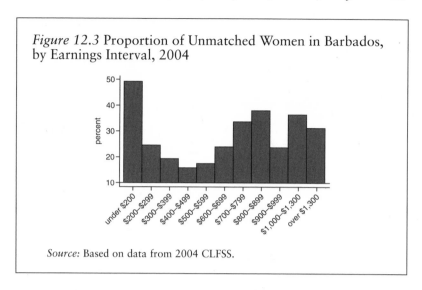

Figure 12.3 Proportion of Unmatched Women in Barbados, by Earnings Interval, 2004

Source: Based on data from 2004 CLFSS.

The last column of table 12.3 includes the full set of matching variables (the five demographic characteristics and the four job characteristics). As shown in the last two rows of that column, only about 3 percent of women and men can be compared when using this set of nine matching characteristics.

Exploring the Unexplained Component of the Gender Earnings Gap

Table 12.4 shows the magnitude of the unexplained earnings gap for different segments of the labor market (and using different sets of matching characteristics). As before, the matching variables are added sequentially but with replacement as one moves to the right of the table.

Regarding age, the evidence seems to be mixed. When using only demographic characteristics, the unexplained gender earnings gap increases with age. When using the full set of matching characteristics, however, the situation is almost reversed.

The results show more consistency regarding education. For all sets of matching characteristics shown in the table, the unexplained gaps are smaller (and in some cases even negative) among university graduates.

With regard to the effect of children in the household, for almost all sets of matching characteristics, the unexplained earnings gaps seem to be larger among workers with no children at home. When considering experience as a matching variable, however, the result is reversed. After accounting for experience (in the last two columns of the table), workers

Table 12.3 Decomposition of Gender Earnings Gap in Barbados after Controlling for Demographic and Job Characteristics, 2004
(percent)

	Demographic set	& Type of employment	& Occupation	& Sector	& Experience	Full set
Δ	18.9	18.9	18.9	18.9	18.9	18.9
Δ_0	20.4	20.4	26.7	14.1	17.8	15.3
Δ_M	-10.4	-2.5	-38.4	-41.1	-27.4	-68.0
Δ_F	11.0	1.8	31.7	45.4	29.1	72.1
Δ_X	-2.1	-0.8	-1.1	0.5	-0.6	-0.5
Percentage of women in common support	73.7	56.8	30.6	35.2	44.6	3.3
Percentage of men in common support	67.7	50.9	24.3	30.5	41.4	2.7

Source: Based on data from 2004 CLFSS.

Note: Δ_M (Δ_F) is the part of the earnings gap attributed to the existence of men (women) with combinations of characteristics that are not met by any women (men). Δ_X is the part of the earnings gap attributed to differences in the observable characteristics of men and women over the "common support." Δ_0 is the part of the earnings gap that cannot be attributed to differences in characteristics of the individuals. It is typically attributed to a combination of both unobservable characteristics and discrimination. The sum of these components equals the total earnings gap ($\Delta_M + \Delta_F + \Delta_X + \Delta_0 = \Delta$).

Table 12.4 Unexplained Gender Earnings Gap in Barbados after Controlling for Demographic and Job Characteristics, 2004
(percent)

	Demographic set	& Type of employment	& Occupation	& Sector	& Experience	Full set
All	20.4	20.4	26.7	14.1	17.8	15.3
Personal characteristics						
Age						
15–24	13.1	14.2	42.1	22.2	12.8	20.4
25–34	8.0	9.7	20.8	6.1	11.8	11.9
35–44	16.3	13.0	19.9	11.0	12.3	25.8
45–54	22.3	23.2	29.1	17.0	32.0	12.1
55–64	38.9	28.1	23.9	32.5	22.9	10.2
Education						
None	40.5	–41.2	55.4	134.1	–41.2	55.4
Primary	47.0	32.8	32.6	39.3	44.5	16.3
Secondary	35.7	31.9	37.7	21.8	34.5	19.4
Tertiary	–0.3	–0.9	9.5	1.0	–1.7	7.5
Presence of children (12 years or younger) in Household						
No	21.8	21.6	27.3	14.4	16.5	15.3
Yes	14.6	13.6	20.6	11.2	19.8	23.9

(continued next page)

Table 12.4 (continued)

	Demographic set	& Type of employment	& Occupation	& Sector	& Experience	Full set
Presence of other household member with labor income						
No	12.0	11.1	19.5	5.9	15.9	26.3
Yes	22.8	22.2	27.6	15.8	17.7	15.2
Stratum (based on socioeconomic development)						
1 (urban)	24.1	17.2	24.3	18.2	21.7	16.2
2 (mixed)	17.1	21.8	21.7	10.8	11.8	13.5
3 (mixed)	9.5	9.2	23.1	7.3	14.3	–3.2
4 (rural)	26.0	28.2	38.9	11.1	25.9	21.2
Job characteristics						
Type of Employment						
Employer		0.0				0.0
Self-employed		23.0				17.3
Public employee		5.9				1.6
Private employee		16.1				24.4
Occupation						
Legislators and senior officials			2.9			0.1
Professionals			5.9			2.7

	Demographic set	& Type of employment	& Occupation	& Sector	& Experience	Full set
Technicians and associate professionals			16.6			4.8
Clerks			13.1			15.5
Service, shop, and market sales workers			43.0			27.5
Skilled agricultural and fishery workers			8.4			8.4
Craft and related trades workers			52.1			23.1
Plant and machine operators and assemblers			76.9			197.7
Elementary occupations			39.0			24.8
Economic sector						
Agriculture and mining				26.4		56.8
Manufacturing				37.7		41.3
Electricity, gas, and water				26.5		26.5
Construction				−14.6		−54.9
Wholesale and retail trade and hotels and restaurants				19.0		22.9

(continued next page)

Table 12.4 (continued)

	Demographic set	& Type of employment	& Occupation	& Sector	& Experience	Full set
Transport, storage, and communication				20.5		20.9
Finance, insurance, real estate, and business services				11.8		21.3
Community, social, and personal services				5.2		1.5
Experience						
Less than 1 year					12.2	24.0
1–5 years					15.1	16.5
6–10 years					15.7	11.2
11–15 years					16.5	28.5
16–20 years					11.9	36.5
20 or more years					19.5	2.3

Source: Based on data from the 2004 CLFSS.
Note: Blank cells appear when the related variable(s) is(are) not used as controls.

living with children at home show larger unexplained earnings gaps than other workers.

The data also suggest that when no other labor income earner lives at home, earnings differences between men and women are smaller. This finding holds true for all sets of matching characteristics except the one that uses the full set of nine variables. The third stratum shows the smallest unexplained gender earnings gaps.

Although type of employment does not explain much of the gender earnings gap in Barbados in the aggregate (see table 12.3), some differences in earnings gaps within types deserve highlighting. Unexplained earnings gaps are larger among the self-employed and private sector employees. They are larger among clerks, craft workers and workers in related trades, plant and machine operators and assemblers, and workers in elementary occupations. Among high-skilled occupations (professionals and senior officials), unexplained earnings gaps are smaller and in some cases close to zero. This finding is consistent with the finding that unexplained gaps are smallest among university graduates.

The economic sectors with the largest unexplained gender earnings gaps are manufacturing, agriculture, and mining. The gender earnings gap among community, social, and personal service workers is almost zero. The construction sector, which is dominated by men in most economies, deserves special mention. In Barbados, 18 percent of men and just 1 percent of women work in construction. The few women who participate in construction, however, have higher earnings than their male peers. One possible explanation for this phenomenon is that the few women who dare work in segments of the labor market dominated by men represent a selected subsample with unobservable traits (such as work ethic, commitment, and motivation) that are rewarded in the market. As a result, these women work as managers.

The differences in unexplained earnings gaps across the experience ladder are mixed. Controlling for the set of demographic characteristics plus experience yields larger unexplained earnings gaps among the most experienced workers. However, when using the full set of control variables, the unexplained gaps among the most experienced workers are the smallest. The interplay of experience with the other demographic and job characteristics should be taken into account when trying to use this variable as an explanatory source for gender earnings gaps.

Jamaica: Women in the Middle, Men at Both Ends

The data employed in the estimation for Jamaica are from the 2003 Labor Force Survey undertaken by the Statistical Institute. These quarterly surveys sample about 1 percent of the population. The sample enumerates households spread across Jamaica's 14 parishes, drawing a representative mix of urban and rural dwellers. The original sample for 2003 contained 22,692 observations; following data cleaning and deletion of observations with missing values, 4,974 observations remained in the final sample; earnings are measured as hourly earnings.

Table 12.5 shows descriptive statistics for Jamaica. Having normalized average women's earnings to 100, average men's earnings can be directly read as the measure of gender earnings gaps. Men's earnings below 100 indicate a negative earnings gap.

On average, women earn more than men in Jamaica. However, the earnings difference is very small (0.8 percent of average women's earnings), and a significance test would fail to reject the null hypothesis of gender equality in earnings. Regarding age, the recurrent pattern for most countries in the region of higher prevalence of men at both extremes of the age distribution is evident in Jamaica. The pattern of earnings progression along the life cycle is also similar to the pattern observed in other countries. In terms of education, 12.3 percent of working women and just 4.5 percent of working men completed university. Earnings for each level of schooling below university show little variation. It is only university graduates, especially men, whose earnings are significantly higher.

The presence of children is much more prevalent among working women than among working men. Whereas for working men there are no earnings differences between men who live with children at home and men who do not, for working women the presence of children is linked to lower earnings. Working women are also more likely than working men to live in urban areas.

Unlike elsewhere in Latin American and the Caribbean, self-employment in Jamaica has higher participation of men than women, and dependent relationships, in both the private and public sectors, are more prevalent among women. As in most countries, the data show no gender earnings differences in earnings in public sector employment; surprisingly, no gender earnings differences are evident in self-employment either. The segments of the labor markets showing earnings disparities in favor of men are private employment and, to a greater extent, employers.

Occupational segregation is also prevalent in Jamaica. Women tend to be overrepresented among professionals, elementary occupations, services, and store and market sales workers. Men tend to be overrepresented among skilled agricultural and fishery workers, craft workers and workers in related trades, and plant and machine operators and assemblers. Women tend to work in wholesale and retail trade; hotels and restaurants; and community, social, and personal services. Men are engaged in agriculture, mining, and construction. The highest-paying occupations for both men and women are in the professional sector. The highest-paying activities for men are electricity, gas, and water; for women, the highest-paying activities are finance, insurance, real estate, and business services.

There are some gender differences in job tenure. Two-thirds of men have been at their job for five years or more; the corresponding figure for

Table 12.5 Demographic and Job Characteristics and Relative
Hourly Earnings of Men and Women in Jamaica's Labor Force, 2003

	Composition (%)		Earnings Index (Base: average women's earnings = 100)	
	Men	Women	Men	Women
All	100	100	99.2	100.0
Personal characteristics				
Age				
15–24	16.9	13.2	84.8	99.3
25–34	28.9	30.4	98.5	107.1
35–44	26.8	30.7	109.7	94.6
45–54	17.7	17.3	102.2	104.6
55–64	9.7	8.4	91.9	85.6
Education				
None	0.2	0.2	64.9	62.0
Primary	26.3	19.7	79.8	73.0
Secondary	69.0	67.8	97.5	87.1
Tertiary	4.5	12.3	240.0	214.8
Presence of children (12 years or younger) in household				
No	70.2	61.6	98.6	106.2
Yes	29.8	38.4	100.6	90.0
Presence of other household member with labor income				
No	49.8	42.0	98.8	107.5
Yes	50.2	58.0	99.6	94.6
Urban				
No	64.1	53.6	84.6	81.1
Yes	35.9	46.4	125.2	121.8
Job characteristics				
Type of employment				
Employer	2.4	1.6	171.8	140.7
Self-employed	42.5	28.7	71.3	70.1
Public employee	9.2	17.1	160.7	156.6
Private employee	45.9	52.5	108.8	96.6

(continued next page)

Table 12.5 (continued)

	Composition (%)		Earnings index (Base: average women's earnings = 100)	
	Men	Women	Men	Women
Occupation				
Armed forces	0.3	0.0	161.3	—
Legislators and senior officials	2.6	7.6	166.5	121.1
Professionals	3.9	10.3	212.6	208.5
Technicians and associate professionals	3.6	5.8	175.8	124.3
Clerks	2.5	12.1	133.5	122.2
Service, shop, and market sales workers	11.1	24.4	108.9	86.3
Skilled agricultural and fishery workers	30.8	8.1	58.1	47.2
Craft and related trades workers	22.2	4.0	116.8	70.5
Plant and machine operators and assemblers	8.5	1.7	113.7	78.6
Elementary occupations	14.4	26.0	74.5	70.2
Economic sector				
Agriculture and mining	34.2	9.7	63.4	50.9
Manufacturing	7.0	4.9	109.2	90.7
Electricity, gas, and water	0.4	0.3	165.6	113.9
Construction	15.8	0.7	116.9	92.7
Wholesale and retail trade and hotels and restaurants	13.8	32.3	94.3	81.9
Transport, storage, and communication	8.0	2.7	119.9	157.1
Finance, insurance, real estate, and business services	4.4	5.7	133.1	177.2
Community, social, and personal services	16.3	43.8	136.1	111.8
Experience				
Less than 3 months	1.9	2.3	84.3	80.2

(continued next page)

Table 12.5 (continued)

	Composition (%)		Earnings index (Base: average women's earnings = 100)	
	Men	Women	Men	Women
3–6 months	2.0	4.4	114.3	76.1
6–9 months	2.3	3.0	82.2	83.0
9–12 months	2.5	3.2	83.0	68.1
1–2 years	6.0	7.7	99.7	91.6
2–5 years	18.5	22.4	97.7	98.1
5 years or more	66.9	57.0	100.7	107.2
Small firm (five workers or less)				
No	41.8	43.4	129.4	134.7
Yes	58.2	56.6	77.5	73.3
Time worked				
Part time	6.0	12.6	99.0	85.7
Full time	72.7	74.6	102.5	105.1
Overtime	21.3	12.8	87.9	84.1

Source: Based on data from the 2003 Labor Force Survey.

women is 57 percent. Gender differences in regular time worked per week are also substantial. Women dominate part-time work, and men dominate overtime work.

The Role of Individual Characteristics in Explaining the Gender Earnings Gap

Tables 12.6 and 12.7 show the earnings gap decompositions exercise. Each column shows one decomposition, based on a set of matching variables. The first table uses only demographic characteristics, adding them sequentially without replacement as one moves to the right. The second table adds job characteristics to the set of demographic ones; in order to avoid the curse of dimensionality, it does so with replacement. The last column of table 12.7 uses the full set of demographic and job characteristics.

The first thing to note is that the –0.8 percent earnings gap in Jamaica for the overall economy masks the fact that women have more schooling than men and are not compensated for it appropriately. When comparing

Table 12.6 Decomposition of Gender Earnings Gap in Jamaica after Controlling for Demographic Characteristics, 2003
(percent)

	Age	+ Education	+ Presence of children in the household	+ Presence of other household member with labor income	+ Stratum
Δ	-0.8	-0.8	-0.8	-0.8	-0.8
Δ_0	0.2	12.2	11.0	9.7	12.0
Δ_M	0.0	-0.1	0.1	0.1	2.2
Δ_F	0.0	-1.8	-2.8	-4.4	-7.8
Δ_X	-1.0	-11.1	-9.1	-6.2	-7.2
Percentage of women in common support	100.0	99.5	98.0	94.8	88.7
Percentage of men in common support	99.9	98.3	96.9	94.3	88.7

Source: Based on data from the 2003 Labor Force Survey.

Note: Δ_M (Δ_F) is the part of the earnings gap attributed to the existence of men (women) with combinations of characteristics that are not met by any women (men). Δ_X is the part of the earnings gap attributed to differences in the observable characteristics of men and women over the "common support." Δ_0 is the part of the earnings gap that cannot be attributed to differences in characteristics of the individuals. It is typically attributed to a combination of both unobservable characteristics and discrimination. The sum of these components equals the total earnings gap ($\Delta_M + \Delta_F + \Delta_X + \Delta_0 = \Delta$).

Table 12.7 Decomposition of Gender Earnings Gap in Jamaica after Controlling for Demographic and Job Characteristics, 2003
(percent)

	Demographic set	& Type of employment	& Occupation	& Sector	& Experience	& Firm size	& Time worked	Full set
Δ	-0.8	-0.8	-0.8	-0.8	-0.8	-0.8	-0.8	-0.8
Δ_0	12.0	15.3	16.5	14.6	11.2	7.9	12.4	16.8
Δ_M	2.2	5.7	6.6	5.9	1.1	3.9	0.9	18.8
Δ_F	-7.8	-15.3	-15.5	-14.0	-6.1	-8.6	-6.4	-24.8
Δ_X	-7.2	-6.5	-8.4	-7.3	-7.1	-4.0	-7.7	-11.6
Percentage of women in common support	88.7	69.4	37.4	41.3	70.7	79.7	72.4	5.8
Percentage of men in common support	88.7	72.6	46.3	52.0	64.9	82.5	74.0	5.5

Source: Based on data from 2003 Labor Force Survey.

Note: Δ_M (Δ_F) is the part of the earnings gap attributed to the existence of men (women) with combinations of characteristics that are not met by any women (men). Δ_X is the part of the earnings gap attributed to differences in theobservable characteristics of men and women over the "common support." Δ_0 is the part of the earnings gap that cannot be attributed to differences in characteristics of the individuals. It is typically attributed to a combination of both unobservable characteristics and discrimination. The sum of these components equals the total earnings gap ($\Delta_M + \Delta_F + \Delta_X + \Delta_0 = \Delta$).

men and women with the same age and education, the unexplained differences in earnings reach 12.2 percent of average women's earnings in favor of men. To a lesser extent, the inclusion of the presence of another labor income earner in the household as a matching variable reduces the explained gender differences in earnings. The addition of other demographic controls does not alter much the unexplained gaps. The measure of the common supports is nearly 90 percent of men and women.

The addition of job characteristics changes the panorama a bit. Two job characteristics that do not greatly change the measure of unexplained earnings gap are tenure and time worked. One variable, firm size, markedly reduces this measure. A hypothetical world in which all gender differences in firm size of workers were eliminated would reduce the unexplained differences in earnings by 4 percentage points. For type of employment, occupation, and economic sector, reduction of gender differences would increase unexplained gender earnings gaps.

Elimination of gender occupational segregation in Jamaica would increase the gender earnings gap by 4.5 percentage points. Jamaica is thus another country in the region in which a reduction of gender occupational segregation seems to be the wrong target for reducing gender earnings gaps. The matching exercise including occupation as a matching variable leads to the smallest measures of the common supports among all job characteristics—that is, gender occupational segregation is a prevalent feature in Jamaican labor markets. However, reducing this segregation may have detrimental effects on gender earnings disparities.

The decomposition exercises for all countries (in this and previous chapters) except Barbados exhibit components caused by the lack of common support that are positive for men and negative for women. Jamaica reveals the same behavior as the rest of the region, with unmatched men and women earnings more than the national average.

The matching decomposition exercise after the inclusion of all demographic and job characteristics is shown in the last column of table 12.7. The results are qualitatively similar to but stronger than the results shown after the inclusion of job variables. The measures of the common supports become smaller: only about 5 percent of men and women are fully comparable under these sets of demographic and job characteristics.

Exploring the Unexplained Component of the Gender Earnings Gap

The exploration of unexplained differences in earnings along the distribution of income reveals a pattern similar to that found in other Latin American and Caribbean countries. The unexplained gap is larger among lower-income workers, suggesting that the problem of earnings gaps is linked to the problem of low income generation and hence poverty. For some intermediary percentiles (10th–20th), the earnings gap attains a minimum and increases thereafter. The original gap is larger than the gap obtained after controlling for observable characteristics from the first to the seventh percentiles. After these percentiles, the situation is as similar to that in other Latin American and Caribbean countries: the controlled earnings gaps is larger than the original one, as women have completed more schooling (figure 12.4).

To conclude the analysis for Jamaica, a description of unexplained gender differences in earnings for different segments of the labor markets is presented (for a complete set of graphs reporting these results, see Bellony, Hoyos, and Ñopo 2010). Some patterns found in Jamaica are similar to those found in other countries. Unexplained gender differences in earnings increase with age (although most of the differences are not statistically significant) and show an inverted *U*-shape with respect to education (where the largest unexplained gaps are found among high school graduates). Workers with young children at home experience larger unexplained gender differences in earnings. The presence of other income earners at home is also linked with larger gender disparities, but the result is not statistically significant.

In some other aspects, Jamaica shows peculiarities with respect to the distribution of unexplained earnings gender differences along segments

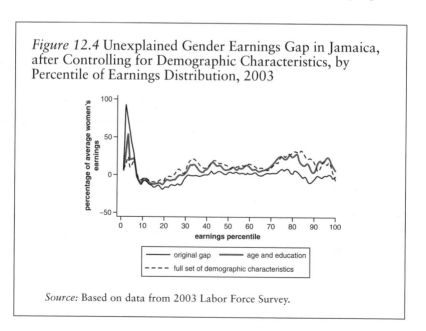

Figure 12.4 Unexplained Gender Earnings Gap in Jamaica, after Controlling for Demographic Characteristics, by Percentile of Earnings Distribution, 2003

Source: Based on data from 2003 Labor Force Survey.

of the labor market. Earnings gaps are similar in urban and rural areas and across types of employment, occupations, economic sectors, firm size, and time worked. Regarding type of employment, however, there is huge heterogeneity within the "employer" category. The only segment of the market for which there seems to be statistically significant differences in earnings is private sector employment. Four occupational categories show statistically positive unexplained gender differences in earnings, and five others are not distinguishable from zero. Among legislators, technicians, and machine operators, gender disparities in earnings are very heterogeneous. Something similar happens across economic sectors, where the only categories with statistically significant earning gaps are agriculture and social services and, to a lesser extent, trade, hotels, and restaurants.

The dispersion of unexplained gender differences in earnings is greater among part-time and overtime workers than among people who work full time. On average, differences in earnings are smaller for part-time and overtime workers than for full-time workers; when dispersion is considered, however, the differences are not statistically significant. Unexplained gender gaps are larger in small firms than in larger firms, as in most countries in the region, but these differences are not statistically significant in Jamaica.

The last point to highlight is job tenure, which seems to have no link to gender differences in earnings. The data show, however, some gender gaps among people with 3–6 months and 9–12 months of job tenure. For workers at the top of the distribution of job tenure (five years or more), the unexplained gender earnings gap is positive and statistically significant. Women are less able to accumulate enough occupational experience, and when they do accumulate that experience, they earn substantially less than their male counterparts.

Summary

This chapter explores gender earnings gaps in two Caribbean economies, Barbados and Jamaica, emphasizing the similarities and differences between the two countries as well as between them and the rest of Latin American and the Caribbean. In both countries, as in most of the region, women's educational achievement is greater than that of men. Jamaica shows lower educational achievement and larger gender disparities than Barbados. Nonetheless, men's earnings surpass those of their female peers. Comparison of earnings for men and women with the same age and education reveals that men earn 25 percent more than women in Barbados and 12 percent more in Jamaica. The unexplained gender earnings gaps after adding extra control variables are larger in Barbados than in Jamaica.

Both countries confirm a finding that is recurrent in the analysis of gender earnings gaps conducted with this matching approach and that challenges some popular beliefs about gender occupational segregation—namely, the notion that elimination of gender occupational segregation would increase rather than reduce gender earnings gaps. Occupational segregation seems to be one of the wrong culprits the literature has emphasized.

Both Barbados and Jamaica show the smallest unexplained earnings gaps among the high skilled and the largest gaps among the low skilled. Regarding segregation by economic sectors, the evidence for Barbados and Jamaica is also in line with what has been found in other countries in the region, and it is mixed. The results indicate that elimination of gender sector segregation would reduce the observed gender earnings gap in Barbados but increase it in Jamaica.

Occupational experience in Barbados and job tenure in Jamaica help explain gender earnings gaps. Elimination of gender disparities in these variables is linked to a reduction of 1–2 percentage points in unexplained earnings gaps.

The data coding of earnings in intervals poses some challenges to the analysis of Barbados. Thanks to the nonparametric nature of the matching approach used, however, most of the analysis can be performed as it is when earnings are coded as a continuous variable. One of the few results that cannot be replicated is the exploration of unexplained earnings gaps along percentiles of the earnings distribution. This result is available only for Jamaica, where gender earnings gaps are larger among low-income workers, as in most of Latin America and the Caribbean. This finding suggests linkages between gender earnings disparities and low income generation (or poverty). Reducing these inequities would also help reduce poverty.

Another issue that calls for further exploration is ethnicity. Some countries in the region have large indigenous and Afro-descendant populations that are worse off in many measures of well-being. Chapter 13 presents an overview of the issue, based on data on Bolivia, Brazil, Chile, Ecuador, Guatemala, Paraguay, and Peru. Chapters 14–16 explore ethnic earnings disparities in Brazil, Ecuador, and Guatemala.

It is suggestive of a problem that among 18 countries with data on gender earnings differences, only 7 have data on ethnic earnings differences. The paucity of data may reflect the invisibility of these populations or the lack of interest in their situation on the part of policy makers. However, the analysis is relevant, as ethnic "minorities" make up an important fraction of the Latin American population and participation of ethnic minorities in the labor market is considerable in most of them. Ethnic minorities in both Bolivia and Brazil make up about half the labor force; they represent more than 30 percent of the working population in Guatemala, Paraguay, and Peru. Ten percent of Ecuador's work force and 5 percent of Chile's are ethnic minorities.

Notes

1. Of the 21 studies in the edited volume of Psacharopoulos and Tzannatos (1992), just one examines a Caribbean country (Jamaica).
2. The CHSS was later changed to the Continuous Labor Force Sample Survey (CLFSS)
3. Stratum 1: St. Michael; Stratum 2: Christ Church, St. Phillip; Stratum 3: St. George, St. James, St. Thomas; Stratum 4: St. John, St. Joseph, St. Andrews, St. Peter, St. Lucy.
4. The curse of dimensionality refers to the fact that the likelihood of finding female-male matches decreases as the number of control variables (the "dimension") increases. This is a problem because researchers would like to use the maximum number of observable characteristics in order to control the scope of the role of unobservable factors in explaining the earnings gap.

References

Bellony, A., A. Hoyos, and H. Ñopo. 2010. "Gender Earnings Gaps in the Caribbean: Evidence from Barbados and Jamaica." RES Working Paper 4683, Inter-American Development Bank, Research Department, Washington, DC.

Brendan, D. 1991. "Male and Female Wage Differentials in Haiti." Graduate School of Public and International Affairs, University of Pittsburgh, Pittsburgh.

Coppin A. 1996. "An Analysis of Earnings in Barbados by Age and Sex." *Economic Review* (Central Bank of Barbados) 23 (3): 14–21.

Hotchkiss, J., and R. Moore. 1996. "Gender Compensation Differentials in Jamaica." *Economic Development and Cultural Change* 44 (3): 657–76.

Hoyos, A., A. Bellony, and H. Ñopo. 2010. "Gender Earnings Gaps in the Caribbean: Evidence from Barbados and Jamaica." IDB Working Paper IDB-WP-210, Inter-American Development Bank, Washington, DC.

Ministry of Education, Youth, and Culture. 2001. "Language Education Policy." Ministry of Education, Youth, and Culture of Jamaica, Kingston. http://www .moec.gov.jm/policies/languagepolicy.pdf.

Olsen, R. N., and A. Coppin. 2001. "The Determinants of Gender Differentials in Income in Trinidad and Tobago." *Journal of Development Studies* 37 (5): 31–56.

Psacharopoulos, G., and Z. Tzannatos, eds. 1992. Vol. 2 of *Women's Employment and Pay in Latin America*. Washington, DC: World Bank.

Scott, K. 1992. "Female Labor Force Participation and Earnings: The Case of Jamaica." In *Case Studies on Women's Employment and Pay in Latin America*, ed. G. Psacharopoulos and Z. Tzannatos, 323–38. Washington, DC: World Bank.

Sookram, S., and P. Watson. 2008. "The Informal Sector and Gender in the Caribbean: The Case of Trinidad, and Tobago." *Journal of Eastern Caribbean Studies* 33 (4): 42–66.

Terrell, K. 1992. "Female-Male Earnings Differentials and Occupational Structure." *International Labor Review* 131 (4/5): 387–98.

UNDP (United Nations Development Programme). 2009. *Human Development Report 2009*. New York: UNDP.

Part III

Ethnic Earnings Gaps

13

Overlapping Disadvantages: Ethnicity and Earnings Gaps in Latin America

Gender earnings gaps have been the subject of much analytical work; the study of ethnic earnings gaps has been somewhat constrained, partly because of limited data, especially in household surveys and national censuses. Only nine countries in Latin America include an "ethnic" question in their national censuses and seven include it in their national household surveys. These questions usually refer to mother tongue or self-identification with an ethnic group (table 2.2 in chapter 2 describes the survey questions used in each country to identify individuals from ethnic minorities). Another important constraint is the number of people belonging to ethnic "minorities" (often majorities) who are not officially registered or lack an identity document. Invisibility in national statistics and systems for delivering public services is a sign of the inferior situation in which ethnic minorities often live. Despite these constraints, studies of ethnic earnings gaps have been made.

Because of the importance of the interplay between ethnic and gender earnings gaps, the analysis in this chapter and the following ones frequently refer to comparisons with information presented in chapters 4–12, on gender differentials. The studies on ethnic earnings gaps try to

This chapter was adapted from the following sources: "New Century, Old Disparities: Gender and Ethnic Wage Gaps in Latin America," Juan Pablo Atal, Hugo Ñopo, and Natalia Winder, RES Working Paper 4640, Inter-American Development Bank, 2009; Evolution of Gender Wage Gaps in Latin America at the Turn of the Twentieth Century: An Addendum to 'New Century, Old Disparities,'" Hugo Ñopo and Alejandro Hoyos, IZA Discussion Papers 5086, Institute for the Study of Labor, 2010.

Juan Pablo Atal is a graduate student in economics at the University of California, Berkeley, and Natalia Winder is a consultant at UNICEF, Division of Policy and Practice, New York. Alejandro Hoyos is a consultant at the Poverty Reduction and Economic Management Network (PREM) at the World Bank.

use the same formats, measures, and methodologies used to analyze gender differentials. However, data on ethnic gaps are available for only 7 of the 18 countries examined elsewhere in this book: Bolivia, Brazil, Chile, Ecuador, Guatemala, Paraguay, and Peru; as usual, earnings are computed as hourly earnings in the main job.

What Does the Literature Show?

Some 28–34 million indigenous people live in Latin America, representing roughly 10 percent of the population (Hall and Patrinos 2006). In all countries, these groups are disproportionately represented among the poor and extreme poor, a situation that has not changed significantly over time. Moreover, since the 1990s, despite decreasing poverty rates in most countries in the region, poverty among indigenous groups either increased or declined at a significantly slower pace than in the rest of the population (Psacharopoulos and Patrinos 1994; Jiménez, Casazola, and Yáñez Aguilar 2006).

On average, 63–69 percent of the indigenous population in the region is economically active. Indigenous people are overrepresented among the self-employed and in the agricultural sector. Despite higher levels of labor force participation over time, in most countries their earnings are significantly lower than those of their nonindigenous peers. This gap narrowed in the past decade, but it remains high in some countries, including Bolivia, Brazil, Chile, and Guatemala (ILO 2007).

Attempts to explain ethnic earnings gaps have analyzed differences in human capital, especially education but also age, migrant status, and the interplay of ethnicity and gender. Despite improvements in educational attainment, indigenous groups earn significantly less than their nonindigenous counterparts (Psacharopoulos 1992). Although low education indicators may explain much of the persistent ethnic earnings differential in some countries, productive characteristics explain only half the earnings gap in other countries (Patrinos 2000). Rangel (1998) explores indicators such as quality of education, measured in terms of certification of teachers, teacher/pupil ratio, and materials, as potential drivers of ethnic earnings differentials in the region. Hall and Patrinos (2006) consider differences in returns by levels of education. None of these studies fully explain pay differentials.

Rangel (1998) shows that indigenous groups tend to be concentrated in low-paid sectors and low-skilled and low-paid jobs. One possible explanation for this concentration could be the impact of social networks, which may have a significant influence on the economic sector, type, and even quality of jobs obtained by indigenous workers, especially migrants. This factor is subject to significant heterogeneity across countries and across ethnic groups within countries (Hall and Patrinos 2006; Fazio 2007).

The literature also examines the impact of proficiency in the dominant language (Chiswick, Patrinos, and Hurst 2000) and regional differences (Contreras and Galván 2003). Important issues, such as the significant share of rural income represented by unsalaried labor and the socioeconomic dynamics of indigenous people in urban zones remain unexplored.

Analysis of many topics has been constrained to country case studies, limiting the conclusions to a specific labor market and earnings structure. Most authors agree, however, that human capital endowments are a critical contributor to earnings differences. Significant narrowing of earnings gaps could be achieved if interventions focus on improving human capital accumulation by indigenous peoples while exploring complementary policies to increase their return on investments in human capital (Hall and Patrinos 2006).

The interplay of ethnicity and gender is of crucial importance: one of the most recurrent stylized facts is that indigenous women appear to fare worst in labor markets. Statistics in this area are unreliable, however, and large discrepancies exist across sources. Indigenous women represent 20–35 percent of the population in Bolivia and Guatemala and 0.2–5.0 percent in Brazil, Ecuador, and Panama. They represent about 25–50 percent of the economically active population in some countries, not including people involved in unpaid work (Calla 2007). Despite increases in female labor force participation and earnings, indigenous women persistently remain at the bottom of the earnings distribution, showing the highest levels of poverty and exclusion (Piras 2004). In Bolivia, for example, being indigenous and female is the most unfavorable condition when entering the labor market and securing earnings (Contreras and Galván 2003).

Latin America also has a large population of African descent: 150 million people. Most of these people live in Brazil (50 percent of the regional total), Colombia (20 percent), and República Bolivariana de Venezuela (10 percent) (Hopenhayn and Bello 2001). Brazil's Afro-descendent population is the largest in the region. It suffers more from unemployment, low earnings, and glass ceilings than the rest of the population.

Occupational differences by race are evident. In 1988 in Rio de Janeiro, 81 percent of Afro-descendent men (and about 60 percent of whites) worked in manual occupations. Among women who worked, the share of domestic workers was 40 percent among Afro-descendents and 15 percent among whites (Rangel 1998, using data from the 1988 Pesquisa Nacional por Amostra de domicílios [PNAD]). Gender earnings gaps are also important among the Afro-descendent population (Hopenhayn and Bello 2001). Despite their achievements in education and occupational attainment, Afro-Brazilian women continue to earn significantly less than men (Lovell 2000).

How Do Ethnic Minorities and Nonminorities in the Work Force Differ?

Wide earnings disparities are evident between minorities and nonminorities in the seven countries for which data were available (table 13.1).

Minorities have significantly lower educational attainment than nonminorities. As in the gender case, disparities are evident in type of employment and occupation. However, ethnic differences in economic sectors are substantially smaller than along the gender divide. Also in contrast to the gender case, there are important ethnic differences in firm size: less than half of nonminorities and almost three-quarters of minorities are employed in firms with five or fewer workers.

The Role of Individual Characteristics in Explaining the Ethnic Earnings Gap

How much of the earnings gap is explained by the striking differences in observable characteristics of minorities and nonminorities just shown? To answer this question, the analysis decomposes ethnic earnings gaps following the strategy developed for gender[1].

In order to make the ethnic earnings gap decompositions comparable to those reported along the gender dimension, it is necessary to decompose the gender earnings gap using only the seven countries used in the ethnic analysis (Atal, Ñopo, and Winder 2009). This subsample of countries displays wider gender earnings gaps than the region as a whole (15.7 percent compared with the 10.0 percent reported in table 4.3 in chapter 4). The wider gaps reflect the fact that gender earnings gaps are large in Brazil, Paraguay, and Peru.

Controlling for ethnicity alone provides little explanation for gender gaps. The results in table 13.2 are qualitatively similar to those reported in table 4.3, with a jump in the unexplained component of the gap after adding education as a matching variable. The set of matching variables and the sequence in which these variables are added follows the same pattern as in the gender decompositions.

The total ethnic earnings gap (37.8 percent) is considerably larger than the gender earnings gap (15.7 percent for this set of countries). The unexplained components of the earnings gap after controlling for gender and age are also larger. However, unlike in the gender analysis, once education is added to the matching variables, the unexplained component of the ethnic gap decreases significantly. The fact that ethnic minorities have considerably lower educational attainment than nonminorities explains the large drop in the unexplained component (from 40 percent of average minorities' earnings to 28 percent) after education is added. A considerable

Table 13.1 Demographic and Job Characteristics and Relative Earnings of Nonminority and Minority Workers in Latin America, Circa 2005

	Composition (percentage)		Earnings index (Base: average minority earnings = 100)	
	Nonminorities	Minorities	Nonminorities	Minorities
All	37.0	36.4	137.8	100.0
Personal characteristics				
Age				
18 to 24			98.4	77.9
25 to 34			133.6	98.2
35 to 44			149.5	109.5
45 to 54			159.8	113.5
55 to 65			151.2	100.1
Education				
None or primary incomplete	14.9	24.8	108.7	74.7
Primary complete or secondary incomplete	38.7	43.0	113.4	90.8
Secondary complete or tertiary incomplete	38.4	27.6	155.7	127.1
Tertiary complete	8.0	4.6	223.7	160.2

(continued next page)

Table 13.1 (continued)

	Composition (percentage)		Earnings index (Base: average minority earnings = 100)	
	Nonminorities	*Minorities*	*Nonminorities*	*Minorities*
Presence of children (12 years or younger) in the household				
No	50.7	45.5	144.7	104.4
Yes	49.3	54.5	130.7	96.3
Presence of other household member with labor income				
No	29.2	34.0	140.5	96.3
Yes	70.8	66.0	136.7	102.0
Urban				
No	15.0	20.2	92.5	68.0
Yes	85.1	79.8	145.7	108.1
Job characteristics				
Type of employment				
Employer	4.5	2.5	264.3	215.4
Self-employed	24.1	28.2	135.0	95.1
Employee	71.5	69.3	130.8	97.8

Table 13.1 (continued)

	Composition (percentage)		Earnings index (Base: average minority earnings = 100)	
	Nonminorities	Minorities	Nonminorities	Minorities
Part time				
No	86.8	85.2	133.0	94.3
Yes	13.2	14.8	169.2	132.7
Formality				
No	47.8	56.6	113.5	83.9
Yes	52.2	43.4	160.0	121.0
Small firm (five workers or less)				
No	50.8	30.0	152.1	113.8
Yes	49.2	70.1	123.0	87.6
Occupation				
Professionals and technicians	13.6	8.5	237.0	180.3
Directors and upper management	4.8	2.3	271.7	211.0
Administrative personnel	9.6	6.5	136.5	114.0
Merchants and sellers	12.4	11.4	117.5	102.2

(continued next page)

Table 13.1 (continued)

| | Composition | | Earnings index | |
| | (percentage) | | (Base: average minority earnings = 100) | |
	Nonminorities	Minorities	Nonminorities	Minorities
Service workers	19.0	24.3	95.0	79.9
Agricultural workers and similar	12.0	16.7	85.3	57.7
Nonagricultural blue-collars workers	27.6	29.0	126.1	102.1
Armed forces	0.0	0.0	409.1	260.1
Occupations not classified above	1.1	1.4	170.3	161.4
Economic sector				
Agriculture, hunting, forestry, and fishing	12.2	16.9	87.6	58.3
Mining and quarrying	0.8	0.7	195.6	144.8
Manufacturing	16.8	14.5	136.9	103.9
Electricity, gas, and water supply	0.6	0.5	178.4	151.3
Construction	7.3	9.6	124.2	94.5
Wholesale and retail trade and hotels and restaurants	24.0	21.9	132.3	102.7
Transport and storage	6.6	5.4	158.2	129.3
Financing, insurance, real estate, and business services	3.7	1.7	196.8	143.4
Community, social, and personal services	28.0	28.8	153.2	112.3

Source: Based on data from national household surveys from circa 2005.

Table 13.2 Decomposition of Ethnic Earnings Gap in Latin America after Controlling for Demographic Characteristics, Circa 2005 *(percent)*

	Gender	+ Age	+ Education	+ Presence of children in the household	+ Presence of other household member with labor income	+ Urban
Δ	37.8	37.8	37.8	37.8	37.8	37.8
Δ_0	40.0	39.5	27.9	26.9	26.2	25.1
Δ_W	0.0	0.0	1.4	2.4	3.6	3.5
Δ_{NW}	0.0	0.0	-0.2	-0.4	-0.8	-0.6
Δ_X	-2.2	-1.7	8.7	8.9	8.8	9.8
Percentage of nonminorities in common support	100.0	100.0	98.0	95.9	93.3	89.6
Percentage of minorities in common support	100.0	100.0	99.7	99.3	98.1	95.7

Source: Based on pooled data from national household surveys from circa 2005.

Note: $\Delta_W (\Delta_{NW})$ is the part of the earnings gap attributed to the existence of nonminorities (minorities) that are not met by any minorities (nonminorities). Δ_X is the part of the earnings gap attributed to differences in the observable characteristics of nonminorities and minorities over the "common support." Δ_0 is the part of the earnings gap that cannot be attributed to differences in characteristics of the individuals. It is typically attributed to a combination of both unobservable characteristics and discrimination. The sum of these components equals the total earnings gap ($\Delta_W + \Delta_{NW} + \Delta_X + \Delta_0 = \Delta$).

portion of the gap still remains unexplained, suggesting that, like educational attainment, returns to schooling are lower for ethnic minorities than for nonminorities.[2] After education, the other demographic variables (presence of children and other income earners in the household) add little to the explanation of ethnic earnings gaps.

Table 13.3 presents the results of the decompositions obtained after adding each of the six job characteristics. To facilitate the comparison of results, the first column of table 13.3 reports the last column of table 13.2, which reports results after matching on the six demographic characteristics. The last column of table 13.3 shows the earnings gap decompositions resulting from matching on the full set of variables (the six demographic and six job characteristics).

The comparison of the six job characteristics reveals that, in contrast with the gender case, occupational segregation plays an important role in explaining ethnic earnings gaps. In fact, occupation is the characteristic that most reduces the earnings gap. When this characteristic is added to the demographic set of matching variables, the unexplained component decreases from 25 percent to 18 percent. Of the other five job-related covariates, three positively contribute to the ethnic earnings gaps but with small effects (2–3 percentage points): type of employment, formality, and economic sector. The other two (part-time and small firm) have almost no effect on ethnic earnings gaps.

However, when all these covariates are considered together (last column of table 13.3), the unexplained component of the ethnic earnings gap diminishes substantially, to just a third of the ethnic gap. Almost one-fourth of the gap can be explained by differences in the distribution of characteristics over the common support (Δ_X), and an important part of the gap can be explained by the component that exists because nonminorities achieve certain combinations of human capital characteristics that minorities fail to reach (Δ_W). Indeed, more than half of the ethnic earnings gap is attributable to the existence of these sorts of access barriers to high-paying segments of the labor markets.

Not surprisingly, when the full set of demographic and job characteristics is used, only 43 percent of nonminorities and 51 percent of minorities lie on the common support of distributions of observable characteristics. Even greater segmentation of the labor market occurs along the gender divide, but with no substantial contribution to earnings gaps. Further analysis of the combinations of characteristics found among nonminorities but not among minorities promises to increase the understanding of ethnic earnings gaps.

Disaggregation of the ethnic earnings gap by country for three sets of control variables reveals high cross-country heterogeneity (table 13.4). In Guatemala, for example, both the total gap and the unexplained gap after controlling for gender and age are more than twice as large as in Chile. The effect of controlling by education differs substantially from country

Table 13.3 Decomposition of Ethnic Earnings Gap in Latin America after Controlling for Demographic, Job, and Full Set of Characteristics, Circa 2005 (percent)

	Demographic set	& Type of employment	& Part time	& Formality	& Sector	& Occupation	& Small firm	Full set
Δ	37.8	37.8	37.8	37.8	37.8	37.8	37.8	37.8
Δ_0	25.1	22.7	25.9	22.4	22.8	18.0	25.1	12.9
Δ_W	3.5	6.5	4.7	4.9	6.1	7.2	4.0	21.2
Δ_{NW}	-0.6	-1.4	-1.4	-0.8	-1.1	-1.0	-1.1	-7.3
Δ_X	9.8	10.0	8.6	11.4	10.1	13.5	9.7	10.9
Percent of nonminorities in common support	89.6	83.5	85.9	84.8	73.2	74.8	85.0	43.0
Percent of minorities in common support	95.7	91.2	92.3	93.1	83.6	85.0	94.4	51.4

Source: Based on data from national household surveys from circa 2005.

Note: $\Delta_W(\Delta_{NW})$ is the part of the earnings gap attributed to the existence of nonminorities (minorities) with combinations of characteristics that are not met by any minorities (nonminorities). Δ_X is the part of the earnings gap attributed to differences in the observable characteristics of nonminorities and minorities over the "common support." Δ_0 is the part of the earnings gap that cannot be attributed to differences in characteristics of the individuals. It is typically attributed to a combination of both unobservable characteristics and discrimination. The sum of these components equals the total earnings gap ($\Delta_W + \Delta_{NW} + \Delta_X + \Delta_0 = \Delta$).

Table 13.4 Decomposition of Ethnic Earnings Gap by Demographic and Job Characteristics in Selected Countries in Latin America, Circa 2005 (percent)

Country	Δ	Gender and age	+ Education	Δ_0	
				+ Presence of children in household, presence of other income earner in household, and urban	+ Part time, formality, occupation, economic sector, type of employment, and small firm
Bolivia	30.8	35.6*	16.5*	12.7*	21.2*
Brazil	38.7	38.6*	30.0*	27.2*	13.9*
Chile	30.8	29.3*	10.6*	8.4*	1.4
Ecuador	30.7	26.7*	3.9	2.6	0.7
Guatemala	67.7	67.4*	23.5*	21.0*	11.4*
Peru	45.5	45.6*	20.9*	17.5*	14.4*
Paraguay	59.6	58.0*	21.8*	12.3*	6.3
Latin America	37.8	39.5	27.9	25.1	12.9

Source: Based on data from national household surveys from circa 2005.

Note: * $p < 0.10$. Δ corresponds to the total earnings gap. Δ_0 is the part of the earnings gap that cannot be attributed to differences in characteristics of the individuals and is typically attributed to a combination of both unobservable characteristics and the existence of discrimination.

to country. In Ecuador, for example, the unexplained component is no longer significantly different from zero after accounting for differences in education, whereas in Brazil it falls from 39 percent to 30 percent. This result is driven by the fact that the gap in educational attainment differs substantially between these two countries. In Ecuador, the percentage of workers with university degrees is 16 percent among nonminorities and 6 percent among minorities. In Brazil, this difference is substantially smaller: 5 percent of nonminority and 4 percent of minority workers have university degrees.[3]

Figure 13.1 presents the four components of the earnings gap (sorted by the magnitude of the unexplained component) for the specification with the full set of control variables. As in the case of the gender gap, there are clear qualitative patterns across countries. First, Δ_X is positive in every

Figure 13.1 Decomposition of Ethnic Earnings Gap in Selected Countries in Latin America after Controlling for Demographic and Job Characteristics, Circa 2005

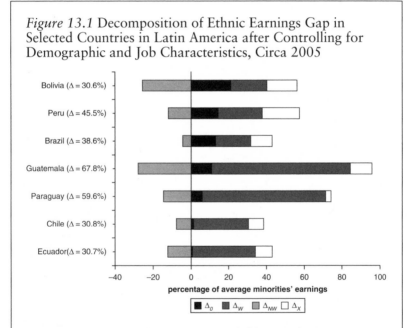

Source: Based on data from national household surveys from circa 2005.

Note: Δ_W (Δ_{NW}) is the part of the earnings gap attributed to the existence of minorities (nonminorities) with combinations of characteristics that are not met by any minorities (nonminorities). Δ_X is the part of the earnings gap attributed to differences in the observable characteristics of nonminorities and minorities over the "common support." Δ_0 is the part of the earnings gap that cannot be attributed to differences in characteristics of the individuals. It is typically attributed to a combination of both unobservable characteristics and discrimination. The sum of these components equals the total earnings gap ($\Delta_W + \Delta_{NW} + \Delta_X + \Delta_0 = \Delta$).

country, meaning that minorities in every country have combinations of characteristics that are associated with lower returns in the labor market (in particular, educational attainment). Second, Δ_W is positive in all countries, and it represents the largest component in most of them, suggesting that in every country, the existence of combinations of characteristics that are achieved only by nonminorities plays an important role in explaining part of the earnings gap. Access barriers—hypothesized here as an explanation for the earnings gaps—prevail in all countries. Unexplained ethnic earnings gaps (Δ_0) are also positive in all countries (although they are not significantly different from zero in Chile, Ecuador, and Paraguay).

Exploring the Unexplained Component of the Ethnic Earnings Gap

Several interesting features are evident in the distribution of the unexplained ethnic earnings gaps across observable characteristics (figure 13.2).

The gap is larger among men. This observation does not contradict the fact that minority women fare worst in labor markets: the earnings gap between minority women and nonminority men reaches an astonishing 60 percent when no control variables are used. Most of this gap cannot be explained on the basis of observable characteristics. Of the components attributable to observable characteristics, the largest is the one explained by combinations of characteristics that white men achieve but minority women do not (tables and figures corresponding to this decomposition are not reported).

The gap is smallest among the youngest cohort. As discussed in the case of gender, where a similar finding was reported, this result may contain good news, but the evidence is not definitive. The good news would be that younger cohorts entering the labor market face less discrimination and therefore get closer to the "equal pay for equal productive characteristics." The word of caution is that this finding may reflect the effect of unobservable characteristics correlated with age, such as experience.

Four other important conclusions, which will not be described as the previous two, are still important. First, *the gap is smaller among workers with other labor income generators in the household than among workers who are the sole income generator at home.* Second, *the gap is smaller in urban areas than in rural ones.* Third, *the gap is smaller and more dispersed among part-time workers than among people who work full time.* Fourth, *the gap is more dispersed at both extremes of the educational attainment distribution.* These results are consistent with previous findings in the gender earnings gaps and are relevant results as well in later chapters.

Figure 13.2 Confidence Intervals for Unexplained Ethnic Earnings Gap in Latin America after Controlling for Demographic and Job Characteristics, Circa 2005

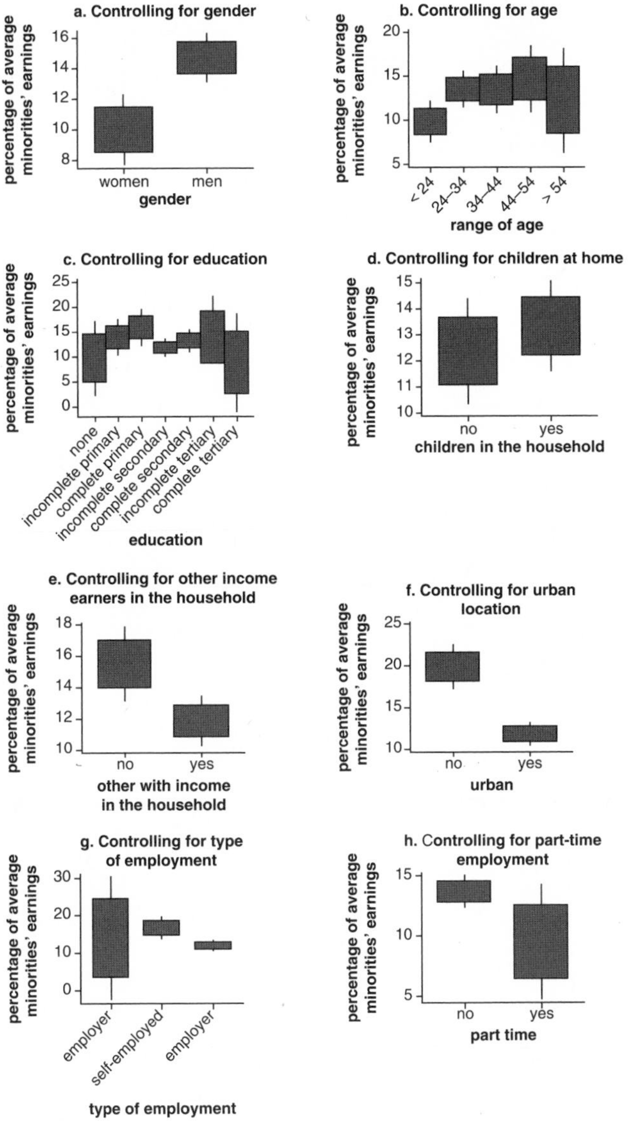

(continued next page)

Figure 13.2 (continued)

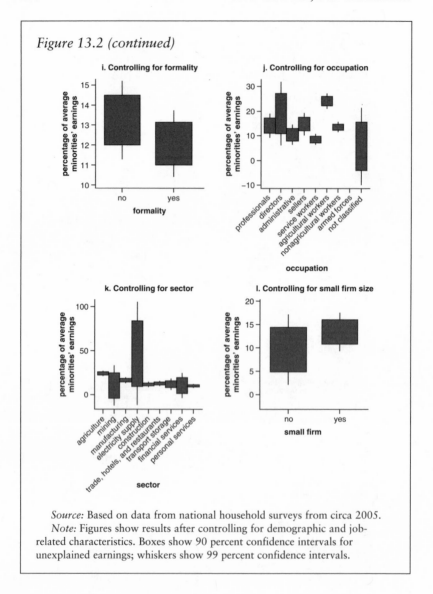

Source: Based on data from national household surveys from circa 2005.
Note: Figures show results after controlling for demographic and job-related characteristics. Boxes show 90 percent confidence intervals for unexplained earnings; whiskers show 99 percent confidence intervals.

Figure 13.3 presents the unexplained ethnic earnings gap by percentile of the earnings distributions of minorities and nonminorities, in order to assess whether the unexplained component is concentrated, as in the case of the gender gap, in particular segments of the earnings distributions. After controlling only for gender and age, the unexplained gap is significantly larger among low-income workers. The gap is more than 100 percent at the

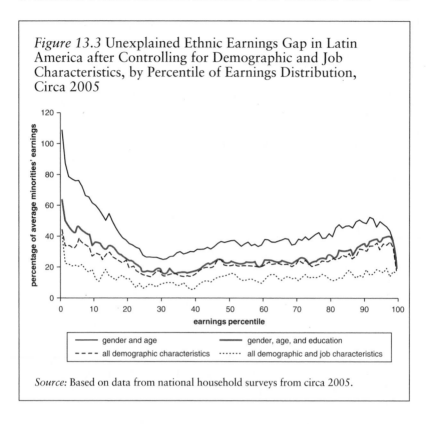

Figure 13.3 Unexplained Ethnic Earnings Gap in Latin America after Controlling for Demographic and Job Characteristics, by Percentile of Earnings Distribution, Circa 2005

Source: Based on data from national household surveys from circa 2005.

bottom of the distributions. It decreases sharply until the 30th percentile, where it is close to 27 percent. The gap then increases slightly, closing altogether only at the very right end of the distribution.

When education is added as a matching variable, this overall pattern is almost maintained, with a reduction in the unexplained component of the ethnic earnings gap. However, the largest reductions in the gap occur at the lower percentiles of the distributions. Thus, educational attainment explains more of the differences in earnings of low-income workers than middle- or high-income workers. After controlling for demographic and job characteristics, the unexplained gap becomes roughly homogenous along the earnings distribution.

A distinctive feature of ethnic earnings gaps is that they are smaller among part-time workers than full-time workers. Although no strong impact of economic sector segregation on earnings gaps was found, there is a link between the ethnic earnings gap and occupational segregation, in contrast with the results for gender earnings gaps. About 21 percentage points of the 39 percentage points of the earnings gap (that is, slightly more than half the earnings gap) is attributable to the existence of nonminorities with combinations of characteristics that are not realized by minorities. These are highly paid profiles of older, educated professionals, directors, or senior managers in specific sectors. In this sense, there is evidence that ethnic minorities in the region are confronted with glass ceilings.

In sum, this chapter provides suggestive evidence that the region still faces major labor market disadvantages based on ethnicity. Policies aimed at reducing these inequalities are still needed, not only because of ethical considerations regarding equality but also as a major strategy to reduce poverty. Policies aimed at boosting school attendance for minorities are welcomed, but they should take into account the lower incentives minorities face to completing school given their lower returns to education in the labor market. Because ethnic minorities and women are particularly disadvantaged, indigenous girls should be given special attention.

The next three chapters analyze ethnic earnings gaps in Brazil, Ecuador, and Guatemala. These countries are important to analyze individually because they are representative of different situations for minorities. In Brazil (chapter 14), there is little difference between the educational attainment of minorities and nonminorities: both groups have poor attainment. In contrast, in Ecuador (chapter 15), minorities have many fewer years of education than nonminorities. Guatemala (chapter 16) has the widest ethnic earnings gaps in the region.

Notes

1. For a description of the methodology used in this chapter, see chapter 2.

2. It could also be the case that lower returns to schooling for ethnic minorities create incentives for them to drop out of the educational system or exert less effort while in school.

3. This is not to say that Brazil has actually been successful in closing the gap in educational attainment between minorities and nonminorities, but that educational attainment is low for both minorities and nonminorities.

References

Atal, J. P., H. Ñopo, and N. Winder, 2009. "New Century, Old Disparities: Gender and Ethnic Wage Gaps in Latin America." RES Working Paper 4640, Inter-American Development Bank, Research Department, Washington, DC.

Calla, R. 2007. "La mujer indígena en Bolivia, Brasil, Ecuador, Guatemala, y Panama: un panorama de base a partir de la ronda de censos de 2000." Serie Mujer y Desarrollo, Consejo Económico para América Latina y el Caribe, Santiago, Chile.

Chiswick, B. R., H. A. Patrinos, and M. E. Hurst. 2000. "Indigenous Language Skills and the Labor Market in a Developing Economy: Bolivia." *Economic Development and Cultural Change* 48 (2): 349–67.

Contreras, D., and M. Galván. 2003. "¿Ha disminuido la discriminación salarial por género y etnia en Bolivia? evidencia del periodo 1994–1999." http://www .depeco.econo.unlp.edu.ar/reunion_desigualdad/trabajo3.pdf.

Fazio, M. V. 2007. "Economic Opportunities." In *Economic Opportunities for Indigenous Peoples in Latin America*, Conference Edition, 9–20. Washington, DC: World Bank.

Hall, G., and H. A. Patrinos, eds. 2006. *Indigenous Peoples, Poverty and Human Development in Latin America*. London: Palgrave Macmillan.

Hopenhayn, M., and A. Bello. 2001. "Discriminación étnico-racial y xenofobia en América Latina y el Caribe." Serie Políticas Sociales 47, Comisión Económica para América Latina y el Caribe (CEPAL), Santiago, Chile.

ILO (International Labour Organization). 2007. *Modelo de tendencias mundiales del empleo*. Geneva: ILO.

Jiménez Pozo, W., F. L. Casazola, and E. Yáñez Aguilar. 2006. "Bolivia." In *Indigenous Peoples, Poverty and Human Development in Latin America*, ed. G. Hall and H. A. Patrinos, 40–66. London: Palgrave Macmillan.

Lovell, P. 2000. "Race, Gender and Regional Labour Market Inequalities in Brazil." *Review of Social Economy* 58 (3): 277–93.

Ñopo, H., and A. Hoyos. 2010. "Evolution of Gender Wage Gaps in Latin America at the Turn of the Twentieth Century: An Addendum to 'New Century, Old Disparities.'" IZA Discussion Paper 5086, Institute for the Study of Labor, Bonn, Germany.

Patrinos, H. A. 2000. "The Cost of Discrimination in Latin America." *Studies in Comparative International Development* 35 (2): 3–17.

Piras, C. 2004. "An Overview of the Challenges and Policy Issues Facing Women in the Labor Force." In *Women at Work: Challenges for Latin America*, ed. C. Piras, 3–24. Washington, DC: Inter-American Development Bank.

Psacharopoulos, G. 1992. "Ethnicity, Education, and Earnings in Bolivia and Guatemala." Policy Research Working Paper 1014, World Bank, Washington, DC.

Psacharopoulos, G., and H. A. Patrinos. 1994. *Indigenous People and Poverty in Latin America: An Empirical Analysis*. Washington, DC: World Bank.

Rangel, M. 1998. "Raza y género en Brasil: las regiones metropolitanas de Rio de Janeiro y de São Paulo." *Acta Sociologica* 23, Universidad Nacional Autónoma de México, Facultad de Ciencias Políticas y Sociales, Mexico City.

14

Promoting Ethnic Equality: Brazil 1996–2006

As in other countries in the region, Brazil's history includes several centuries of slavery involving both indigenous peoples and Afro-descendents. The legacy of slavery persists in more and less subtle forms of discrimination. Although grassroots movements have denounced these problems for decades, only recently has the federal government launched an innovative and coordinated National Policy for the Promotion of Gender and Race Equality. For the first time, the multiyear plan for 2004–07 included "social inclusion and reduction of social inequalities" in its goals. The central objective of the national policy is to reduce gender and ethnic inequalities in Brazil, with emphasis on the Afro-descendant population. The policy's success will depend on coordinated action and commitment by all spheres of government and society.

This chapter uses data from the Pesquisa Nacional por Amostra de Domicilios (National Survey of Sample Households, PNAD) for 1996–2006 to analyze and decompose the ethnic earnings gap based on the methodology described in chapter 2.[1] Attention is restricted to people 15–65 years old with positive earnings at the primary occupation (measured as hourly earnings).

What Does the Literature Show?

López-Calva and Lustig (2009) report a decline in inequality across Latin America. They focus on four countries: Argentina, Brazil, Mexico, and Peru.

This chapter was adapted from "Gender and Racial Wage Gaps in Brazil 1996–2006: Evidence Using a Matching Comparisons Approach," Luana Marquez Garcia, Hugo Ñopo, and Paola Salardi, RES Working Paper 4626, Inter-American Development Bank, 2009.

Luana Marquez Garcia is a young professional at the Inter-American Development Bank. Paola Salardi is a research fellow in the Economics Group at the University of Sussex, in Brighton, United Kingdom.

In Brazil, they report a steady fall in the Gini coefficient since 1998 and a decline in poverty and extreme poverty between 2001 and 2007.[2,3] During this period, annual per capita income of the poorest grew at a much faster rate (7.0 percent) than per capita income of the richest decile (1.1 percent), which defines Brazil's growth pattern as pro-poor. Reductions in overall inequality and poverty are caused by the decline in labor income inequality, which occurred thanks to an accelerated expansion of access to education in Brazil and a drop in the returns to education. Labor earnings differentials by education level have declined at all levels in Brazil, particularly for secondary and tertiary education (López-Calva and Lustig 2009). Changes in education account for half the reduction in labor income inequality; the other half is accounted for by a number of factors, among which Barros et al. (2009) include changes in gender and ethnic discrimination and labor force participation rates. A popular perception in Brazil is that racism does not affect a person's life and that study, hard work, and initiative are the main factors leading to success. There is an emerging popular belief, however, that class differences prevent people from progressing.

Research suggests that earnings gaps between whites (nonminorities) and nonwhites (minorities) were about 50 percent for men and 45 percent for women in the mid-2000s (that is, white men earned 50 percent more than Afro-descendant men, and white women earned 45 percent than Afro-descendant women [De Carvalho, Néri, and Britz do Nascimento Silva 2006; Guerreiro 2008]). Race and gender significantly affect income, even when education, experience, and labor market characteristics are taken into account.

One of the most comprehensive analyses of gender and ethnic earnings differentials in Brazil is Soares (2000). He documents that, since the 1980s, ethnic earnings gaps have been larger than gender earnings gaps. White women earn 79 percent and Afro-descendant men only 46 percent of white men's earnings.

Using the Blinder-Oaxaca decomposition yields very different patterns for gender and ethnic differentials in earnings Although gender earnings gaps decreased over time, ethnic differentials remained constant. Most of the earnings differentials by race can be explained by differences in observable characteristics between ethnic groups, whereas the unexplained component by gender is constantly larger than the explained component.

De Carvalho, Néri, and Britz do Nascimento Silva (2006) analyze gender and ethnic earnings gaps by applying the Blinder-Oaxaca decomposition and correcting for selection bias as proposed by Heckman (1979).[4] Correcting for labor market participation reduces the unexplained component of the ethnic gender gap from 37 percent to 30 percent and the unexplained component of the gender gap from 33 percent to 18 percent. It increases the earnings gap between white men and Afro-descendant women, however, from 78 percent to 95 percent.

Lovell (1994, 2000, and 2006) analyzes gender and ethnic differences in earnings using census data instead of national household surveys. In her empirical applications, she adopts a modified version of the standard Blinder-Oaxaca decomposition as proposed by Jones and Kelly (1984). Drawing on sample data from the 1960 and 1980 censuses, Lovell (1994) finds that gender earnings gaps are larger than ethnic earnings gaps.

Lovell and Wood (1998) highlight how the unexplained component of both gender and ethnic earnings gaps has increased. Lovell (2000) focuses on regional differences in earnings gaps, considering only the states of São Paulo and Bahia. The wealthier state, São Paulo, shows larger earnings differentials and a larger unexplained component.

Lovell (2006) focuses on earnings gaps in São Paulo, covering a longer time period. Her finding that ethnic differentials are stable whereas gender differentials diminished over time is in line with previous studies. She finds that the unexplained component of both gaps increased.

Calvalieri and Fernandes (1998) also report earnings gaps that are larger along gender than ethnic lines. Using the PNAD for 1989, they estimate earnings equations. They find that after controlling for a large set of characteristics, the gender earnings gap becomes larger than the ethnic earnings gap, probably because of the greater variation in the ethnic earnings gap than in the gender earnings gap, which is captured by regional dummies included in the regression equations.

The 1980 study by Silva represents a pioneering analysis of ethnic earnings gaps using the Blinder-Oaxaca decomposition technique. He employs a 1.27 percent subsample of the 1960 census, restricting his analysis to male workers living in the Rio de Janeiro area. He examines three ethnic groups: whites; "mulattoes" (people of brown complexion, presumably of mixed European and African ancestry); and "negroes" (darker-skinned people appearing to be primarily or exclusively of African ancestry). Silva finds a larger earnings gap for negroes than for mulattoes with respect to white male workers and finds that the explained component is larger than the unexplained component.

Silva's seminal work was not updated until 2004, when Arias, Yamada, and Tejerina examined the entire earnings distribution, using the quantile regression methodology developed by Koenker and Bassett (1978). Their findings support the importance of examining different points of the earnings distribution, not simply average values, as in the Blinder-Oaxaca decomposition technique. They find that the bottom decile of nonwhites earns 24 percent less than comparable whites, whereas the top decile of nonwhites earns 56 percent less. Overall, nonwhites earn 46 percent less than whites, and people of mixed race earn 42 percent less. The earnings of people of mixed race at the bottom of the earnings distribution are similar to those of nonwhites. In contrast, the earnings of people of mixed race at the upper end of the income distribution are similar to those of whites.

Arcand and D'Hombres (2004) enrich the study of ethnic earnings differentials based on the Blinder-Oaxaca decomposition and quantile regression by considering the selection bias correction for occupational attachment. The explained component accounts for most of the gaps for both nonwhites and people of mixed race; the unexplained component is larger for nonwhites.

Expanding on Soares (2000), Campante, Crespo, and Leite (2004) focus on differences between the North-East and South-East regions. In the South-East, the ethnic gap exceeds the national average, and the unexplained component tends to be larger than elsewhere in Brazil.

Leite (2005) shows that the unexplained component is higher in the South-East than the North-East. This finding holds after controlling for the endogeneity of individuals' schooling, which reduces the size of the unexplained component.

Reis and Crespo (2005) show how ethnic earnings differentials are not constant over time, as claimed by previous studies. They decompose the unexplained component into age, period, and cohort effects and show that ethnic earnings gaps are smaller for younger cohorts.

Taking as a point of departure Campante, Crespo, and Leite (2004) and Soares (2000), Guimarães (2006) adds controls for region and sector of activity. She finds that unexplained differences represent 30 percent of total differentials and that pay gaps between whites and nonwhites are larger in the North and North-East regions than elsewhere.

In summary, ethnic earnings gaps in Brazil were larger than gender earnings gaps in recent decades (Soares 2000); only before the 1980s were gender earnings gaps more important (Lovell 1994; Lovell and Wood 1998). Gender earnings gaps tend to be more homogenous across regions than ethnic gaps (Calvalieri and Fernandes 1998). Ethnic gaps are wider in the South-East region than in the North-East; they are also wider in urban than rural areas (Lovell 2000; Campante, Crespo, and Leite 2004; Loureiro, Carneiro, and Sachsida 2004; Leite 2005).

Over time, gender earnings gaps have decreased significantly; ethnic gaps have not. Nonetheless, work on cohorts by Reis and Crespo (2005) finds that ethnic earnings gaps are shrinking for the younger generation. The explained component of the ethnic gap is smaller for nonwhites than for people of mixed race; people of mixed race also earn more than nonwhites (Arcand and D'Hombres 2004; Arias, Yamada, and Tejerina 2004).

How Do Ethnic Minorities and Nonminorities in the Work Force Differ?

Age tends to be homogeneous across people who matched and people who do not (that is, people in and out of the "common support" [see chapter 2]), as well as over time (table 14.1). Among whites (nonminorities) who do not match nonwhites(minorities), the share that had more than 15 years of schooling was 19.9 percent in 1996 and 28.3 percent in 2006; among unmatched nonwhites, these shares were just 2.8 percent in 1996 and

Table 14.1 Demographic and Job Characteristics of Matched and Unmatched Samples of Whites and Nonwhites in Brazil, 1996 and 2006 *(percent)*

	1996			2006		
	Unmatched nonwhites	*Unmatched whites*	*Matched whites and nonwhites*	*Unmatched nonwhites*	*Unmatched whites*	*Matched whites and nonwhites*
Personal characteristics						
Age						
15–24	28.9	23.2	28.3	24.1	19.2	25.3
25–34	27.4	27.7	30.3	28.1	25.3	28.9
35–44	23.0	24.8	24.6	23.1	24.5	25.8
45–54	13.7	16.0	12.4	16.7	20.5	14.9
55–65	7.0	8.3	4.4	8.1	10.5	5.1
Years of education						
Less than 4	39.6	19.4	31.9	30.0	13.1	21.7
4–10	56.4	56.9	61.4	62.9	52.0	64.7
11–15	1.1	3.9	0.7	1.8	6.6	1.8
More than 15	2.8	19.9	6.0	5.4	28.3	11.9

(continued next page)

Table 14.1 (continued)

	1996			2006		
	Unmatched nonwhites	Unmatched whites	Matched whites and nonwhites	Unmatched nonwhites	Unmatched whites	Matched whites and nonwhites
Gender (male)	70.1	64.9	58.1	70.0	63.1	54.7
Urban	87.8	90.6	83.2	87.1	92.4	86.5
Regions:						
North	19.8	4.0	4.4	26.0	6.1	10.5
North-East	39.9	9.2	31.5	35.1	9.8	31.4
South-East	18.4	33.2	42.8	16.8	30.1	35.4
South	4.4	42.5	12.1	4.9	42.0	12.6
Central West	17.5	10.8	9.2	17.4	12.1	10.2
Job characteristics						
Type of occupation:						
Professionals	7.1	14.9	10.7	16.1	38.2	18.3
Intermediate	43.3	52.0	44.8	41.7	35.7	45.7
Blue collar	49.6	33.2	44.6	42.2	26.1	36.1

Table 14.1 (continued)

	1996			2006		
	Unmatched nonwhites	Unmatched whites	Matched whites and nonwhites	Unmatched nonwhites	Unmatched whites	Matched whites and nonwhites
Formal	49.1	51.9	45.7	47.2	50.9	48.2
Agriculture	9.4	7.3	14.9	9.1	6.0	11.7
Construction	11.1	5.6	7.1	11.0	5.5	7.1
Social services	35.2	35.8	44.6	25.3	28.1	41.2

Source: Based on data from 1996 and 2006 PNAD.

271

5.4 percent in 2006. Unmatched nonwhites are more likely to be men. There seems to be a geographical concentration of unmatched nonwhites in the North-East and of unmatched whites in the South. This pattern reflects Brazilian regional disparities by ethnic groups.

Reflecting educational attainment patterns, unmatched whites are more likely to be professionals: in 2006, 38.2 percent of unmatched whites—and just 16.1 percent of unmatched nonwhites and 18.3 percent of matched white and nonwhites—were professionals. Unmatched nonwhites are employed mainly as blue-collar workers and are more likely to work in the informal sector. For economic activities, differences in and out of the common support are smaller for race than for gender, although unmatched nonwhites are more likely to work in sectors with a higher density of low-skilled workers, such as agriculture and construction.

The Role of Individual Characteristics in Explaining the Ethnic Earnings Gap

This subsection describes the matching conducted, based on six sets of human capital and job characteristics. The first set includes only the number of years of schooling. The second set adds age and education, and the third set adds the region.[5] Job variables are then added.

The ethnic earnings gap in Brazil is large, and it has been decreasing slowly (figure 14.1). Starting from a value of 96 percent in 1996, it declined from 18 percent to 78 percent in 2006. The unexplained component, the part of the earnings gap that cannot be attributed to differences in characteristics of the individuals, is small: after controlling for the wider set of characteristics, Δ_0 accounts for about 18 percent of the total gap. The bulk of the gap is given by the explained component, Δ_X—the part of the earnings gap attributed to differences in the observable characteristics of whites and nonwhites over the common support. The unexplained component is responsible for most of the drop in the total gap between 1996 and 2006 (15.2 percentage points of the 18.0 percentage point decline), however.

For unmatched individuals, Δ_{NW} represents the portion of the earnings gap for which there are nonwhites who cannot be matched with whites, and it is negative. Interestingly, Δ_W (the part of the earnings gap attributed to the fact that there are whites with characteristics that are not matched by nonwhites) is larger than Δ_X and fairly stable over time. This result may reflect that fact that a consistent portion of white workers has stronger human capital characteristics than nonwhites and may hold very high-paid positions.

Exploring the Unexplained Component of the Ethnic Earnings Gap

Table 14.2 reports ethnic earnings gaps by various demographic and job characteristics, considering only the first year (1996) and the last year (2006) of the period under study.[6] Ethnic earnings gaps increase with age and education; they are large for high-paid positions. The gap for the youngest age group is far smaller than the gap for other groups. The

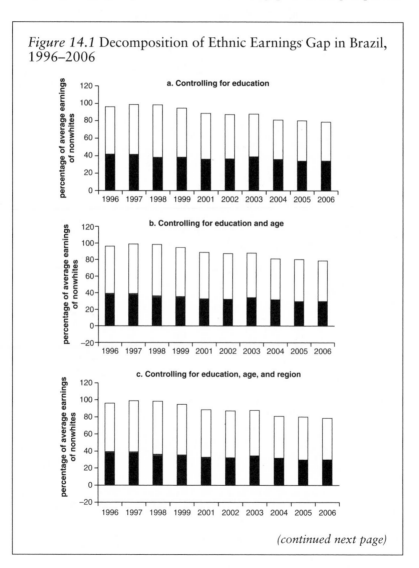

Figure 14.1 Decomposition of Ethnic Earnings Gap in Brazil, 1996–2006

(continued next page)

Figure 14.1 (continued)

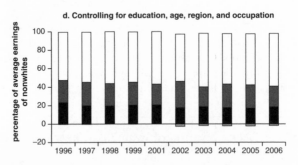

d. Controlling for education, age, region, and occupation

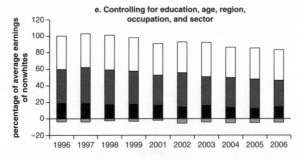

e. Controlling for education, age, region, occupation, and sector

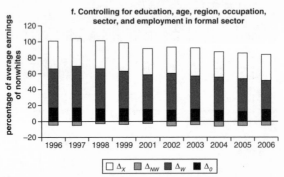

f. Controlling for education, age, region, occupation, sector, and employment in formal sector

$\square$ Δ_X $\blacksquare$ Δ_{NW} $\blacksquare$ Δ_W $\blacksquare$ Δ_0

Source: Based on data from the 1996–2006 PNAD.

Note: Δ_W (Δ_{NW}) is the part of the earnings gap attributed to the existence of whites (nonwhites) with combinations of characteristics that are not met by any nonwhites (whites). Δ_X is the part of the earnings gap attributed to differences in the observable characteristics of whites and nonwhites over the "common support." Δ_0 is the part of the earnings gap that cannot be attributed to differences in characteristics of the individuals. It is typically attributed to a combination of both unobservable characteristics and discrimination. The sum of these components equals the total earnings gap ($\Delta_W + \Delta_{NW} + \Delta_X + \Delta_0 = \Delta$).

Table 14.2 Original and Unexplained Ethnic Earnings Gaps in Brazil, by Demographic and Job Characteristics, 1996 and 2006 *(percent)*

	1996		2006	
	Δ	Δ_0	Δ	Δ_0
Demographic characteristics				
Age groups:				
15–24	33.85	8.26	25.53	5.53
25–34	91.31	20.42	67.44	15.29
35–44	125.98	22.76	88.43	15.05
45–54	141.84	20.92	121.05	26.26
55–65	109.8	12.23	123.72	19.21
Years of education:				
Less than 4	26.38	6.08	17.52	3.81
4–10	41.78	16.21	29.29	8.47
11–15	75.21	52.15	54.73	38.98
More than 15	146.09	61.25	130.35	80.91
Men	114.19	20.22	94.74	15.45
Urban	99.77	20.28	81.07	16.6
Regions:				
North	71.86	7.16	53.8	16.01
North-East	74.5	8.7	53.15	9.47
South-East	106.91	28.17	87.75	19.83
South	82.39	17.87	70.38	19.85
Central West	92.71	16.36	84.33	12.54
Labor characteristics				
Type of occupation:				
Professionals	153.41	23.92	130.55	45.17
Intermediate	118.81	19.65	29.48	7.83
Blue collar	43.88	13.52	40.32	11.06
Formal	80.27	19.57	61.81	14.93
Agriculture	64.81	10.84	60.68	8.43
Construction	64.48	15.39	49.78	16.14
Social services	99.19	13.95	90.8	16.06

Source: Based on data from 1996 and 2006 PNAD.

Note: Δ is the total earnings gap. Δ_0 is the part of the gap attributed to differences between whites and nonwhites that cannot be explained by observable characteristics.

geographical distribution of ethnic earnings gaps, which are larger in the
South-East, confirms the crucial role played by this variable.

The analysis is enriched by considering unexplained earnings differentials in individual income. Data sets were pooled, rescaling earnings
so that the average earnings of ethnic minorities are normalized to 100
in each year. In this way, changes in earnings in the economy over time
are ignored, in order to focus on earnings gaps. At each percentile of the

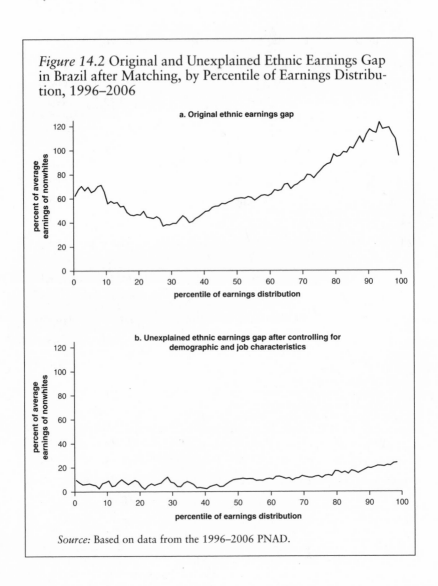

Figure 14.2 Original and Unexplained Ethnic Earnings Gap
in Brazil after Matching, by Percentile of Earnings Distribution, 1996–2006

Source: Based on data from the 1996–2006 PNAD.

earnings distribution of whites and nonwhites, the earnings of representative individuals in each distribution are compared and the gap between the two is computed (figure 14.2).

The difference between the total gap and the gap that remains after controlling for the full set of observable characteristics is large. The total gap increases at the upper end of the earnings distribution. Although the unexplained gap is considerably smaller than the total, it shows larger differentials for better-paid workers, a result similar to that found by Crespo (2003).

Ethnic earnings gaps are significantly larger than gender gaps; after controlling for observable individual characteristics, however, the situation is reversed. Observable individual characteristics play an important role in explaining earnings differentials between whites and nonwhites but a smaller role in gender earnings gaps. Among these characteristics, education plays a prominent role; labor market characteristics (occupation, economic sector, and formality) are also significant in explaining ethnic earnings differentials. The data suggest that the way in which these labor market characteristics operate takes the form of some sort of access barrier (as the Δ_W components are largest). Almost half of the ethnic earnings differential can be explained by the fact that whites have greater access to certain occupations, in certain sectors, with a certain degree of formality than nonwhites. Education matters, but segregation in labor markets does too.

Unexplained ethnic earnings gaps increase with workers' age and education; they are larger among professionals and in the South-East. Unexplained gaps increase monotonically, albeit only slightly, with income.

Notes

1. For 2000, census data were used. Asians and unnidentified ethnic minorities were dropped because of their negligible sample sizes.

2. The Gini coefficient is a measure of inequality in a society. A Gini coefficient of 0 expresses perfect equality; a Gini coefficient of 1 expresses perfect inequality.

3. Extreme poverty is the absence of one or more factors enabling individuals or households to assume basic responsibilities and enjoy fundamental rights.

4. This study also controls for the use of complex sample surveys without finding any significant alterations in the estimated coefficients.

5. The regions are North (Rondônia, Acre, Amazonas, Roraima, Parà, Amapà, Tocantins); North-East (Maranhão, Piauì, Cearà, Rio Grande do Norte, Paraiba, Pernambuco, Alagoas, Sergipe, Bahia); South-East (Minas Gerais, Espìrito Santo, Rio de Janeiro, São Paulo); South (Paraná, Santa Catarina, Rio Grande do Sul); and Central-West (Mato Grasso do Sul, Mato Grosso, Goiás, Distrito Federal).

6. Only the results for the first and last year are reported, because the trend over the decade is stable and smoothly decreasing. For all subsamples of the population, both explained and unexplained earnings gaps decreased over time.

References

Arcand, J. L., and B. D'Hombres. 2004. "Racial Discrimination in the Brazilian Labour Market: Wage, Employment and Segregation Effects." *Journal of International Development* 16: 1053–66.

Arias, O., G. Yamada, and L. Tejerina. 2004. "Education, Family Background and Racial Earnings Inequality in Brazil." *International Journal of Manpower* 25 (3/4): 355–74.

Barros, R., F. H. G. Ferreira, J. Molinas Vega, and J. Saavedra Chanduvi. 2009. *Measuring Inequality of Opportunities in Latin America and the Caribbean.* Washington, DC: World Bank.

Calvalieri, C., and R. Fernandes. 1998. "Diferenciais de salarios por genero e por cor: uma comparação entre as regiões metropolitanas Brasileiras." *Revista de Economia Politica* 18 (1): 158–15.

Campante, F. R., A. R. V. Crespo, and P. G. Leite. 2004. "Desigualdade salarial entre raças nomercado de trabalho urbano Brasileiro: aspectos regionais." *Revista Brasileira de Economia* 58 (2): 185–210.

Crespo, A. 2003. "Desigualdade entre racas e generos no Brasol: uma analise com simulacoes contra-factuais" Dissertação de mestrado, Pontifícia Universidade Católica do.

De Carvalho, A. P., M. Néri, and D. Britz do Nascimento Silva. 2006. *Diferenciais de saláriospor raça e gênero no Brasil: aplicação dos procedimentos de Oaxaca e Heckman em pesquisas amostrais complexas.* Rio de Janeiro: Instituto Brasileiro de Geografia e Estatística.

Guerreiro, R. 2008. "Is All Socioeconomic Inequality among Racial Groups in Brazil Caused by Racial Discrimination?" Working Paper 43, International Policy Centre for Inclusive Growth, Brasilia.

Guimarães, R. 2006. "Desigualdade salarial entre negros e brancos no Brasil: discriminação ou exclusão?" *Econômica* 8 (2): 227–51.

Heckman, J. 1979. "Sample Selection Bias as a Specification Error." *Econometrica* 47 (1): 153–61.

Jones, F. L., and J. Kelley. 1984. "Decomposing Differences between Groups. A Cautionary Note on Measuring Discrimination." *Sociological Methods and Research* 12: 323–43.

Koenker, R., and G. Bassett. 1978. "Regression Quantiles." *Econometrica* 46 (1): 33–50.

Leite, P. G. 2005. "Race Discrimination or Inequality of Opportunities: The Brazilian Case." Universität Göttingen Discussion Paper 118, Göttingen, Germany.

López-Calva, L. F., and N. Lustig, 2009. "The Recent Decline of Inequality in Latin America: Argentina, Brazil, Mexico and Peru." Working Paper 140, ECINEQ (Society for the Study of Economic Inequality), Palma de Mallorca, Spain.

Loureiro, P. R. A., F. G. Carneiro, and A. Sachsida. 2004. "Race and Gender Discrimination in the Labor Market: An Urban and Rural Sector Analysis for Brazil." *Journal of Economic Studies* 31 (2): 129–43.

Lovell, P. 1994. "Race, Gender and Development in Brazil." *Latin American Research Review* 29(3): 1–35.

——. 2000. "Race, Gender and Regional Labour Market Inequalities in Brazil." *Review of Social Economy* 58 (3): 277–93.

——. 2006. "Race, Gender, and Work in São Paolo, Brazil, 1960–2000." *Latin American Research Review* 41 (3): 63–87.

Lovell, P., and C. H. Wood. 1998. "Skin Colour, Racial Identity and Life Chances in Brazil." *Latin American Perspectives* 25 (3): 90–109.

Marquez Garcia, L., H. Ñopo, and P. Salardi. 2009. "Gender and Racial Wage Gaps in Brazil 1996–2006: Evidence Using a Matching Comparisons Approach." RES Working Paper 4626, Inter-American Development Bank, Research Department, Washington, DC.

Reis, M. C., and A. R. V. Crespo. 2005. "Race Discrimination in Brazil: An Analysis of the Age, Period and Cohort Effects." IPEA Texto para Discussão 1114, Instituto de Pesquisa Econômica Aplicada, Rio de Janeiro.

Silva, N. D. V. 1980. "O preço da cor: diferenciais raciais na distribuição de renda no Brasil." *Pesquisa e Planejamento Econômico* 10 (1): 57–67.

Soares, S. D. S. 2000. "O perfil da discriminação no mercado de trabalho: homens negros, mulheres brancas e mulheres negras." IPEA Texto para Discussão 769, Instituto de Pesquisa Econômica Aplicada, Brasilia.

15

No Good Jobs and Lower Earnings: Ecuador 2000–07

Within Latin America, Ecuador can be regarded as paradigmatic, with one of the largest shares of indigenous people and a very high incidence of poverty among them and Afro-descendants. Despite the economic potential that this cultural diversity and social capital could represent, socioeconomic differences persist.

The empirical analysis of ethnic earnings gaps reported in this chapter was conducted using annual data from the national labor survey (Encuesta de Empleo, Desempleo, y Subempleo [ENEMDU]) collected by the Instituto Nacional de Estadísticas y Censos de Ecuador (INEC) for 2003–07. The sample includes labor income earners and the self-employed reporting positive earnings (measured in hourly earnings) who were 15–65 years old and lived in the coastal, highland, and Amazon regions of Ecuador.

What Does the Literature Show?

García-Aracil and Winter (2006) measure the extent to which earnings differentials can be attributed to differences in human capital or to discrimination for labor income earners 12–65 years old. They identify indigenous people as people who live in a household in which there is at least one inhabitant who speaks an indigenous language. They use variables such as age and family composition (number of older and younger siblings in the household) as instruments for labor market participation in order to reduce bias caused by selection into the labor markets. Their decomposition results, using the nonindigenous pay structure as reference, yield a

This chapter was adapted from "Ethnic and Gender Wage Gaps in Ecuador," Lourdes Gallardo and Hugo Ñopo, RES Working Paper 4625, Inter-American Development Bank, 2009.

Lourdes Gallardo is an investment officer at the Inter-American Development Bank.

total earnings difference of 104 percent between indigenous and nonindigenous workers, of which 46 percent reflects difference in endowments and 58 percent reflects "unexplained" differences.

Larrea and Montenegro (2005) calculate separate regressions of labor earnings for indigenous (minorities) and nonindigenous (nonminorities) workers using data from the 1998 Survey on Living Conditions (Encuesta de Condiciones de Vida [ECV]), which approximates ethnicity through language. Using traditional Blinder-Oaxaca decompositions, they report a total earnings differential between indigenous and nonindigenous workers of 69 percent, of which 17.4 percent reflects endowment differences and 82.6 percent is unexplained. The difference between García-Aracil and Winter (2006) and Larrea and Montenegro (2005) is considerable given that both use data from the same source, collected only one year apart.

The language-based definition of ethnicity used by both García-Aracil and Winter (2006) and Larrea and Montenegro (2005) has a limitation, as it includes Spanish-speaking indigenous workers among nonindigenous workers. Doing so could underestimate earnings differentials, because the lower earnings of indigenous workers narrow the earnings gap as well as the differences caused by endowments and the differences that are left unexplained. Furthermore, this language-based approach includes other minority groups, such as Afro-descendants and people of mixed race who are Spanish speakers. There is consistent anecdotal evidence that points to discriminatory treatments of these people in everyday activities, possibly leading to biases and underestimates in the decomposition outcomes. Including nonindigenous people with indigenous language speakers within indigenous households will likewise negatively bias estimates of differences.

Both studies use monthly earnings as the dependent variable. It can be argued that monthly earnings do not accurately capture the return to productivity based on each worker's human capital endowments, because they are affected by workers' decision on how many hours to allocate to their job throughout a month, not just the return to their labor. Monthly earnings are useful when measuring income inequality between two groups. Hourly earnings are a better measure of pay differentials between groups, as they are compensation rates per unit of time worked. In this way, differences in hourly earnings can show pay differentials for equal productivity.

Gallardo (2006) analyzes labor market differentials of the indigenous and Afro-descendant population in Ecuador. Unlike the previous two studies, this study uses ethnic self-identification, as reported in the 2000 Household and Childhood Measurement Indicators Survey (Encuesta de Medición de Indicadores sobre la Niñez y los Hogares [EMEDINHO]) survey. Another difference between this study and the other two is the extended earnings differential decomposition model for labor income earners, based on the traditional Blinder-Oaxaca methodology and a system of simultaneous equations. This extension contributes to the analysis by recognizing that ethnicity and the intergenerational transmission of human capital may influence educational investments, sector of employment, and area of residence (Black, Devereux, and Salvanes 2003). By decomposing these three variables separately using the Blinder-Oaxaca method, Gallardo captures direct and indirect paths through which discrimination may affect earnings in the labor market.

Gallardo finds that low levels of educational attainment accompany higher rates of informal sector employment and that returns to education in the labor market for both indigenous and Afro-descendant labor income earners are lower than those of the mixed-race and white populations. The author also finds evidence that the transmission of human capital from parents to children has negative education and labor market outcomes for the indigenous and Afro-descendant populations. Among male workers, the direct effect on earnings differentials between indigenous, Afro-descendant, and mixed-race employees and white employees with similar endowments accounts for 27.1 percent of overall earnings differences. Indirect channels through schooling, sector of employment, and area of residence account for 39.9 percent of the earnings differential. For women, unexplained differences in pay account for 23.5 percent of the difference in earnings between the two ethnic clusters, and indirect channels account for 56.9 percent.

Ethnic minorities in Ecuador are concentrated largely in rural areas, where they are employed mostly in the agricultural sector; on-farm employment constitutes the main source of income for most indigenous families (World Bank 2004). Poverty in Ecuador affects predominantly rural areas. Ethnic minorities still have limited or no access to land ownership and work mostly low-productivity land (De Ferranti et al. 2003). This unequal distribution of land reflects the historical and institutional legacy dating back to colonial times.

MacIsaac and Rama (1997) find that the largest earnings gap in Ecuador is between workers in agriculture and workers in the rest of the economy. The income of rural poor indigenous workers is still tied to agriculture, a sector characterized by lower economic outcomes for all workers than other sectors of the economy. The authors also find that ethnic minorities in Ecuador are overrepresented in agriculture and in informal nonunionized activities and that hourly earnings in agriculture are 30 percent lower than in the informal sector.

How Do Ethnic Minorities and Nonminorities in the Work Force Differ?

Table 15.1 presents the proportion of the Ecuadorian population that reports being indigenous or Afro-descendant (black or mulatto). These

Table 15.1 Ethnic Minorities in Ecuador, by Gender, 2003–07
(percent)

National	2003	2004	2005	2006	2007
Men	14.5	12.1	12.3	12.5	12.8
Women	14.0	11.7	12.4	12.6	11.4
Urban					
Men	9.4	7.2	8.4	8.3	9.1
Women	8.7	6.9	7.8	7.6	8.0

Source: Based on data from 2003–07 ENEMDU.

populations are referred to as *ethnic minorities.* One of the traditional concerns attending the use of self-identification rather than native language to determine ethnicity is the "self-whitening" phenomenon, in which minorities deny their "indigeneity." This phenomenon leads to statistical underreporting. In recent years, underreporting seems unlikely, as the identity of the indigenous population has been empowered in Ecuador through social mobilization and political events.

Ethnic minorities in Ecuador have traditionally been predominantly rural; in 2003, 63 percent of the indigenous population was concentrated in rural areas. Based on the ENEMDU/EMEDINHO data, Gallardo (2006) estimates that about 78 percent of the indigenous population was concentrated in rural areas in 2000. This figure declined to 58 percent by 2007. The proportion of ethnic minorities also declined nationally and in urban settings, possibly influenced by the effects of the 1999 financial crisis, which stimulated internal and international migration.

Both the reduction of the proportion of ethnic minorities and their growing concentration in urban areas are important for understanding the evolution of these populations' well-being in Ecuador. Many observers believe that these phenomena have generated new forms of discrimination against emigrants and their families in Ecuador, many of them, indigenous. Ecuadorian society views emigrants and their families who stay behind as irrational, unproductive, and dysfunctional for the national economy. The families who stay behind usually consist of households headed by women, as men have higher emigration rates. Furthermore, emigrants' children have lower educational outcomes than nonemigrant children. They are inclined to leave the countryside as their parents did, which encourages dropping out of high school and university (Soruco, Piani, and Rossi 2008). If emigration-based discrimination spills over to labor markets, women and indigenous people related to emigrants could suffer adverse labor outcomes as a consequence of this phenomenon.

The ethnic educational gap is still wide, particularly at higher levels of education, but it has been narrowing, because enrollment of ethnic minorities in secondary and higher education has slightly increased while enrollment of nonminorities has stayed roughly constant (table 15.2).

Between 2003 and 2007, the percentage of ethnic minorities with no education also declined slightly. This trend suggests that there were higher enrollment rates for ethnic minority children, as total net primary enrollment in 2006 was 94.3 percent, up from 90.3 percent in 1999.

The participation of ethnic minorities in low-income occupations such as day work, domestic employment, and self-employment, which predominantly includes informal sector workers, is high (table 15.3). However, between 2003 and 2007, male labor force participation in self-employment decreased considerably, and male participation as day laborers increased. Meanwhile, the relative proportions of the self-employed decreased from 39 percent women versus 30 percent men in 2003 to 36 percent women versus 25 percent men in 2007. Among the self-employed, the proportion of women is higher among ethnic minorities than nonminorities. Women from ethnic minorities are highly concentrated in domestic employment and self-employment.

Unemployment is particularly high among Afro-descendants. According to the INEC, in 2007, the unemployment rate in Ecuador was 7.9 percent for the general population, 11.0 percent for Afro-descendants, and 17.5 percent among women. Among the indigenous population, the unemployment rate was 6.0 percent.

The Role of Individual Characteristics in Explaining the Ethnic Earnings Gap

Figure 15.1 illustrates the ethnic earnings gap decompositions for four combinations of observable characteristics used as controls.[1] The first combination includes area (rural or urban), education, gender, and age. The second adds to the previous list a dummy variable that identifies whether the respondent is the head of household. The third combination builds on the second one by adding occupation (coded at the one-digit level). The fourth combination adds a variable that reports whether the respondent's income is complemented by remittances from abroad.

The earnings difference between ethnic minority and nonminority groups fluctuated around 45 percent during the period of analysis. The Δ_W (the portion of the earrings gap attributed to characteristics of nonminorities that are not met by minorities) is positive and larger when the occupation variable is introduced, suggesting the existence of glass-ceiling effects in the form of barriers to access to certain human capital profiles. Furthermore, nonminorities with combinations of observable characteristics that are not

Table 15.2 Educational Attainment in Ecuador's Labor Force, by Gender and Minority Status, 2003 and 2007 (percent)

Year/education level	Men			Women		
	Ethnic minorities	Nonminorities	Total	Ethnic minorities	Nonminorities	Total
2003						
None	12.4	4.1	5.3	21.9	5.4	7.8
Pre-school	0.7	0.2	0.3	0.9	0.2	0.3
Basic	61.5	50.6	52.2	54.3	47.3	48.3
Bachillerato[a]	20.4	30.2	28.7	17.9	30.7	28.8
Tertiary	5.0	15.0	13.5	5.0	16.3	14.7
2007						
None	9.0	3.4	4.1	17.2	4.5	6.1
Pre-school	0.8	0.2	0.3	1.4	0.2	0.4
Basic	63.4	51.8	53.3	56.7	48.9	49.9
Bachillerato[a]	21.2	28.5	27.5	18.6	28.9	27.6
Tertiary	5.6	16.2	14.8	6.1	17.4	16.0

Source: Based on data from 2003–07 ENEMDU.
a. Equivalent to last three years of high school.

Table 15.3 Occupational Distribution in Ecuador, by Gender and Minority Status, 2003 and 2007 (percent)

Year/employment status	Men			Women		
	Ethnic minorities	Nonminorities	Total	Ethnic minorities	Nonminorities	Total
2003						
Government employee	5.7	9.4	8.9	7.4	14.7	13.6
Private employee	21.9	28.9	27.8	16.2	27.3	25.8
Day laborer	26.8	27.2	27.1	12.5	5.9	6.8
Boss or employer	3.8	6.0	5.6	3.2	3.9	3.8
Self-employed	41.4	28.4	30.2	47.6	37.8	39.2
Domestic employee	0.5	0.2	0.3	13.1	10.4	10.7
2007						
Government employee	6.7	9.2	8.9	9.4	14.1	13.5
Private employee	24.5	34.1	32.9	23.1	32.0	31.0
Day laborer	32.0	26.1	26.8	12.2	5.7	6.5
Boss or employer	3.1	6.4	6.0	1.7	3.9	3.7
Self-employed	33.4	23.8	25.0	42.3	35.2	36.0
Domestic employee	0.3	0.3	0.3	11.2	9.1	9.3

Source: Based on data from 2003–07 ENEMDU.

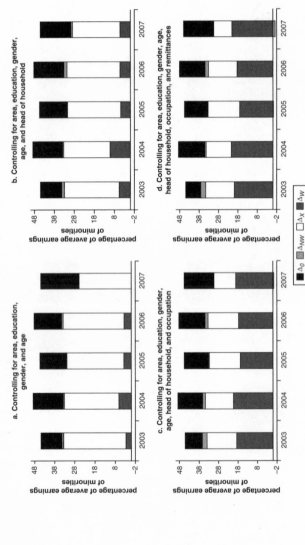

Figure 15.1 Decomposition of Ethnic Earnings Gap in Ecuador, 2003–07

Source: Based on data from 2003–07 ENEMDU.

Note: Δ_W (Δ_{NW}) is the part of the earnings gap attributed to the existence of nonminorities (minorities) with combinations of characteristics that are not met by any minorities (nonminorities). Δ_X is the part of the earnings gap attributed to differences in the observable characteristics of nonminorities and minorities over the "common support." Δ_0 is the part of the earnings gap that cannot be attributed to differences in characteristics of the individuals. It is typically attributed to a combination of both unobservable characteristics and discrimination. The sum of these components equals the total earnings gap ($\Delta_W + \Delta_{NW} + \Delta_X + \Delta_0 = \Delta$).

matchable to those of ethnic minorities have earnings that are, on average, higher than in the rest of the economy. The Δ_{NW} (the portion of the earnings gap attributed to characteristics of minorities that are not met by nonminorities) is small and almost negative; whether positive or negative, they do not play an important role.

The part of the gap attributable to differences in observable characteristics, Δ_X, becomes smaller as variables are added to the matching, particularly in the occupational category, which is also associated with an increase in Δ_W. This tendency accounts for the fact that certain combinations of human capital characteristics are achieved by nonminorities but not ethnic minorities. Decompositions controlling for whether the household received remittances from abroad do not change the earnings gap decompositions between these two groups.

The unexplained component of the decomposition, Δ_0—the part of the earnings gap that cannot be attributed to differences in characteristics of the individuals—accounts for about a fifth of the difference in earnings between minorities and nonminorities. Δ_0 is smaller when matching comparisons are used than when the traditional Blinder-Oaxaca methodology is used. This finding is relevant, as the Blinder-Oaxaca methodology has been found to overestimate the unexplained earnings differences because of its failure to take into account differences in the supports of the distributions of observable characteristics (see chapter 2). Differences in the supports account for an important part of the gap (in the full set of characteristics, it accounts for almost one-third of the total gap).

Exploring the Unexplained Component of the Ethnic Earnings Gap

Figure 15.2 shows the unexplained component of the ethnic earnings gap for different percentiles of the income distribution of minorities and nonminorities when the pooled data set for the five years under study is used and the earnings each year are normalized such that average earnings of minorities are constant over time. At the lower deciles of the income distribution, occupation is the most important variable explaining earnings differentials, accounting for almost a third of the difference. This outcome likely reflects the facts that ethnic minorities are clustered in agriculture and in informal sector employment and that the largest earnings gaps in Ecuador are still between jobs in agriculture and in the rest of the economy. Moreover, the income of ethnic minority workers is tied to agricultural output in a sector characterized by lower economic outcomes than in other sectors of the economy. Unexplained differences in earnings between the two groups decrease as income increases; Δ_0 is smallest between the 50th and 90th percentile of the distribution. Occupation itself does not account

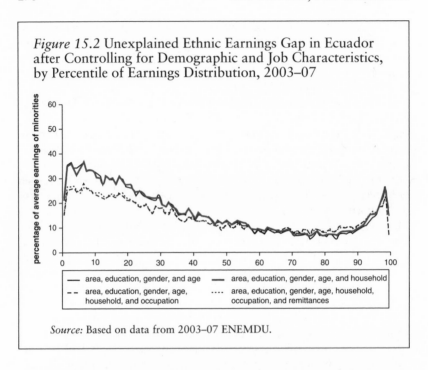

Figure 15.2 Unexplained Ethnic Earnings Gap in Ecuador after Controlling for Demographic and Job Characteristics, by Percentile of Earnings Distribution, 2003–07

Source: Based on data from 2003–07 ENEMDU.

for any more of the earnings difference than area, education, gender, and age within those percentiles. However, toward the high end of the income distribution, Δ_0 increases; none of the control variables seems to account for the ethnic earnings gap.

In general, results for Ecuador are similar to those found in Brazil. In both countries, ethnic gaps are larger than gender gaps, and ethnic earnings gaps are larger among men than among women. Whereas differences in human capital characteristics help explain almost half of ethnic earnings gaps, they account for only a very small fraction of gender earnings gaps. Likewise, occupational segregation is important for explaining ethnic but not gender earnings gaps. Ethnic minorities in Ecuador are concentrated in agricultural and informal employment, segments of the labor markets with lower productivity than the rest of the economy. Both gender and ethnic earnings gaps are more pronounced at the lower percentiles of the earnings distribution.

On the basis of these results, it can be inferred that policies aimed at reducing ethnic and gender disparities in earnings should also reduce poverty.

Note

1. For a description of the methodology used in this chapter, see chapter 2.

References

Black, S. E., P. J. Devereux, and K. G. Salvanes. 2003. "Is Education Inherited? Understanding Intergenerational Transmission of Human Capital." Norwegian School of Economics and Business Administration, Oslo, and Institute for the Study of Labor, Bonn, Germany.

De Ferranti, D., G. E. Perry, F. H. G. Ferreira, M. Walton, D. Coady, W. Cunningham, L. Gasparini, J. Jacobsen, Y. Matsuda, J. Robinson, K. Sokoloff, and Q. Wodon. 2003. *Inequality in Latin America and the Caribbean: Breaking with History?* Washington, DC: World Bank.

Gallardo, M. L. 2006. "Ethnicity-Based Wage Differentials in Ecuador's Labor Market." Master's thesis, Cornell University, Department of Economics, Ithaca, NY.

Gallardo, M. L., and H. Ñopo, 2009. "Ethnic and Gender Wage Gaps in Ecuador." RES Working Paper 4625, Inter-American Development Bank, Research Department, Washington, DC.

García-Aracil, A., and C. Winter. 2006. "Gender and Ethnicity Differentials in School Attainment and Labor Market Earnings in Ecuador." *World Development* 34 (2): 289–307.

Larrea, C., and F. Montenegro Torres. 2005. "Ecuador." In *Indigenous Peoples, Poverty and Human Development in Latin America: 1994–2004*, ed. H. A. Patrinos and G. Hall, 67–105. Washington, DC: World Bank.

MacIsaac, D., and M. Rama. 1997. "Determinants of Hourly Earnings in Ecuador: The Role of Labor Market Regulations." Policy Research Working Paper 1717, World Bank, Washington, DC.

Soruco, X., G. Piani, and M. Rossi. 2008. "What Emigration Leaves Behind: The Situation of Emigrants and Their Families in Ecuador." Latin American Research Network Working Paper R–542, Inter-American Development Bank, Washington, DC.

World Bank. 2004. *Ecuador Poverty Assessment.* World Bank: Washington, DC.

16

Ethnic Earnings Gaps for Large Minorities: Guatemala 2000–06

Guatemala is one of the countries with the highest ethnic diversity, not only in Latin America but also in the world. However, the economic well-being of the different ethnic groups is far from homogenous.

Indigenous groups represent 41 percent of Guatemala's population. They are concentrated in rural and poor areas. Furthermore, the incidence of poverty in Guatemala is twice as high among indigenous people (72 percent) as nonindigenous people (36 percent) (Sauma 2004). Along the same lines, the indigenous population amounts for less than one-quarter of national consumption (Fazio 2007).

As Guatemalans generate about 90 percent of their family income in labor markets (Fazio 2007), the analysis of the role of ethnic differences in earnings is important for an understanding of Guatemalans' general well-being. To some extent, earnings gaps reflect differences in human capital characteristics. Indeed, differences in average human capital characteristics (age, education, marital status, migrant status) between indigenous and nonindigenous groups explain a little more than half of the ethnic earnings gap (Romero 2007).

This chapter analyzes ethnic earnings gaps in Guatemala using data from the 2000 and 2006 National Survey of Living Conditions (Encuesta Nacional de Condiciones de Vida [ENCOVI]) and the 2004 National Survey of Employment and Income (Encuesta Nacional de Empleo e Ingresos [ENEI]). The population under consideration is all employed individuals between the ages of 18 and 65; earnings are measured as hourly earnings in the main occupation.

This chapter was adapted from the following source: "Gender and Ethnic Wage Gaps in Guatemala from a Matching Comparisons Perspective," Hugo Ñopo and Alberto Gonzales, RES Working Paper 4587, Inter-American Development Bank, 2008; and Hugo Ñopo and Alberto Gonzales, "Brechas salariales por género y etnicidad," in *Más crecimiento, más equidad*, ed. Ernesto Stein, Osmel Manzano, Hector Morena, and Fernando Straface, Banco Interamericano de Desarrollo, 265–98, 2009.

Alberto Gonzales is a PhD student in the department of economics at the University of Virginia, Charlottesville.

The ethnic variable comes from individuals' self-identification in surveys. Surveyed individuals were asked "To which of the following ethnic groups do you belong?" The list included 22 ethnic indigenous Mayan and 2 non-Mayan groups. Respondents who reported belonging to one of these ethnic groups were regarded as indigenous. *Mestizos* (Ladinos) and foreigners were considered nonindigenous.

How Do Ethnic Minorities and Nonminorities in the Work Force Differ?

Real earnings of the indigenous (minorities) population remained roughly constant during the period under review, while real earnings of nonindigenous (nonminorities) people fell slightly, especially in urban areas (figure 16.1). The earnings gaps favored nonindigenous workers in both urban and rural areas, but the gap was larger in urban areas: whereas in urban areas, the average earnings of nonindigenous people were twice those of indigenous people, in rural areas they were 1.4 times as great (for graphs reporting on urban and rural areas, see Ñopo and Gonzales 2008).

The earnings gap between low-educated and better-educated workers is enormous. The average earnings of a person with higher education is four times the average earnings of a person who did not complete secondary education. Table 16.1 shows the average years of education for indigenous and nonindigenous workers for 2000–06. Nonindigenous workers have about three more years of education than indigenous workers.

Figure 16.1 Real Monthly Earnings of Indigenous and Nonindigenous Workers in Guatemala, 2000–06

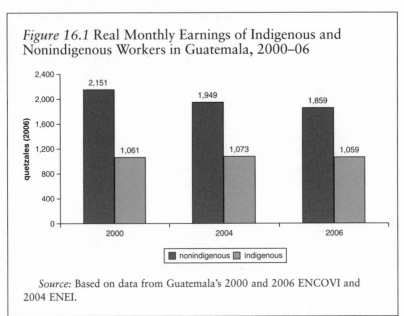

Source: Based on data from Guatemala's 2000 and 2006 ENCOVI and 2004 ENEI.

Table 16.1 Highest Educational Level Begun or Completed by Indigenous and Nonindigenous Workers in Guatemala, 2000, 2004, 2006
(*percent*)

Education	2000		2004		2006	
	Nonindigenous	*Indigenous*	*Nonindigenous*	*Indigenous*	*Nonindigenous*	*Indigenous*
Average years	6.6	3.4	6.5	3.8	7.3	4.6
Level						
Less than high school	74.8	91.5	67.1	84.3	76.8	89.0
University degree or more	5.2	1.1	4.6	1.4	3.3	0.7

Source: Based on data from Guatemala's 2000 and 2006 ENCOVI and 2004 ENEI.

In rural areas, where the majority of the population is indigenous, educational levels achieved are systematically lower than in the urban areas. Whereas in rural areas the schooling gap by ethnicity is about one year, in urban areas it is nearly four years. During the period studied, almost 9 out of 10 indigenous workers and 7 out of 10 nonindigenous workers had not completed secondary education. These figures were higher in rural than in urban areas. Thus, the ethnic gap in education is wider in urban areas. The share of indigenous workers with higher education is very low, at just 1 percent nationally and virtually zero in rural areas.

The Role of Individual Characteristics in Explaining the Ethnic Earnings Gap

Based on these figures, one would expect earnings gaps to be at least partly explained by differences in human capital characteristics of different groups. The rest of the chapter analyzes the decomposition of the ethnic earnings gap, in order to identify the part of the gap that results from educational gaps and other differences in characteristics between indigenous and nonindigenous populations.[1]

Matching is done based on four combinations of characteristics. The first combination includes age, marital status, and years of education. The second combination adds gender to the variables set. The third combination adds migrant status. The fourth combination adds whether the person lives in the capital or not.

The gaps are measured as percentages of the average earnings of the lowest income group (in this case, the indigenous group). Δ_W denotes the component of the gap that can be explained by the existence of certain profiles of nonindigenous workers that cannot be met by indigenous workers. Δ_{NW} denotes the component of the gap caused by the presence of certain profiles of indigenous workers that cannot be met in the sample of nonindigenous workers. Figure 16.2 shows the decomposition at the national level, using the full set of matching characteristics.

Ethnic gaps are 50–80 percent of average indigenous earnings—that is, on average, nonindigenous workers earn 50–80 percent more than indigenous workers with the same characteristics. In rural areas, the unexplained earnings gap is larger. Δ_{NW} plays a significant role in both urban and rural areas: the existence of certain human capital profiles present only in the indigenous population increases the ethnic earnings gap by about 10 percentage points.

Exploring the Unexplained Component of the Ethnic Earnings Gap

Figure 16.3 reports the unexplained component of the ethnic earnings gap that cannot be attributed to differences in characteristics of the individuals

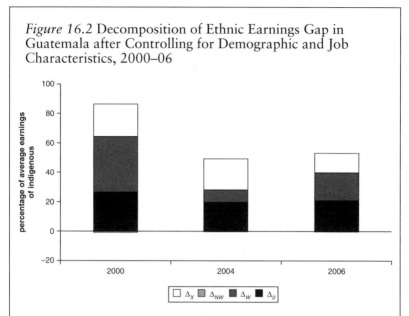

Figure 16.2 Decomposition of Ethnic Earnings Gap in Guatemala after Controlling for Demographic and Job Characteristics, 2000–06

Source: Based on data from Guatemala's 2000 and 2006 ENCOVI and 2004 ENEI.

Note: Δ_W (Δ_{NW}) is the part of the earnings gap attributed to the existence of nonindigenous (indigenous) with combinations of characteristics that are not met by any indigenous (nonindigenous). Δ_X is the part of the earnings gap attributed to differences in the observable characteristics of nonindigenous and indigenous over the "common support." Δ_0 is the part of the earnings gap that cannot be attributed to differences in characteristics of the individuals. It is typically attributed to a combination of both unobservable characteristics and discrimination. The sum of these components equals the total earnings gap ($\Delta_W + \Delta_{NW} + \Delta_X + \Delta_0 = \Delta$).

(Δ_0) by percentile of the income distribution after controlling for the full set of observable characteristics. The unexplained gaps are larger for low-income workers; the decline in Δ_0 related to higher income percentiles reverts in the highest income decile, where Δ_0 increases.

Table 16.2 reports the unexplained earnings gaps for different segments of the working population. Unexplained ethnic earnings gaps are smaller for younger workers (ages 18–25). They are larger for married workers, more educated workers, and men.

This exploration of earnings gaps in Guatemala yields several results, suggesting some guidelines for policy discussion (see next chapter). Earnings gaps favoring men and nonindigenous workers are very large in Guatemala (Chong and Ñopo [2007] report that they are among the highest in Latin America). Differences in observable human capital

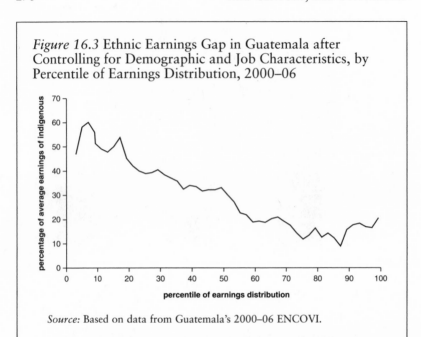

Figure 16.3 Ethnic Earnings Gap in Guatemala after Controlling for Demographic and Job Characteristics, by Percentile of Earnings Distribution, 2000–06

Source: Based on data from Guatemala's 2000–06 ENCOVI.

Table 16.2 Unexplained Ethnic Earnings Gap in Guatemala Controlling for Demographic Characteristics, 2000–06 *(percent)*

Characteristics	Age, education, and marital status	+ gender	+ migrant condition	+ residence
Age				
18–25	17.2	17.7	17.5	15.6
26–35	25.7	29.0	27.9	24.4
36–45	20.2	25.6	26.3	23.8
46–55	24.3	31.1	30.7	27.7
56 or more	24.8	26.6	21.5	19.8

(continued next page)

Table 16.2 (continued)

Characteristics	Age, education, and marital status	+ gender	+ migrant condition	+ residence
Education				
Nothing	22.1	20.8	20.3	19.5
Primary	21.9	25.6	24.3	22.6
Secondary	21.0	26.1	25.7	22.2
Tertiary	73.9	80.4	78.8	45.4
Marital status				
Married	22.9	26.9	26.7	23.7
Separated	10.1	10.7	12.7	11.8
Single	19.6	18.2	17.4	15.3
Migrant condition				
Nonmigrant	20.8	23.6	24.1	21.4
Migrant	15.3	21.9	21.3	19.5
Residence				
In capital city	18.6	21.2	20.7	21.4
Outside of capital city	9.8	14.8	19.5	20.3
Gender				
Women	17.3	17.5	15.4	12.7
Men	24.5	25.6	26.1	23.2
Area				
Urban	19.8	24.0	23.9	20.2
Rural	24.6	26.3	22.3	22.8
Total sample	21.2	24.3	23.9	21.3

Source: Based on data from Guatemala's 2000, 2006 ENCOVI and 2004 ENEI.

characteristics of workers, particularly education, explain about half of these earnings gaps in Guatemala. According to Latinobarometro, a polling organization, Guatemalans believe that lack of education is the principal cause of discrimination. This result is in line with the findings reported in chapter 3: educational gaps in Guatemala are among the highest in Latin America.

Note

1. For a description of the methadology used in this chapter, see chapter 2.

References

Chong, A., and H. Ñopo. 2007. "Discrimination in Latin America: An Elephant in the Room?" Research Department Working Paper 614, Inter-American Development Bank, Washington, DC.

Fazio, M. V. 2007. *Economic Opportunities for Indigenous Peoples in Guatemala.* Conference Edition. Washington, DC: World Bank.

Ñopo, H., and A. Gonzales. 2008. "Brechas salariales por género y etnicidad en Guatemala desde una perspectiva de comparaciones emparejadas." RES Working Paper 4588, Inter-American Development Bank, Research Department, Washington, DC.

———. 2009. "Brechas salariales por género y etnicidad." In *Más crecimiento, más equidad*, ed. Ernesto Stein, Osmel Manzano, Hector Morena, and Fernando Straface, 265–98. Banco Interamericano de Desarrollo.

Romero, W. 2007. "Los costos de la discriminación étnica en Guatemala." In *Diagnóstico del racismo en Guatemala*, vol. 1, 69–95. Vicepresidencia de la República de Guatemala, Guatemala City.

Sauma, P. 2004. "Las desigualdades étnicas y de género en el mercado de trabajo de Guatemala." Working Paper 27/2004, International Labour Organization, Geneva.

Part IV

Policy Options

17

Policy Options

Despite substantial improvements in human capital indicators during the past few decades, women and ethnic minorities still lag men and whites in labor markets, especially in labor earnings. Women, indigenous people, and Afro-descendants are participating more in labor markets and bringing greater human capital to their jobs—but labor markets still fail to reward them appropriately.

This book documents the extent to which earnings disparities correspond to gender and ethnic differences in observable demographic and job characteristics in Latin America and the Caribbean. The first result it highlights is the role of education in explaining earnings differentials. Despite completing more years of schooling than men, women still earn less. In fact, earnings gaps for men and women the same age and with the same number of years of schooling are actually wider than the gaps observed in the data overall. Regarding ethnicity, the situation is even more problematic, as indigenous people and Afro-descendants still lag the rest of the population in years of education.

Another variable that plays an important role in the analysis of gender earnings gaps is part-time work. Including this variable increases the gender earnings gap significantly. Comparing earnings of men and women with the same demographic and job characteristics reveals that the gender earnings gap was 34 percent in the 1990s and 30 percent by the mid-2000s. These values are more than twice as high as the unconditional gender earnings gap.

These average gender earnings gaps mask considerable heterogeneity. The gap is more pronounced among poor and low-educated workers, workers employed by small firms or self-employed, people working part time, and people without formal labor contracts. The good news is that the segments of the labor market in which gender disparities are

This chapter was adapted from the following source: "Pushing for Progress: Women, Work and Gender Roles in Latin America," Hugo Ñopo, *Harvard International Review* 33 (2): 315–28, 2011.

more pronounced have experienced the largest reductions in the earnings gaps. Brazil, for example, has the widest gender earnings disparities in the region, but it also experienced the largest declines. Ethnic earnings disparities have also declined over the past few decades.

Gender and ethnic gaps are narrowing, particularly in countries where they are—or were—widest. The pace at which they are doing so, however, does not seem commensurate with the pace at which women, indigenous people, and Afro-descendants have been acquiring education and human capital. Much work remains to be done to close these gaps.

Policies aimed at reducing these disparities are still needed. Policies that do so should also reduce poverty, as earnings differentials are larger among the poor. Four sets of policies may be effective.

Investing in Education Early in Life

Girls' educational attainment is at least as strong as boys' in most countries in the region. Attainment by minorities is well below that of nonminorities, however. More needs to be done to improve the educational attainment of minorities by providing equal access to education. Inclusive educational methods in the region have included bilingual education (in Bolivia, Ecuador, and Honduras); the expansion of physical access and use of innovative teaching methods that allow people with disabilities to attend regular classes (in Mexico's Inclusion in Higher Education program); the incorporation and adaptation of curricula to emphasize multicultural heritage and the contributions of indigenous groups and people of African descent to national culture and history (in Colombia); and the linkage of education and school attendance with programs aimed at eradicating the worst forms of child labor (in Central America), Márquez et al. (2007). Policy makers could consider adopting any of these interventions.

The earlier in the life cycle an intervention is made, the more effective it is (Carneiro and Heckman 2003; Heckman 2011). For this reason, some researchers and policy experts support interventions that stimulate development in early childhood—through, for example, conditional cash transfers complemented by quality and quantity improvements in education.

Gender and ethnicity have a synergistically negative effect on individuals' labor market performance. Consequently, it makes sense for a long-run strategy to focus on indigenous girls, who underperform boys on a series of educational indicators. Policy needs to create incentives for household heads to send their girls to school, and increases in enrollment have to be paired with improvements in the supply of educational services.

Policies aimed at boosting school attendance and improving the quality of education for minorities should take into account the lower incentives to completing schooling the labor market provides them, because of their concentration in agriculture and informal labor activities, where the returns to education are lower than in other sectors. Although training in the skills required by the modern economy may induce workers to move out of these sectors, it is not clear that labor markets will absorb the workers in the short or medium run if their quality of education is not improved.

Boosting Productivity and Reducing Labor Market Segregation

Ethnic earnings gaps—and their unexplained component—are larger in rural areas than in urban areas. To address this problem, it is necessary to boost productivity in underperforming rural sectors, by facilitating stronger links with other participants in production chains and adding value to them. Localities need to develop skills relevant to their environment and respect local customs. Investments are necessary not only in infrastructure but particularly in individuals' accumulation of human capital.

Additionally, for workers at the bottom of the earnings distribution, policies aimed at reducing occupational segregation seem to be effective in reducing ethnic and gender earnings gaps. This reduction of segregation would not only reduce disparities; it would also make better use of human capital resources, improving overall economic productivity (Hsieh et al. 2012). Labor intermediation services and information campaigns (in both labor and education markets) have proven fruitful in both the developed and the developing world. Expansion of these types of programs would be useful (Autor 2009).

Fostering a More Equitable Division of Household Responsibilities

Unequal relations between men and women within households have important social consequences. More evenly balanced bargaining power increases employment opportunities for women and improves the nutritional status of household members (Calderón 2007).

Part of the gender gap in earnings stems from women's dual roles as workers and homemakers, which reduces their labor market attachment and bargaining power at work. Family-friendly policies may have the potential to reduce this gap. Policy makers could, for example, expand early childhood development facilities and extend school schedules for primary school students. Longer schools days would not only allow more women to work full time, but they would also increase the human capital of the next generation, improving its labor market outcomes.

Most countries in the region have antidiscriminatory laws and legal protections for women. Such legislation is full of good intentions—but most of these laws incentivize behaviors that reduce rather than increase gender parity. A law that mandates equal pay for men and women performing the same job, for example, may encourage employers to avoid hiring or promoting women, who are more likely than men to leave the work force. Legislation promoting parity should therefore be analyzed for both intended and unintended consequences.

Equalization of maternity and paternity leave could help level the playing field regarding hiring decisions for men and women. It could also have positive consequences outside the labor market. Encouraging men and women to devote the same amount of time to their newborns could help create more harmonious households, with more equitable intrahousehold bargaining and decision making. Such a rebalancing could help nurture more equitable divisions of responsibilities, time, and opportunities within households. Over time, equalization of leave following the birth of a child, together with a host of other measures, could help create a more egalitarian society.

Diminishing Stereotyping

The findings in this book that gender disparities in earnings are widest among the self-employed suggest that employer discrimination may not be a major factor accounting for such disparities in the region. To the extent that employers do discriminate, however, information can reduce it. Altonji and Pierret (2001) pioneered this notion by positing that discrimination declines with job tenure, a hypothesis they validated with U.S. data. Job tenure reveals information about a worker's real productivity, which leads people to abandon assessments of capabilities based on stereotypes.

Torero, Castillo, and Petrie (2008) show that in the absence of other information, people in Peru—like people elsewhere—use observable characteristics, such as gender, skin color, and height, as proxies for productivity. When information about actual productivity is revealed, they replace these proxies with data. Information thus displaces discrimination.

Initiatives to improve information on labor markets (employment bureaus and job intermediation, for example) can help change attitudes, stereotypes, and social norms. These instruments can and should compensate for the disadvantages women and minorities face, particularly in terms of network building and the development of core competencies.

Information can also be used to effect cultural and attitudinal changes. One fruitful avenue in this regard has been the tying of job placement with mentoring and networking programs. The entrance of women into the workplace has helped change the perceptions of (male and female) employers and coworkers, replacing stereotypes with facts.

Tools that reach mass markets are also needed. Chong and La Ferrara (2009) illustrate how the subtle introduction of role models in Brazilian soap operas over the course of decades induced changes in fertility and divorce rates in Brazil's middle class. Mass media campaigns that make people more aware of misperceptions about gender roles may also play an important role. But egalitarian values take time to be nurtured. Such nurturing has to start at home, during the early years, and continues at school.

School systems can nurture gender stereotypes. Researchers found that two-thirds of the images of children in fourth and sixth grade textbooks in Peru were of boys (GRADE 2005). In addition, images of women were related largely to leisure and domestic work, whereas images of men were linked to work and schooling. This subtle, and most likely unconscious, communication of stereotypes needs to be eliminated.

Changes in attitudes may take more than a generation to effect. Ensuring that they do so will require the active participation of current and future members of society, not only employers and job seekers.

References

Altonji, J., and C. Pierret. 2001. "Employer Learning and Statistical Discrimination." *Quarterly Journal of Economics* 116 (1): 313–50.

Autor, David H., ed. 2009. *Studies of Labor Market Intermediation.* Chicago: University of Chicago Press.

GRADE (Grupo de Análisis para el Desarrollo). 2005. *Educación de las niñas: lecciones del proceso peruano.* http://educacion-nosexista.org/repo/educdelas niaslecionesdelprocesoperuano.pdf.

Calderón, M. C. 2007. "Discrimination, Marital Bargaining Power and Intrahousehold Allocation in Guatemala." Population Studies Center, University of Pennsylvania, Philadelphia.

Carneiro, P., and J. Heckman. 2003. "Human Capital Policy." IZA Discussion Paper 821, Institute for the Study of Labor, Bonn, Germany.

Chong, A., and E. La Ferrara. 2009. "Television and Divorce: Evidence from Brazilian Novelas." RES Working Paper 4611, Inter-American Development Bank, Research Department, Washington, DC.

Heckman, J. 2011. "The Economics of Inequality. The Value of Early Childhood Education." *American Educator* 35 (1): 31–47.

Hsieh, C.-T., E. Hurst, C. Jones, and P. Klenow. 2012. "The Allocation of Talent and U.S. Economics Growth." http://klenow.com/HHJK.pdf.

Márquez, G., A. Chong, S. Duryea, J. Mazza, and H. Ñopo, eds. 2007. *¿Los de afuera? patrones cambiantes de exclusión en América Latina y el Caribe. Informe de progreso económico y social en América Latina.* Washington, DC: Inter-American Development Bank.

Ñopo, H. 2011. "Pushing for Progress: Women, Work and Gender Roles in Latin America" *Harvard International Review* 33 (2): 315–28.

Torero, M., M. Castillo, and R. Petrie. 2008. "Ethnic and Social Barriers to Cooperation: Experiments Studying the Extent and Nature of Discrimination in Urban Peru." RES Working Paper 3246, Inter-American Development Bank, Research Department, Washington, DC.

Index

Boxes, figures, notes, and tables are indicated by b, f, n, and t following the page number.